Collaborative Worldbuilding for Writers and Gamers

Also published by Bloomsbury

Composition, Creative Writing Studies, and the Digital Humanities,
Adam Koehler
Creative Writing in the Digital Age, Michael Dean Clark,
Trent Hergenrader and Joseph Rein
Creative Writing Innovations, Michael Dean Clark,
Trent Hergenrader and Joseph Rein

Collaborative Worldbuilding for Writers and Gamers

Trent Hergenrader

BLOOMSBURY ACADEMIC
LONDON • NEW YORK • OXFORD • NEW DELHI • SYDNEY

BLOOMSBURY ACADEMIC
Bloomsbury Publishing Plc
50 Bedford Square, London, WC1B 3DP, UK
1385 Broadway, New York, NY 10018, USA

BLOOMSBURY, BLOOMSBURY ACADEMIC and the Diana logo are trademarks
of Bloomsbury Publishing Plc

First published in Great Britain 2019

Cover design by Toby Way and Eleanor Rose
Cover image © Tithi Luadthong / Shutterstock

A catalogue record for this book is available from the British Library.

A catalog record for this book is available from the Library of Congress.

ISBN: HB: 978-1-3500-1667-5
       PB: 978-1-3500-1666-8
       ePDF: 978-1-3500-1668-2
       eBook: 978-1-3500-1669-9

Typeset by RefineCatch Limited, Bungay, Suffolk

To find out more about our authors and books visit www.bloomsbury.com
and sign up for our newsletters.

To Greyson and Anders—
May the worlds you build be better than the one you inherited.

Contents

Figures

Tables

Examples of Building Tal-Vaz

Acknowledgments

I would like to thank my professional colleagues who have made this work better, many of whom I met through the Games+Learning+Society conference, the primary venue where I presented the key concepts for this book over a number of years. This includes Stephen Slota, Roger Travis, Kevin Ballistrini, Michael Young, Jeremy and Kate Sydik, and Ian Schreiber. I am also indebted to James Ryan, Shelly Jones, Todd Wellman, Stephen Garabedian, and Jeremy Sydik for their valuable feedback on an early draft of this book.

I must also thank my colleagues at the Rochester Institute of Technology for their support of my research in general and this book in particular. This includes both my colleagues in the Department of English for allowing me to develop courses on worldbuilding and game-based approaches to fiction writing, and to Dean Jamie Winebrake and the College of Liberal Arts for providing research funds for this book and the worldbuilding card deck. I also wish to extend special thanks to the College for the Paul A. and Francena L. Miller Research Fellowship, which allowed me time to write this book. Finally, I wish to thank Nick Paulus of the RIT Scholarly Publishing Studio for providing me with student workers to help with this project, and to Jeff Lee, the designer responsible for the timeline graphs, forms, and the layout of the worldbuilding cards. I also must thank Paolo Orso-Giacone for the artwork that adorns the worldbuilding cards.

Finally, I must thank my family, starting with my partner Amy Mueller, who holds our world together in more ways than I can count. I also want to thank our parents, Bob and Marti Hergenrader and Bob and Karen Mueller, for their unwavering support. And of course I wish to thank my two sons, Greyson and Anders, who are my inspiration.

Abbreviations

GM   game master
NPC   non-player/non-perspective character
NPOV   neutral point of view
PC   player/perspective character
RPG   role-playing game

Part One

Collaborative Worldbuilding Concepts and Terminology

Introduction to Collaborative Worldbuilding

This book is a practical guide for anyone who is eager to build a large-scale fictional world with other people. Most concepts herein apply to a single-authored worldbuilding project as well, but collaborative worldbuilding has an advantage in that you can tap into other people's imaginations and, together, you can quickly build an enormous world full of details, quirks, and surprises. The book is divided into two parts. Part One covers collaborative worldbuilding concepts and terminology. Part Two puts those concepts into practice and leads you through the collaborative worldbuilding process.

There are many reasons to participate in a collaborative worldbuilding project. Storytellers of all kinds can use a collaboratively built world to write a series of linked short stories or novels; they might create their own episodic online video series; they could write webcomics using the created world as the backdrop. Tabletop role-playing gamers can create complex worlds as campaign settings, and game designers can develop a rich and nuanced environment for digital or tabletop games. Or the project can just be a fun writing exercise, something to stretch your creative muscles with friends. For educators, collaborative worldbuilding projects can also serve as great teaching tools. Writing instructors can use this methodology for a connected class project, and teachers of history and literature can use collaborative worldbuilding exercises as a way to encourage students to think critically about forces at play in different kinds of fictional worlds. In every case, collaboratively built worlds require the contributors to act as a team and exchange ideas as they work through complex questions about how worlds work, including our own. This book will be your guide to help ensure that the world your group creates is as diverse, complex, and fully realized as possible.

As Mark J.P. Wolf notes in *Building Imaginary Worlds: The Theory and History of Subcreation*,[1] sprawling fictional worlds are more common than ever before, and the stories set in these worlds appear in a variety of different narrative media. You might be asking: is this how authors like J.R.R. Tolkien or George R.R.

Martin developed their popular fictional universes? The answer is a resounding no, it is not. Novelists tend to have their own idiosyncratic processes for developing their fictional worlds, and more often than not, they do this work alone. Writers often stew over ideas for months or even years, mentally revising and connecting ideas before committing a single word to paper. They never need to explain to anyone how their imaginary world works because, once they figure out the details, they reveal the nuances of their world through their fiction. Thus the processes by which most writers develop their fictional worlds are locked in a black box inside the author's head. A collaborative writing project simply can't work like that because the process from beginning to end is defined by sharing. No one can be sure what's going on in someone else's head, at least not until ideas are put into language. Once verbalized, those ideas can be debated and critiqued, adopted, modified, or discarded. A collaborative worldbuilding project operates much more like a team of screenwriters or game designers brainstorming concepts for a major project than a single fiction writer working on a novel.

This book describes a structured approach to building a large-scale fictional world using a step-by-step process that takes you from a broadly sketched high-level vision to the granular details that make the world teem with story-making potential. I've developed this process over several years in different environments—in classrooms, in writing workshops, and in gaming groups—and I've helped hundreds of writers build fictional worlds in many different genres: alternate history, post-apocalyptic fiction, epic fantasy, urban fantasy, steampunk, cyberpunk, deep space science fiction, and more. In my experience, people overwhelmingly enjoy themselves when they're engaged in the creative act of building worlds together.

While the focus of this book is creating unique new worlds, the process is flexible enough to be adapted for other purposes as well. For example, a group could take a fanfiction angle and create a new planet in the *Star Wars* galaxy, a new region in J.R.R. Tolkien's Middle-earth or George R.R. Martin's world of Westeros, or branch out from any other media franchise that sparks the group's imagination. It can also be used to model different historical time periods. You can use the system to create a model of Ancient Greece or China during the Ming Dynasty; you could even add some fantastical or science fictional elements to warp these historical worlds and run some alternate history thought experiments. I have worked with writers who have used this process to kick-start old worldbuilding projects that have sat dormant in notebooks and hard drives for years. They've used the process described in the book to fill in the details of what they know about their world, and then they invited others to round out details, add greater nuance, and offer their own new unique perspectives on how the world might work.

By following the process described in this book, you and some collaborators will wind up with a compelling project that everyone in your group finds satisfying and engaging. There's leeway in how your group approaches the process, but overall in this book, you will find a proven method for producing interesting, complex, and coherent worlds.

The Case Against Worldbuilding?

In the last few years, it has become popular to knock worldbuilding. In a widely cited complaint, award-winning fiction writing M. John Harrison writes: "Worldbuilding is dull. Worldbuilding literalises the urge to invent. Worldbuilding gives an unneccessary [sic] permission for acts of writing (indeed, for acts of reading)."[2] Lincoln Michel asserts something similar, objecting to superfluous details about the world, stating that "the goal of the writer is not to clutter the path with every object they can think of, but to clear the way for the reader's journey."[3] Michel also writes that "the focus on worldbuilding has moved far beyond simply creating some interesting backstories and complex politics to increase the drama of the tale, to expecting a writer to have mapped out every detail of a world as if they were producing an encyclopedia instead of a story."[4] Both of these writers are correct in a narrow sense that pure worldbuilding is not good storytelling, but they miss a broader question: does every form of creative writing always need to be in the service of a story?

When conceptualized this way, the problem is less with the act of worldbuilding and more with the novice writer who confuses the work of worldbuilding with the work of storytelling. Contrary to what Michel says, sometimes producing an encyclopedia is exactly what writers need to be doing in order to lay the groundwork for stories that will come later. The encyclopedia isn't wasted writing, but rather is an act of learning about the world and filling a repository for story-making material that can be selectively drawn from. Consider this quote from China Miéville, one of the most accomplished fantasy writers of the last two decades:

> Probably one of the most enduring influences on me was a childhood playing RPGs: *Dungeons and Dragons* and others. I've not played for sixteen years and have absolutely no intention of starting again, but I still buy and read the manuals

occasionally. There were two things about them that particularly influenced me. One was the mania for cataloguing the fantastic: if you play them for any length of time, you get to know pretty much all the mythological beasts of all pantheons out there, along with a fair bit of the theology. I still love all that—I collect fantastic bestiaries, and one of the main spurs to write a secondary-world fantasy was to invent a bunch of monsters, half of which I'm sure I'll never be able to fit into any books.[5]

Miéville refers to "the mania for cataloguing the fantastic" and fueling his own encyclopedic impulse to create beasts he knows might never find a home in his novels. The overproduction of material is intentional, an exercise in imagination and possibility. The difference between an amateur fiction writer and Miéville is that the latter knows not to dump in everything he's created into every novel he writes. Again, this is a problem of clumsy storytelling, not a problem with the act of worldbuilding.

Imagine the collaborative worldbuilding process as the creation of an enormous story-generating machine. In this view, the act of worldbuilding is distinct and separate from conventional storytelling. The process outlines steps to follow, checkpoints to reach, schedules to keep, and quotas to meet that will keep your project focused and on track. A proper collaborative worldbuilding project becomes an intense exercise in seeing the world from many different points of view. This ability to see a world through the eyes of many different diverse characters is a skill that all storytellers, regardless of their medium of choice, need to develop. By the time you're coming to an end of the process, you and your contributors will be bursting with potential story ideas.

What You Need to Get Started

Getting a collaborative worldbuilding project started is easy: all you need is one or more people willing to write with you. A collaborative worldbuilding project can, in theory, support a limitless number of contributors, but in the early stages of a project, you'll want a smaller group of writers so you have an easier time staying focused. While an essential part of the worldbuilding process is the sharing of a diversity of ideas, it can also be a case of too much of a good thing if you start with too many ideas too soon. On the other hand, you need other people involved to benefit from the different perspectives they can offer.

The ideal number tends to be between four and six people. Fewer than four and the world can lack diversity; with more than six people serving as primary contributors to the world, you can spend just as much time fielding ideas and struggling to gain consensus than actual worldbuilding. With experience, the process can expand to accommodate much larger groups. The largest groups I've facilitated have had as many as twenty-five contributors, but groups that size present serious challenges in managing the number of ideas shaping the world. It's best to start small for the first time through the process, at least until you better understand a worldbuilding project's natural ebbs and flows.

For your first collaborative worldbuilding project, it's usually best if you both know the other participants and have a good relationship with them. The process involves a significant amount of discussion that revolves around sensitive topics like political views and spiritual beliefs. Disagreements are sure to arise, but discussing and working through these different viewpoints is absolutely necessary—this is a feature of the process, not a bug. Listening and learning from each other is an important part of collaborative worldbuilding, and contributors will have to make peace with the fact that they won't always get their way. In a classroom or workshop environment, an instructor can moderate such disagreement, but it can be more difficult in less structured environments, and it can be doubly difficult to read people whom you've only recently met. The chance for misunderstanding increases exponentially when you're writing online. Tone, sarcasm, and irony can be difficult to detect unless you have a good sense of someone's personality. This is all to say: choose your collaborators wisely.

This book assumes that all project contributors will have regular access to computers and a reliable Internet connection so they may access online tools like wikis and digital maps. This allows for people to work on the project asynchronously, and the entire world is always up to date for everyone, day or night. While it's theoretically possible *not* to use a computer, it isn't recommended. Work can always be done offline, either in notebooks or on notecards, but it is good practice to move everything online as quickly and as often as possible.

This book's website, collaborativeworldbuilding.com, features a number of forms and resources that, while not strictly required for a collaborative worldbuilding project, are highly recommended. They are designed to work with the process described in each chapter and provide some additional scaffolding to help you through the various stages of your worldbuilding project.

The Stages of Collaborative Worldbuilding

A collaborative worldbuilding project happens in two distinct stages: 1) building a *foundation*; and 2) populating a *catalog* with people, places, and things. Each stage has several steps that should be completed in chronological order, and each step should be recorded on a shareable online document or on a wiki so all contributors have access to it. The first stage is the most intensely collaborative period where writers must be in constant contact, ideally meeting face-to-face as much as possible. The second stage is more individualized, where the group designs templates for different types of catalog entries, and then each person is responsible for creating entries that populate the world with story-making material.

The process described in the book should be followed in chronological order. Resist the temptation to skip ahead. For example, don't create characters before you figure out the social structures of the world. This can lead to a sense of inauthenticity, where the world seems to exist only to serve a single character's interests. It will feel much more organic if the characters are born into an existing world rather than having a world shaped around them. However, this doesn't mean the process runs in only one direction. With each step, you will be finding out new details about the world that will need to be incorporated into earlier parts of the process. A collaborative worldbuilding project will constantly ask you to rethink, revise, and refine different aspects of the fictional world.

Completing both stages of the collaborative worldbuilding project usually takes about one to two months, but it depends on the number of contributors you have and how much time they can devote to the project on a regular basis. The group size often dictates the pace at which you move through the stages too. A smaller group will usually be able to crank through the foundational aspects of the world relatively quickly as it's easier to gain consensus with fewer people, but populating a substantial catalog may take them more time. In contrast, a larger group may need more to time to sort through all the ideas for the world's foundations, but the catalog of people, places, and things can expand very quickly.

When does a worldbuilding project end? That's entirely up to the group. There will be a point when the details of the world have reached critical mass and you will feel the temptation to start telling stories rather than further describing the features of the world. When you reach this point, the group should wrap up the worldbuilding project and spend some time exploring the world through other forms of storytelling. Different contributors may have different plans for what they want to do with the world and in what form of media they want to tell their stories. One of the most gratifying parts of collaborative worldbuilding is watching the diverse range of stories emerging from the project, and witnessing your individual contributions being used by other collaborators in ways you never imagined. After everyone creates some new stories and, ideally, shares them with each other for critique and enjoyment, the group can reconvene to develop the world further. You might move to a different part of the world or shift to a different time period, either earlier in history or sometime into the future. You could also start a new project, perhaps with a few new contributors to get some fresh perspectives.

Project Overview and Key Terminology

This book draws on concepts from several sources including media theory, literary theory, critical theory, narrative theory, writing studies, game studies, and role-playing games. Each of them has their own specialized jargon and technical terms, which in many cases have been modified or simplified for the purposes of this book. Key terms are set in italics and appear in the glossary at the back of the book. This section introduces you to the broad concepts of the collaborative worldbuilding process. All the concepts, terms, and processes below are discussed in greater detail in later sections of the book.

While we sometimes use the word *world* to mean our planet Earth, it also can mean some narrower aspect of human life, for example, "the *world* of Wall Street bankers." We also commonly refer to conditions in a historical period, such as "the *world* of the Aztec Empire." To confuse matters more, we also talk about worlds that exist only in the human imagination like "the *world* of Middle-earth." To differentiate these different types of worlds, this book will use the term *primary world* to describe our reality in which we have not (perhaps yet) discovered alien life, explored distant planets, or traveled through time or faster than the speed of light; likewise we cannot cast spells, summon the dead, and monsters such as ogres and fire-breathing dragons have never existed.

For the purposes of this book, *worldbuilding* will be generally understood to mean the act of creating a fictional world. *Fictional worlds* created during the collaborative worldbuilding process come in many different shapes and sizes, but the majority of worlds tend to be varieties of *speculative fiction*, where some rules of the primary world have been altered in some fundamental way. Speculative fiction is an umbrella term for the *genres* of *science fiction, fantasy,* and *horror,* each of which has multiple subgenres. For example, post-apocalyptic fiction is a subgenre of science fiction and sword and sorcery is a subgenre of fantasy. *Genre-blending* occurs when a world draws from two or more genres, such as a zombie apocalypse or a Western setting that features both cowboys and magic. Representations of the primary world of the past that feature no speculative element are *historical worlds,* and fiction that is faithful to the historical record is called *historical fiction.*

Collaborative worldbuilding is when more than one person works on a collaborative worldbuilding *project* for a specific *audience* and in a recognizable *genre* of speculative fiction. The writers in the *group* are interchangeably referred to as *writers, collaborators,* and *contributors.* The goal of a collaborative worldbuilding project is to create a world that is convincingly *coherent,* which means each individual piece of the world must make logical sense in the context of the world's rules. It should also be *consistent,* meaning that all these pieces of the world are compatible with each other. Ensuring both coherence and consistency requires a significant amount of negotiation and compromise of differing, and sometimes competing, viewpoints of the contributors. In your first meetings, you should set up a *wiki* and/or online *document sharing* files for notetaking and ensure that all contributors understand how to access those resources.

The *first stage* of the collaborative worldbuilding process is building the world's *foundation.* The foundational work begins with the contributors determining the intended *audience* and choosing a genre for the worldbuilding project. Next comes establishing the *framework* for the fictional world, which happens in five steps:

1. Determine the world's *scope,* which includes the world's *breadth* (its physical space) and *depth* (level of detail about the world), as well as identifying potential *focal points* (individual *locations* and *sublocations* that feature the greatest depth of detail).
2. Arrange the world's *sequence,* where you chart a *timeline* for your world, including the timeline's *termination points* in the past and future, *historical events* of monumental importance, and the *point of the present,* or when on the timeline you anticipate the "now" of the world to be.
3. Choose a *perspective* from which to describe the world, or who is telling the story of your world. This could be anything from a *neutral point of*

view (NPOV) to a highly subjective narrative told from a *first-person perspective.*

4.   Define the *map* of the world, and pin down the location of the focal points.
5.   Finally, write a *metanarrative lead* that describes the world's framework in a short fictional narrative that serves as an introduction to the world.

With the framework established, the group moves on to developing the *structures* of the fictional world. There are four *structural categories* and 14 *substructures* that fit beneath those four categories. The four structural categories and their 14 substructures are:

- *governance*, which deals with issues of *government presence, rule of law*, and the provision of *social services*;
- *economics*, which includes the world's *economic strength, wealth distribution*, and levels of *agricultural production and trade*;
- *social relations*, which describes inequalities or tensions that relate to *race relations, class relations, gender relations*, and *sexual orientation relations*; and
- *cultural influences*, which accounts for the degree of importance for *military influence, religious influence, technology influence*, and the influence of the *arts and culture* in the fictional world.

Once the foundational work is completed to the group's satisfaction, the contributors use the framework and social structures to begin writing a longer, more detailed *metanarrative*, or a story of the fictional world. The metanarrative presents a broad, multifaceted picture of the world as a whole in terms of its governance, economics, social relations, and cultural influences, both from a historical perspective as well as the state of the world in the point of the present. When the metanarrative has been completed, the group has finished the first stage of the collaborative worldbuilding process.

The *second stage* of the process is populating a *catalog* with entries from different *categories* that include *historical events, characters, locations, items*, and *groups*. Each catalog entry is comprised of two sections: the categorical information found in the *stat block*, and a *narrative description* section that provides a more subjective summary about how the entry fits in the world. The stat block also includes information on entry *types*, which help ensure there's sufficient diversity of entries in each category. When the group has completed and agreed upon a number of catalog entries, they move on to drawing stories set in their shared fictional world and the collaborative worldbuilding project draws to a close, at least temporarily.

Examples of Fictional Worlds: Middle-earth, the *Star Wars* Galaxy, Westeros, and More

To illustrate the concepts of frameworks and structures, this book draws on three exemplary large-scale fictional worlds: J.R.R. Tolkien's Middle-earth, George Lucas's *Star Wars* galaxy, and George R.R. Martin's Westeros and the Known World from his *A Song of Ice and Fire* series. The second stage of the collaborative worldbuilding process is explicitly modeled after role-playing game catalogs, so many examples are also drawn from *Dungeons & Dragons* rulebooks and supplemental materials, and the digital role-playing game *Fallout 4*.

These examples were chosen because they would be widely familiar to most readers, and there's little doubt that Tolkien, Lucas, and Martin loom large in the minds of people interested in creating their own massive worlds. These works are far from the *only* worlds that serve as good examples, and all of them fall under the umbrella of fantasy (or perhaps science fantasy in the case of *Star Wars*). The process described in this book, however, is adaptable for any kind of worldbuilding project. In fact, readers are encouraged to think about the concepts set forth in relation to their own favorite large-scale worlds. The examples could have used J.K. Rowling's *Harry Potter* series, Isaac Asimov's *Foundation* series, Ursula Le Guin's *Hainish Cycle*, Frank Herbert's *Dune* series, Stephen King's *Dark Tower* series, Octavia Butler's *Parable* series and many others. Outside print fiction, other possibilities include Robert Kirkman and Tony Moore's *The Walking Dead* comics and the television adaptation, any of the series in the Marvel and DC comics universes and their films, as well as many videogames series such as *Final Fantasy* and *Mass Effect* that feature long-established, enormous fictional worlds.

In addition to thinking about their favorite large fictional worlds, readers should check out fan-run wikis that inventory their favorite fictional worlds. For the example worlds used, the wikis referenced are the Tolkien Gateway[6] and Encyclopedia of Arda[7] for Tolkien's Middle-earth, Wookieepedia[8] for the *Star Wars* galaxy, A Wiki of Ice and Fire[9] for Martin's Known World, and The Fallout Wiki[10] for the *Fallout* series. Each provides an excellent model for how a large-scale fictional world can be broken down into different types of catalog entries for the different categories of historical events, items, locations, characters, and groups.

Collaborativeworldbuilding.com

The companion website for this book can be found at collaborativeworldbuilding. com. The site contains a number of resources, including a downloadable set of collaborative worldbuilding cards, worldbuilding worksheets, and other supplemental resources designed to work with this book. The website also provides a number of commercial products you may find useful in your worldbuilding endeavors, including lists of books, games and game supplements, and online software.

Additional collaborative worldbuilding resources are in development, such as a character-building and story-building system that can either be used as standalone products or in conjunction with the worldbuilding materials referenced in this book. Check collaborativeworldbuilding.com often for updates and join the mailing list for news and announcements.

2

Worlds, Worldbuilding, and Collaborative Worldbuilding

Before you get started with a worldbuilding project, it's worth taking time to review some seemingly straightforward questions. What do we mean when we talk about a *world*? What do we mean when we talk about *worldbuilding*? How is *collaborative worldbuilding* any different?

On the face of it, the answers to these questions might seem obvious: a world is a place where people (or fictional characters) live and breathe and act, worldbuilding is the process by which an artist creates a detailed imaginary world, and collaborative worldbuilding is when more than one person is involved in making an imaginary world. While each of these answers is generally true, they don't tell the whole story. The purpose of this chapter is to unpack these terms and reveal some of the complexities that come with talking about worlds and worldbuilding. Turning over such questions in your mind isn't merely an academic exercise. The better you understand the intricacies of answering these questions, the more likely you are to create a more nuanced representation of a world in a more mindful and intentional way.

What Is a World?

Often when we use the word *world* we simply mean planet Earth. When we say "Manchester United is the biggest sports team in the world" no one bothers to ask which world we're talking about. Yet we use the word in other ways too, especially when we're referring to smaller, more specific subsets of human culture. We use terms like "the world of professional football players" or "the fashion world" all the time; we might talk about what daily life was like in "the world of the Aztec Empire." When using the word world in this sense, we actually mean some specific aspect of life on our planet, not some totalizing picture of all reality. Thus it can be said that our lone planet (i.e., Earth) holds an infinite number of worlds within it, and that when we talk about worlds, we are in fact talking about something much more compact: a general description that attempts to capture a given place at a given time. For example, "the world of the Aztec Empire" is generally understood to mean the region in and around the Valley of Mexico in the early fifteenth to early sixteenth centuries. Historians and anthropologists can say a number of things that are generally true about this place in time in regards to geography, the flora and fauna, and cultural aspects of the Aztec people. However, if we talk about an earlier or later time, or if we move our focus further north or further south, the conditions change to the point where we are no longer talking about the Aztec Empire as the generalizations we can make about that world no longer hold true. We are in fact crossing over into describing a different world.

Worlds are deceptively complex and we must be aware that our natural inclination is to generalize lived experiences. We do this in order to get a grip on our bewilderingly complex planet and the many different people who live, or have ever lived, on planet Earth. Such generalizations can be useful for understanding differences between places and times. For example, we know that the people living in the world of central Mexico in 1450 would have experienced life very differently than those who lived in the world of central France or the world of central China at that same time. Each of these worlds naturally had its own unique political hierarchy, economic systems, social relations, and cultural values, which can be compared and contrasted in meaningful ways. Yet it can also be said that significantly different experiences existed within those groups as well. The people in those cultures who lived near inland mountains would have experienced life very differently from those who lived closer to the coastline. People from different regions would have spoken differently, eaten different foods, and even followed different religious practices, just as people do today. Worlds change over time as well. People living at the start of an empire would have experienced a very different world than those who lived in an era of imperial decline. How we distinguish between worlds, what we identify as the rules of different worlds, and how social forces operate in a given world are all matters of importance.

Some aspects of human existence, however, are consistent across time or cultures. These broad, generally uncontroversial facts about human life describe what this book refers to as the *primary world*. For example, gravity works the same in Bangalore, Brussels, or Boston and has throughout human history. Our species has never been able to move forward or backward in time, travel faster than the speed of light, or stop the aging process. Humans have always required oxygen, food, and water to survive. In the primary world, people can't shoot fireballs from their fingertips, we have not discovered alien life, and we cannot resurrect the dead. We do, however, have a broad comprehension of how human cultures have changed over time, and how certain historical events have shaped the course of world history. Thus, we can understand the broad scope of world history as the story of our primary world. However, we don't have to go very far into the finer details of any historical period to encounter a number of competing and contested perspectives about how life was experienced by people at that time.

What Is Worldbuilding?

Worldbuilding is the process of creating a representation of a fictional world. It encompasses more than just the setting where a story takes place. It includes the political and social forces at work, logistical questions pertaining to geography and economics, and much, much more. As writer Chuck Wendig says:

> It's easy to think [worldbuilding] means "setting," but that's way too simple—worldbuilding covers everything and anything inside that world. Money, clothing, territorial boundaries, tribal customs, building materials, imports and exports, transportation, sex, food, the various types of monkeys people possess, whether the world does or does not contain Satanic "twerking" rites.[1]

Worldbuilding means all of the available information about the fictional world, and how all those pieces fit together. People praise a story's worldbuilding when the many details of the fictional world work in harmony and feel natural. They criticize the worldbuilding when blatant contradictions or logic gaps break their sense of immersion in the narrative, or when the minute details of the world's workings take precedence over characters and plot.

However, just as artists cannot hope to capture the totality of the reality of the primary world, it is equally impossible (and foolish) to attempt this in a work of fiction. Good fiction writers don't begin by exhaustively describing every minute aspect of a world. Instead, they build worlds within worlds and let their characters explore the juxtapositions and frictions within the society. Characters who live in a fictional world should possess different opinions, different value systems, and even harbor different assumptions about the way their world works. Their attitudes and beliefs should come under scrutiny and cause conflicts. These differences in worldviews often become the basis for compelling plots. If you don't create a diversity of perspectives among your characters, your world will feel contrived and your stories will seem either forced or stale.

Creating a large-scale fictional world is a daunting prospect even for accomplished writers. The volume of material J.R.R. Tolkien created over the course of his life at times paralyzed him, as he struggled to find the shape of his world's story.[2] George Lucas could be accused of developing too little of the *Star Wars* galaxy, leading to a number of logic gaps and inconsistencies in his film saga,[3] and George R.R. Martin seems to have lost a handle on his ever-growing fictional world in his *A Song of Ice and Fire* series. Even as his global fan base demands the next installment, Martin has confessed he can't quite find the threads of the story he wants to tell,[4] possibly because he has so many characters spinning off in so many different directions.

Creators of imaginary worlds must balance worldbuilding and storytelling. They must develop complexity on one hand, but incorporate only the details that a plot demands on the other. As mentioned in the introduction, this book strives to keep the two as separate as possible. First, build a sufficiently complex world that will serve as an engine for different types of storytelling. Second, use that engine to drive stories told from the perspective of specific characters, who will view the world in different ways and will face different challenges based on their position in society. While storytelling itself presents a number of daunting challenges—plotting, pacing, using evocative language, requiring characters to grow and change—the goal of this book is to ensure that your worldbuilding process is efficient, fun, and rewarding.

What Is Collaborative Worldbuilding?

In a cursory way, we've established that any description of a world is not a universal truth, but rather a broad interpretation of a specific location in a given moment in time, and that worlds are open to a multitude of subjective, individual experiences within them. We've also established that worldbuilding is the process by which an author creates an imaginary world that takes into account the varied social and cultural forces at play, how these forces work in concert as a coherent system, and how in a work of fiction the details of the imaginary world often emerge by way of a narrative. The fictional worlds of contemporary narratives tend to be both very big and very complex. Many of us are enthralled by these massive settings and are eager to begin building our own vast imaginary worlds.

This book argues that *collaborative worldbuilding* can assist a group of writers in creating their own large, complex worlds and they won't have to spend years of their lives doing it. One of the most obvious advantages of collaborative worldbuilding is that the world can grow very quickly. It can take a lone writer several days to write 10,000 words of history for a world, where it might take ten writers a few hours at most. Secondly, collaborative worldbuilding projects are naturally diverse and complex, as a world built by ten writers draws from ten different imaginations and ten different perspectives on the world. Collaborative worldbuilding requires the participants to work through the mechanics of how worlds work, including discussing how our shared primary world works. This intellectual exercise gives us a richer sense of how different people might experience our world. Thirdly, from a pragmatic angle, collaborative worldbuilding gives you a built-in critique group for your writing. A worldbuilding project belongs both to everyone and to no one. Participants share a sense of ownership and pride in their co-created world, and contributors are eager to see how other writers build off their inventions and provide each other with feedback to help improve it.

In short, a collaborative worldbuilding project allows a group of writers to reduce the time to create a vast, yet complex, imaginary world that has both breadth and depth for use as a shared environment for storytelling. Constructing a world with other people requires critical thinking skills as well as creativity, and contributors will have much to learn from each other as the group navigates questions about how worlds work. Collaborative worldbuilding projects engage contributors intellectually, creatively, and socially in ways that sole authorship does not. While many writers will choose to create their own worlds and tell their own stories in the media of their choice, it is my hope that participating in a collaborative worldbuilding project will help deepen each contributor's understanding of the complexity and sophistication of imaginary worlds, and that they will be able to apply these lessons to their future artistic projects, regardless of whether they collaborate with others or work on their own.

3

Audience and Genres

In a collaborative worldbuilding project, the *audience* refers to the intended group of readers for whom you are writing. Being clear about your intended audience for your worldbuilding project is something that should be determined before you write a single word. The dividing line is between the *contributors* (those people who are creating the world) and the audience (the people who are reading about the world).

A *closed project* is one where the contributors themselves are the only intended audience, and no one outside the immediate *group* will have access to the *collaborative worldbuilding project*. All worldbuilding is kept behind-the-scenes and anyone outside the immediate group of contributors will learn details about the world through the stories set in it. This is the most common approach for commercial artists who build fictional worlds for books, films, games, etc. In this case, it's up to fan wikis to reverse engineer the closed fictional world by painstakingly cataloging every person, place, and thing described, or even alluded to, in stories set in the fictional world. For a closed collaborative worldbuilding project, the group sets up a password-protected wiki site where only contributors have access and all other public viewing is denied. In some cases, the public audience may never know that the collaborative worldbuilding site even exists.

Alternately, an *open project* may function as a publicly viewable reference document. In this approach, stories set in the fictional world may contain explicit links to the collaborative worldbuilding wiki. For example, a character name or a location may be linked to its wiki catalog entry, inviting the audience to dip in and out of the story and delve into a character's backstory or learn more about some facet of the world. In this scenario, the worldbuilding project exists in parallel to the creative work and can be explored by the audience in a non-linear fashion. Some projects might begin as closed worlds but are later opened up to public readership once the stories begin being published. Another option is to publicize the creation of the wiki worldbuilding site from the beginning so an audience can see the evolution of the project as it happens.

A third option is where the collaborative worldbuilding project is a creative product itself and the contributors have no intent to advance to the storytelling phase. Building worlds together can be invigorating writing exercises that can fuel other creative endeavors or it can just be done for fun among friends. These are also the types of worlds built at workshops, conferences, and conventions where a group of strangers may only have an hour or two to sketch out some broad concepts for a fictional world. In this scenario, the question of audience is put to the side since it is less about the final product and more about demonstrating the intellectual and creative exercise of collaborative worldbuilding.

Finally, for groups designing worlds for use in games or campaign settings, a world may have *limited access*. This means that while all the contributors in the group will be involved in building the foundation and populating the catalog with people, places, and things, some knowledge will be restricted for those who plan on serving as game master for a role-playing game campaign. For example, a haunted mansion could be a location all contributors know about, and the catalog entry might contain broad information that people in the world would conceivably know. More detailed information, such as the exact floor plan and a list of the traps and monsters inside, would be visible only to game masters. This preserves suspense and surprise for the players, who will only have limited knowledge of the world. In this scenario, contributors will want to be very clear on what knowledge is intended to be common knowledge versus what's secret information only known to the game master.

Regardless of which approach your group takes, make sure everyone understands the project's intended audience from the start. You may also wish to establish some ground rules about how contributors should use the wiki. For example, should people leave notes for the other contributors explaining their rationale or asking questions about entries? Is creating half-finished or placeholder entries acceptable, or is the wiki only for posting completed drafts? There are no right or wrong answers to these questions, just ones that should be answered with the project's intended audience in mind. If you intend to share your world with a broad audience, you might not want it cluttered with notes and half-finished entries. On the other hand, you might not mind exposing the rough edges of the creative process.

Worldbuilding Genres

Worldbuilding projects can focus on worlds that are either very similar to, or very different from, our primary world. This book assumes that most groups will be creating speculative worlds where the differences between their fictional worlds and our own reality will be pronounced. The broad term *speculative fiction* covers any kind of story that features at least one aspect of our world that diverges from our commonly understood sense of what is real or possible in our primary world. Most collaborative worldbuilding projects are likely to fit under the broad categories of fantasy, science fiction, or horror, and each of these genres contains additional factors that should be considered when building the foundation of your fictional world. There's also the possibility of *genre-blending*, where you take elements of two or more genres and combine them. Genres are notoriously slippery to define and the below offerings make no attempt to provide clear boundaries between them. Rather, the purpose is to get you thinking about prominent features of different speculative fiction genres and how you might incorporate (or resist) them when building your foundation. For more comprehensive definitions, check out the free online *Encyclopedia of Science Fiction*[1] and its companion site, the *Encyclopedia of Fantasy*.[2]

Fantasy Worlds

When many people hear the word *fantasy*, they often think of quasi-medieval worlds with primitive levels of technology—swords and catapults, not pistols and cannons—as well as magical spells, monsters such as dragons and trolls, and races of elves, orcs, and dwarves. This is the fantasy tradition popularized by J.R.R. Tolkien and his legion of imitators, and it's also the default setting for *Dungeons & Dragons* and their popular *Forgotten Realms* resources. The popularity of George R.R. Martin's *Song of Ice and Fire* series suggests that this type of fantasy still has a large, and perhaps growing, fan base. The subgenres of this type of fantasy include epic fantasy, high fantasy, heroic fantasy, and sword and sorcery. Each carry a slightly different connotation but are often used synonymously. For all but the diehard fans, the distinctions between them are slight and tend to be present at the level of narrative—for example, whether a story's protagonist is more chivalrous or self-interested and opportunistic— rather than at the level of worldbuilding. Stories in these subgenres often feature characters on quests who are required to traverse wild, perilous terrain and who struggle against evil forces that threaten to overrun the world.

Though magic, monsters, and medievalism might be what most people think of when they hear the word fantasy, it is only one type of the genre. Other kinds of fantasy fiction are settings much closer to our primary world but include fantastic elements. These include the retelling of fairy tales and myths and fables, known as mythic fiction and fabulism respectively, which often take place in ancient, medieval, or otherwise non-modern yet historical times. One exception is urban fantasy, which incorporates elements of magic and fantastical creatures and places them in our primary world, usually in major metropolitan areas. Characters in these worlds often worry as much about mundane realities of modern life, struggling to balance their checkbooks as much as they strive to master new spells. Monster fiction, dark fantasy, and supernatural horror are also commonly set in our primary world, from H.P. Lovecraft's cosmic Cthulhu mythos to all manner of vampires, zombies, ghosts, and other undead or otherworldly threats that walk our streets.

Aspects of Fantasy of Worlds

Magic is a staple of fantasy worlds. If you're building a fantasy world, you'll need to decide whether it exists or not. If it does, you'll need to determine its prevalence in the world, who is able to use it, the extent of its power, what people need to do to make magic work, and more. The nature and mechanics of magic can either be central to the world's operation, such as in Ursula Le Guin's *Earthsea* series or Patrick Rothfuss's *Kingkiller Chronicle*, or it can be rare and shrouded in mystery as it is in Tolkien's Middle-earth and Martin's *A Song of Ice and Fire*. If the setting is our primary world, then you need to decide whether it is a matter of common knowledge, such as in Joanna Clarke's *Jonathan Strange & Mr. Norrell*, or only known to secret societies, as in Lev Grossman's *The Magicians*. Working out intricate details about how magic operates can be time-consuming but worthwhile if magic is important to your world, either as a commodity, or if it has specific religious or cultural value, or if magic use is either celebrated or shunned. In urban fantasies in particular, how the presence of the magic is concealed from the mundane world is often a key concern.

After the presence of magic, the presence of fantastical creatures is another hallmark of fantasy worlds. Often the creatures are inspired by classical myth, such as giants, gorgons, and centaurs; of course, Tolkien's use of orcs, ogres, and dragons helped cement a central place for them in the fantasy genre. In some fantasy worlds, fantastical creatures are capable of rational thought and can speak with humans. In others, they are wild and often a chief danger to civilized society, and there are fictional worlds in which they are both. Fantastical creatures can also be a common part of daily life, or they can be rare, reclusive, or even an endangered species.

In fantasy worlds, the word race is often used interchangeably with species. At a minimum, you must decide how many races/species exist, how the groups interact, and how familiar they are with each other. Failing to distinguish between a race and a species can flatten what should be a more nuanced way of thinking about social relations among humans and non-humans and diminish our vocabulary for discussing potential biases or tensions that exist within each group. For example, if we say a fantasy world has deep racial tensions, does this mean that humans harbor biases against elves and orcs, or does it mean that humans are equally biased against other humans who have different skin color or ethnic backgrounds, or both? Would a human character of a certain race be more apt to trust elves more than humans of another race? No answers are necessarily right or wrong, or better or worse; rather, these are questions that need to be carefully worked through by the group.

A wild, rugged natural world is also common in fantasy worlds. Often large portions of fantasy worlds have not been settled, meaning wild beasts roam forests, jungles, and mountains. Fantasy worlds are often sparsely populated outside of a few major cities or ports. Crude road systems link those outposts of civilization, and the wilderness between them is often unkind to travelers, who are exposed to harsh weather and can expect to be attacked by all manner of feral animals, monsters, and brigands.

Science Fiction Worlds

The genre of science fiction is an umbrella term that covers a number of very different genres, but ones that generally eschew the supernatural in favor of scientific theories and rational thought experiments based on our understanding of the primary world. Thus a franchise like *Star Trek* features equipment such as phasers and teleportation machines whose workings are extrapolated from modern science rather than being explained as being magical or supernatural. Common subgenres of science fiction include space opera, or adventures occurring on a grand scale on distant planets featuring alien species. Military science fiction often takes the theme of deep space exploration and adds elements of combat and military strategies.

Some science fiction subgenres can take place in settings very similar to our primary world, such as those dealing with alien invasion and first contact with alien species. The subgenre of hard science fiction is also very close to our primary world, as this subgenre deals with technological innovations we suspect may be coming to us in the near future, such as self-driving cars, the prevalence of virtual reality environments, or the ubiquity of neural implants. Other science fiction genres that are often intensely concerned with connections to our primary world are apocalyptic and post-apocalyptic fiction, which deal with the destruction of the primary world as we know it and consider how people would go about rebuilding society. Dystopian fiction can either use our primary world or an entirely fictional world as its setting and usually features some form of an oppressive government or other totalitarian system running the society.

The genres of cyberpunk and steampunk are both usually set in our primary world but focus on technology, whether it's digital information technologies in cyberpunk or steam-powered gadgetry in steampunk. Cyberpunk stories tend to be set in vast futuristic metropolises in the near or far future, and steampunk stories frequently occur in the Victorian era in the United Kingdom, though each has spawned a number of subgenres within them. Varieties of cyberpunk include biopunk (dealing with biotechnologies such as genetic manipulation of human beings), nanopunk (dealing with technology operating at the microscopic level) and works dealing with cyborgs or mechanically augmented humans. Varieties of steampunk can be set in environments other than the UK—from the American West to the Far East—and in different time periods, such as clockpunk (Renaissance-era setting), or further into the twentieth century with dieselpunk (from the turn of the century through World War II) and *atompunk* (the Atomic Age of the 1950s and 1960s). The "punk" suffix should not be overlooked. At the core of these subgenres is an implicit critique of hegemonic societal norms, and the plots of stories set in these worlds often revolve around attempts to overturn social and cultural hierarchies.

Aspects of Science Fiction Worlds

Whereas magic tends to be part of the bedrock of much of the fantasy genre, technology is usually a major part of science fiction. One immediate question is how the technology in the fictional world compares to the technology in our primary world. It could be far advanced to what we see today or comparable to what we have today, or it's possible that future technological advancements grew at different rates. For example, microcomputing and biomechanics could be far more advanced than our world, but developments in aeronautics and space exploration could have stagnated or declined.

The reliability of technology is also necessary to consider. While faster-than-light travel is common in science fiction, the hyperdrive that often makes such travel possible can be notoriously fickle, breaking down at the most inopportune times. Cutting-edge technology, no matter how advanced, should always be susceptible to failures and malfunctions. Software programs crash or glitch, robots behave inappropriately, communication devices malfunction, and so forth. Usually, the reliability of a technology relates to how long it has existed. The same questions pertain to less advanced technologies, such as steampunk contraptions or rigged devices pieced together from found materials.

Another factor to consider is technology accessibility and/or availability. Sophisticated tech may exist in a fictional world, but it might also be prohibitively expensive for the average consumer. In plenty of science fiction narratives, particularly in the case of cyberpunk, we see the protagonists having to scrimp or hustle to acquire the necessary components to make their futuristic technology work. It's also common that the most advanced technologies may be the property of secretive government agencies, unscrupulous empires, or amoral corporations. For worlds with scarce resources, such as post-apocalypses, scavenging also becomes a central activity for many characters and items that were once considered junk become newfound treasures.

Reliability and accessibility relate to a general sense of technology familiarity among the populous. The awe of a new technology wears off quickly and soon becomes commonplace. A decade ago, the touchscreen features of most mobile devices would have seemed an improbable marvel, yet today hardly anyone thinks twice about them. Some new technologies might be capable of astonishing characters in fictional worlds, but things the audience finds extraordinary might seem trivial or mundane to a character in the fictional world. A Mars colony seems like a remote possibility to readers in 2017, but perhaps not for a character who lives in a world where three generations of settlers have already lived and died on the planet. Of course, the reverse can also be true, where a piece of technology we find mundane today might seem strange, exotic, or the stuff of lore for characters in worlds unlike ours. For example, a simple calculator would be astonishing for people living in the Middle Ages, and a now-obsolete phonograph could be a wonder for characters living in a distant post-apocalyptic future.

Finally, a technology's emergence must make sense in the context of the world. A new technology doesn't fall from the sky but rather comes into being by specific parties for specific reasons. For example, improvements in interstellar travel could be motivated by an imperialistic government seeking conquest, a cultural desire for connection to other sentient species, a corporation wishing to expand economic trade or some other factor. We also know from the history of our primary world that a technology may begin with one intended use but wind up being used for another, which can add an interesting twist to a fictional world. Along with this, a technology must make sense within the situation of the wider world. For example, a nineteenth-century mobile phone couldn't exist without a whole host of other existent technologies, including networks, microprocessors, and cell towers. This isn't to say that those technologies couldn't exist two centuries ago, but rather it would be logical for other technologies in addition to the mobile phone to have evolved in parallel to it as well.

The presence of non-humans and altered humans raise interesting questions for social relations in science fictional worlds. This includes alien species, genetically modified humans, clones, cyborgs, and robots. The presence of non-humans adds a layer of complexity in terms of privileges or discrimination that might exist in the political and economic systems of the science fictional society. There's the question of how common the non-human entity is in the society, and also whether there are hierarchies within these groups. For example, alien species might have alliances or hold grudges with other species, or one model of sentient robots may resent an earlier version for being inferior.

Worlds Like Ours: Post-apocalypses, Dystopias, and Alternate Histories

Post-apocalypses, dystopias, and alternate histories are often very similar to our primary world with a few significant changes. These subgenres, as well as any subgenre that uses the primary world as its base model, require some additional consideration.

The timeline can get tricky with such fictional worlds. For starters, you need to determine the moment of the world-changing event, for example when the apocalypse happened, when a totalitarian dictator assumed power, or the point when the historical record becomes altered. You also need to think about the distance in time between our current present in the primary world and the present in the fictional world, as well as considering how much time has elapsed in the fictional world since the world-changing event.

Another important factor would be the nature of the world-changing event. For example, it matters whether an apocalypse is the result of nuclear or chemical warfare, a widespread social collapse, a global epidemic of viral disease, or catastrophic natural disasters. Whereas a nuclear war would flatten buildings and irradiate the environment, a chemical attack or biological warfare would leave the infrastructure more or less unharmed. Having said that, modern buildings require constant upkeep to prevent them from falling into ruin. Without regular maintenance, urban environments would become danger zones: buildings can become deathtraps; plant and animal life would soon overtake cities and roads; waters would flood homes and streets; water supplies can become stagnant and poisoned, and food supplies can spoil; sinkholes, live electrical wires, and other structural hazards would all be serious dangers.

Changing fundamental aspects of our primary world would likely have a dramatic impact on the human population too. Post-apocalyptic worlds tend to be severely depopulated due to the cataclysmic event itself claiming lives in an instant, or more slowly as people perish due to starvation or exposure in the wake of the disaster. For dystopias and alternate histories, conditions might differ greatly between different segments of society. The society's elite may be able to shield themselves from many hardships by stockpiling resources, leaving the masses to fight over the scraps. A world with many survivors but scant resources would quickly turn violent as people compete for adequate food and shelter. The level of depopulation will also shape social interactions. In a sparsely populated world, it could be possible not to see another human being for months or years at a time. Running into a random stranger could be a very exciting or very frightening possibility.

Genre-Blending

Genre-blending is the combining of two (or possibly more) genres to create a new world that draws on elements of both. This can produce some unique and exciting results if done with care, but it can also lead to a confusing mess if you're not careful as you need to account for two or more sets of genre-specific factors. Some examples of genre-blending are zombie apocalypses (combination of post-apocalypse and horror), dark fantasy (varieties of fantasy blended with supernatural horror), Weird West (the Western genre with magic, robots, aliens, etc.), post-apocalyptic steampunk (where scavengers craft original devices from pieces of pre-apocalyptic technology), gaslamp fantasy (historical fiction and fantasy), superhero fiction (blending all kinds of fantasy and science fiction), science fantasy (fantasy elements in science fictional world or vice versa) and more.

At its best, genre-blending produces fresh new takes on familiar genres. At its worst, the world becomes a muddled mess or an assemblage of clichés. While it can be fun to explore genre mashups, recognize that some genres blend more easily than others. Making a world by combining high fantasy with cyberpunk would almost certainly be too jarring to pull off; however, a high fantasy steampunk could work (something similar to the Dwemer in the *Elder Scrolls* videogame series) as would a post-apocalyptic high fantasy—think of a medieval world devastated by dragon fire or ruined by marauding demons from an alternate dimension. Many high fantasy settings successfully genre-blend by making use of monsters such as vampires, werewolves, demonic possession, and other elements drawn from dark fantasy.

Other Types of Worlds

Most collaborative worldbuilding projects are entirely new worlds that incorporate some speculative element, but the system is suitable for other purposes as well. One fun approach is to work on a collaborative fanfiction project. In this case, the group would select some preexisting world and choose to add elements to it. This would include any fictional world that exists in any form (or multiple forms) of media, whether it's novels, films, comics, or games. For example, a group might develop the eastern portions of the world in either Tolkien's Middle-earth or Martin's Known World. The eastern sections of their world maps are labeled but audiences know comparatively little about them. For franchises like *Star Wars* and *Star Trek*, groups could build new worlds or whole new galaxies. The same idea applies for the worlds of *Harry Potter*, *The Hunger Games*, the Marvel and DC comic book universes, or popular videogame series such as *Halo*, *Assassin's Creed*, *Fallout*, *Gears of War*, or many others. One of the biggest benefits of working in a preexisting world is that much of the groundwork has already been laid for you. Fan wikis already describe different aspects of the world in great detail, so your group might model your site's aesthetic and catalog templates similar to those used by the fan wiki. Another bonus is that many franchises have licensed role-playing games, which will provide a detailed catalog of people, places, and things that you can use without remaking the proverbial wheel.

Another approach that works especially well in classrooms is building models of literary worlds. This is equivalent to being a very esoteric form of fanfiction but with a more concentrated focus on a literary work. For example, the group could be charged with building a model that accurately represents the world of *The Odyssey*, *Beowulf*, *Hamlet*, *Frankenstein*, *Huckleberry Finn*, or any of Jane Austen's novels set in early nineteenth-century England. These literary world models tend to be tightly focused on the setting of the chosen novel, but collaborative worldbuilding exercises can help readers tease out the impact of different social forces at play in the world. After the group has established the historical and cultural forces at play in the world, they can generate their own characters and have them face challenges similar to those confronting the protagonists. Building historical worlds works in a similar manner, where a group could reconstruct a specific era or time period based on primary sources. Such projects require close reading and attention to detail, and it takes mastery of the material to tell plausible works of historical fiction that attempt to faithfully represent the primary world of the source material.

From Genres to Frameworks

Understanding the conventions of your world's genre is important as you move to establishing the *framework* for your worldbuilding project. Establishing the framework requires you to set some parameters for the creative space you'll be working in, and specific genres lend themselves to different kinds of frameworks. For example, the collapsed infrastructure of post-apocalyptic worlds often limits the possibility of long-distance travel, so these worlds tend to be limited to a single urban environment or region. At the other extreme, if your world allows people to travel at light speed, the expectation is that they will travel to distant corners of the galaxy. While you shouldn't let your choice of genre dictate all the decisions pertaining to your worldbuilding project, it helps to keep the genre in the forefront of your mind as you build the framework for your fictional world.

4

Frameworks of Fictional Worlds

This chapter begins outlining concepts and defining terminology that will be used throughout this book. It is important for the contributors to the worldbuilding project to be familiar with these terms so they can be used effectively to facilitate different steps of the worldbuilding project. This chapter focuses on describing the elements of the *framework* with examples from a number of different types of stories. It also features an extended analysis of the frameworks of J.R.R. Tolkien's Middle-earth, George Lucas's *Star Wars* galaxy, and George R.R. Martin's Known World and continent of Westeros from *A Song of Ice and Fire*. The chapter ends with a transition from the concepts of the framework to those of the *structures* present in the world. The structures must fit within the confines of the established framework in order for the world to be coherent.

Think of establishing the framework as a process of creating boundaries for the creative space so the project doesn't spin out in all directions over space and time. As an analogy, imagine that you're playing a game of soccer with a dozen friends in a park. In order for the game to function, the players need to agree to the boundaries of play and what constitutes the sidelines and goals. If more players join, you can lengthen or widen the field to make space to accommodate them, or if players leave you can condense the field of play. Establishing a framework for a collaborative worldbuilding project works in a similar way. You're defining an area that can grow or shrink depending on what works for the project and the current number of contributors, but before you can do anything the group must agree on the boundaries of your imaginary world.

The framework consists of three core concepts: *scope*, which includes the entirety of the world's physical space; *sequence*, or the entirety of the world's past and present, and some possible future(s) on a timeline; and *perspective*, or the point of view from which information about the world is communicated to the intended audience. These concepts provide clear boundaries so you can pick a specific place in a specific moment in time and a specific viewpoint(s) from which you may begin your project. This chapter concludes with extended examples from Middle-earth, the *Star Wars* galaxy, *A Song of Ice and Fire*, and *Dungeons & Dragons* that explain how scope, sequence, and perspective help define the space of these large fictional worlds.

Scope

How big does your fictional world need to be? Like most creative writing advice, the answer is: it depends. There are two aspects to scope: *breadth* and *depth*. *Breadth* is the physical extent of your world or the space that lies within in its borders. A fictional world's breadth may span a galaxy, a planet, a country, a region, or could be as condensed as a single metropolis. *Depth* relates to the level of detail that describes the fictional space. Some locations are inherently more interesting, more complex, or more central to the action of the world, whereas other areas may not demand the same level of elaboration. *Focal points* are specific locations that have the greatest depth of detail and function as "worlds within the world." Focal points can operate at many different levels within the world's scope. For example, focal points could be the most significant planets in a galaxy, the most important cities on a continent, or the most diverse neighborhoods in a metropolis.

Striking the right balance between breadth and depth is essential for a successful worldbuilding project. It's easy to create an enormous, sprawling universe with too little depth where every location feels the same and is overly simplistic. On the other hand, it's equally easy to get lost in describing the minutiae of daily life without thinking through how it might ever be relevant to the rest of the world. Happily, fictional worlds come in all shapes and sizes, and that includes different breadths and depths as well. The key is being intentional from the onset about setting up your world's boundaries and committing to filling that space with interesting material.

Some worlds might have a narrow breadth but feature deeply detailed focal points. One example of this is China Miéville's extraordinary 700-page novel *Perdido Street Station*. The novel takes place almost entirely in the sprawling city of New Crobuzon. The city holds numerous districts, each one of them its own focal point, and the novel's plot often details with situations where radically different species come in contact with each other in the confines of the densely populated metropolis. The world of New Crobuzon is so deep and rich there's no need to explore other parts of the continent, which he does in both *The Scar* and

Iron Council, both of which are set in the same world. Scott Lynch's *The Lies of Locke Lamora* works in a similar fashion, where the 500-page book takes places in the city of Camorr, which is modeled after medieval Venice and has many colorful districts and landmarks. Mervyn Peake goes even narrower in his 500-page book *Titus Groan,* which takes place in a single labyrinthine castle. In all of these books, the breadth of the wider world gets a brief mention while the majority of the deep descriptive worldbuilding happens within a smaller physical area. Within that area multiple focal points—the worlds within worlds—that play by different rules separate from the rest of the society. For Miéville and Lynch, the focal points are different locations within a large city, whereas for Peake they are rooms and wings of an enormous castle. In all cases, these locations are fleshed out to the extent that they feel more like fully developed characters than places, with each focal point exuding its own characteristics and personality.

Massive universes like that of *Star Trek* work in the opposite direction—the breadth, or physical space, of the fictional world is far greater and spans whole galaxies. In *Star Trek* and other space travel series, specific locations generally have a far shallower depth of detail. Entire planets are often boiled down to a single focal point and are represented by a single alien species or single culture. Given the fictional world's enormous breadth, characters rarely dwell too long in one location as part of the appeal of *Star Trek* and likeminded narratives is exploration and how the characters are always encountering something new and noteworthy on their travels. *Star Trek's* ship, the U.S.S. *Enterprise,* serves as its own focal point where we get an enormous depth of detail. The ship effectively acts as a portable world that comes into contact with a variety of other worlds. While exploring large universes like this can be exhilarating, worldbuilders should be wary of the tendency to collapse an exotic species or society into a single, simplistic hegemonic group.

A third type of world splits the difference between a narrow fictional world (e.g., a metropolis) and the expansive one (e.g., a universe) by presenting a world that's roughly the size of a continent in our primary world. The fictional land mass usually has several distinct regions and each region has a few well-developed focal points. The broader details of worlds of this sort are often revealed over time in different storytelling episodes, in which characters are compelled to travel across the map. This allows them to experience diverse cultures and reflect on the differences between the places they've seen. Tolkien is the obvious example, but others include Mid-World of Stephen King's *Dark Tower,* where the protagonist Roland Deschain travels to different regions across different books in the series. The readers gradually learn of locations such as the post-apocalyptic city of Lud, the village of Hambry in the region of Mejis, the capital city of Gilead, and so on. Others series that have similar structures include J.K. Rowling's *Harry Potter* and Ursula LeGuin's *Earthsea*, where the breadth and depth of the world increase over time. This can be a very effective way to develop a worldbuilding project, where the group agrees to develop a handful of focal points in one region to start with and, once these locations reach critical mass, they later expand outward and begin working on a new region.

Broad and shallow, narrow and deep, or somewhere in-between? No strategy for determining the scope is necessarily better than the others. Rather, the scope of the fictional world needs to support the types of stories the author wishes to tell and the type of creating the contributors are most interested in. Using the strategies in this book will help you establish the best scope for your worldbuilding project and help you sidestep the most common pitfalls when it comes to building large-scale fictional worlds.

Sequence

Stories happen in time. The concept of "today" presumes the existence of both yesterday and tomorrow. Time moves inexorably forward as today morphs into yesterday, then becomes a day last week, then into an anonymous day last year. Worldbuilding requires fixing your world in a given point in time, which places it in a *sequence* of events. In the story of your world, there are events in the world that happened in the past, events that are currently happening, and events that seem likely to happen in the future.

Imagine a *timeline* of your favorite story as a series of moments that proceed from left to right in time, from the beginning of the story to its end. If we followed the imaginary timeline to the left past the beginning of the story, we would pass the birth of the characters and head toward ancient history and the beginning of all time; if we followed the timeline to the right, we'd travel beyond the story's conclusion and the eventual deaths of the protagonists as we head forward into an unknown future. Collaborative worldbuilders must contemplate not only how their world works in the present, but how it came to be, and to consider different directions in which it may be heading in the future.

When beginning a worldbuilding project, it helps to determine some functional start and end points in the timeline called *termination points*. The distance between these termination points constitutes the length of your worldbuilding timeline. That length could span decades, centuries, or millennia. The leftmost marker represents the last relevant point in the past; the rightmost marker indicates what's known about the future. Imagine vertical markers along this length, where each marker represents a *historical event* of major significance. Historical events could be anything from the discovery of the wheel, to the spread of the bubonic plague, to the entirety of the Thirty Years War. Milestone historical events can be spread out along the timeline at intervals or clustered around events of primary significance in times of great change. The last consideration for the timeline is establishing the *point of the present*, or the default "now" of the worldbuilding project. Usually, this will be very close or aligned with the termination point on the far right of your line. The characters in your world won't know for certain what will happen in the future, and neither should the creators—at least not with any certainty.

Establishing a commonly agreed upon sequence of events is essential for a collaborative worldbuilding project. All the collaborators should have a solid sense of the major historical events in the timeline and the temporal distance between them. This keeps everyone working toward a common goal and developing the same time period, and thus increases the likelihood of finding connections between people's individual creations.

Perspective

Perhaps the least obvious aspect of worldbuilding is that of perspective, especially because it is such a slippery issue even in traditional forms of fiction writing.[1] An inattentive reader can easily mistake the protagonist for the narrator, confusing who is telling the story versus who is a participant in it. Sometimes the narrator and protagonist are the same person, but often they are not. At the most basic level, the three options for telling a story are *first person* (I walked to the store), the less common *second person* (you walked to the store), and *third person* (she walked to the store). There is also the question of narrative distance between the narrator, the world, and the characters who inhabit it. An omniscient narrator knows every thought and emotion of every character in the world (i.e., a godlike viewpoint), whereas a third-person limited perspective, also known as a close third, only provides information from a single character's point of view. Storytellers have employed to all kinds of various narrative techniques and tricks, such as the opinionated unreliable narrator, with Chief from Ken

Kesey's *One Flew Over the Cuckoo's Nest* being one notable example of many. Another is the near-omniscient narrator of Cormac McCarthy's *Blood Meridian* who dispassionately describes gruesome acts of violence without judgment.

For a collaborative worldbuilding project, the easiest strategy is to adopt something similar to Wikipedia's style, which their site refers to as a *neutral point of view* (NPOV). Wikipedia strives to maintain an objective, third-person viewpoint that they describe as "representing fairly, proportionately, and, as far as possible, without editorial bias, all of the significant views that have been published by reliable sources on a topic."[2] Most worldbuilding projects use some variation of the third-person near-omniscient perspective—that is, a disembodied narrator who ostensibly knows everything about everything that's important. Both Wikipedia and collaborative worldbuilding projects rely on contributors to do their honest best to fairly represent a wide range of viewpoints without passing judgment upon them.

As with many aspects of worldbuilding, there is no definitive right or wrong way to choose a perspective for your project. The most important part is that the group makes an intentional choice and that everyone agrees to adopt this as the style. Reviewing Wikipedia pages can also be useful in terms of understanding how knowledge of a given topic is collaboratively constructed and multiple viewpoints presented. For example, at the time of writing, the Wikipedia page for World War II[3] has been edited over 24,000 times by 7,600 authors and maintains an air of objectivity about the major events of the conflict. This sense of objectivity is reached by acknowledging different perspectives. For example, the page on "Causes of World War II" begins with a qualified statement:

> Some long-term causes of World War II appear in the conditions preceding World War I – historians may see these as common causes for both World Wars. Supporters of this view paraphrase Carl von Clausewitz, seeing World War II as a continuation of World War I by the same means. In fact, World Wars had been expected before Benito Mussolini and Adolf Hitler came to power and Japan invaded China.[4]

These opening statements soften what could be construed as hard, inarguable truths. Phrases such as "some long-term causes" (not necessarily all long-term causes), and "supporters of this view" (suggesting there are others who oppose this view) qualify the statement. The writers of the wiki entry do not need to delve into other causes or extrapolate on alternatives, but the inclusion of qualifiers open up space for the possibility of other perspectives and more deeply nuanced discussions of the topic. Those competing viewpoints and perspectives can be a rich vein of storytelling potential for characters committed to forwarding counter-narratives from the "official" recorded history.

Example Frameworks of Fictional Worlds

It helps demystify the framework if you keep the concepts of *scope, sequence,* and *perspective* in mind when you're reading books, watching movies, or playing story-driven games. Think about how the creators establish the framework for the narrative—the world's breadth and depth that define the scope, the sequence of historical events referenced by characters, and from whose perspective you come to learn about the world. The below examples come from some of the most popular fictional worlds of the last century in Tolkien's Middle-earth, Lucas's *Star Wars* galaxy, and Martin's Westeros and the Known World from *A Song of Ice and Fire*. Each of these works serves as an example of how the concepts of scope and sequence show up in the stories told in those worlds. For perspective, the different viewpoint characters in these works help us see the world through different eyes, but an even better example for worldbuilding purposes come from *Dungeons and Dragons* role-playing game books, where information about the fictional world is presented in different styles with different effects.

The Scope of Middle-earth

The initial breadth of Middle-earth literally couldn't be any bigger, as the first portion of *The Silmarillion* describes the creation of the universe and everything in it.[5] However, after only a few pages, that enormity is narrowed down from all existence to a single planet called Arda. Once we reach the stories of the people who live on Arda, the scope has narrowed again to focus on a specific region, that being the northwest portion of the continent known as Middle-earth. So while the initial scope of Tolkien's work is an entire universe, for all intents and purposes, the breadth of his fictional world (i.e., its physical space) across his body of work winds up being no bigger than a large continent.

Most of the events of the First Age of Middle-earth as described in *The Silmarillion* occur in the westernmost portion of the continent, in a region known as Beleriand. The stories cycle between a number of focal points, including: the realm of Doriath and its subterranean fortress of Menegroth ruled by King Thingol; the broad plain of Dor-Lómin overseen by Fingolfin and his son Fingon; the hidden mountain stronghold of Gondolin governed by King

Turgon; the riverside caves of Nargothrond ruled by Finrod Felagund; and then the dwelling of Morgoth, Middle-earth's antagonist, who establishes himself in the Iron Mountains to the far north with the twin dungeon fortresses of Utumno and Thangorodrim. Other broader geographic features such as mountain ranges, major rivers, and the plains where the battles played out also serve important functions in the narrative.

Where Tolkien truly distinguished himself as a worldbuilder is less for the breadth of his world and more for the tremendous depth of detail he provides about it. *The Silmarillion* provides a dizzying array of characters and locations, many of which go by more than one name. It becomes a serious challenge for the first-time reader to keep them all straight. Each of the focal points acts as a unique world within the wider world of Beleriand. The local cultures of the elvish kingdoms are shaped by both their environments—for example, whether they were situated in the mountains, deep in the forest, or along coastlines—as well as the temperaments of their leaders. Some family sagas revolved around specific focal points while others like the tale of Beren and Lúthien, which is one of the longest and most important stories in Tolkien's fictional universe, follows the couple as they travel through several of the world's most important locations on their quest to be united in marriage.

The wars at the conclusion of the First Age are of such magnitude that they literally break the earth and send the entire region of Beleriand crashing to the bottom of the sea. In fact, the far western coast that Frodo travels to in *The Lord of the Rings* corresponds to what was the far eastern portion of Beleriand, and the events of *The Hobbit* and *The Lord of the Rings* are set in what's left of Middle-earth. *The Hobbit* follows Bilbo on his travels from the northwest of Middle-earth almost due east across the width of the continent.[6] In *The Lord of the Rings*, the journey of Frodo and the fellowship tracks east and southeast, beginning again in the Shire in the northwest but bending down to Mordor in the southeastern corner of the continent.[7] The two novels share some focal points but also introduce completely new ones as well. What follows is a list of focal points and sublocations within them as described in *The Hobbit* and *The Lord of the Rings*.

The story of *The Hobbit* begins in 1) the Shire, which is the novel's first focal point, and then follows the party of Bilbo and the dwarves as they travel along the Great East Road to 2) the elven kingdom of Rivendell. From there, they make several unscheduled stops, including in 3) Goblin-town beneath the Misty Mountains, 4) at the hall of the skin-changer Beorn, a side adventure in 5) the enchanted forest of Mirkwood, and then suffer imprisonment in 6) the elvish king Thranduil's Woodland Realm. After a daring escape, they next arrive in

7) the human settlements of Lake-Town and Dale before reaching their final destination, 8) the dwarvish ancestral home of Erebor, the Lonely Mountain. The characters spend a chapter or more in each focal point location, which allows Tolkien ample time to flesh out each place with specific details that differentiate the races and their customs, details that the sheltered Bilbo always finds curious and remarkable. Much of the wonder in the book derives from Bilbo coming into contact with worlds that differ from his home in the Shire and his remarks on the contrasts.

The Lord of the Rings covers more ground than *The Hobbit*, both in the length and detail of the narrative but also in terms of the distances traveled by the characters. The characters visit more focal points on the map and more information is given for each location. Like *The Hobbit*, *The Lord of the Rings* begins in 1) the Shire but it contains a prologue that delves into much deeper detail about the regional differences between hobbits and their local communities. As in *The Hobbit*, the party heads off for Rivendell but they are waylaid in 2) the Old Forest, the first focal point outside the Shire. There they meet the mysterious Tom Bombadil and have a harrowing encounter with wights in the barrow-downs. As the party continues east, they arrive in 3) Bree-land, a cluster of four villages where hobbits and men mingle—another focal point that represents a "world next door" that is similar but somewhat different from the Shire. The group eventually passes through the wilderness to arrive at 4) Rivendell. The characters dwell here for weeks, and the nature of the kingdom and its inhabitants are described in much greater detail than they are in *The Hobbit*.

Before long the group takes to the road once more and they arrive at a number of other focal points. They travel south through 5) the Misty Mountains and 6) the abandoned dwarven kingdom of Khazad-dûm, also known as Moria. The party passes through the mountain to the kingdom of 7) Lothlórien, which is described as being much older than Rivendell and, in contrast, feels much more foreign for the travelers. The group is sundered shortly afterward, sending the characters wide and far across Middle-earth, including visits to 8) the horse lord's kingdom of Rohan, with major events occurring in locations of the throne room in Edoras and in the fortress of Helm's Deep. Another group continues to 9) Gondor, the largest kingdom of Man, and its two primary cities Osgiliath and Minas Tirith. Readers also get to see the wizard Saruman's 10) realm of Isengard and his Tower of Orthanc; the ominous 11) Fangorn Forest, home to the tree people named Ents; and of course the hellish terrain on the road to 12) Mordor that includes trips through locations of the Dead Marshes, the pass of Cirith Ungol, and the slopes of Mount Doom itself.

What makes Tolkien's fictional project noteworthy is the depth of the cultures of this world and how they connect to specific points in his world's timeline. Each of the major regions—the Shire, the Misty Mountains, the two elvish kingdoms, the two kingdoms of Men, and the realm of Sauron—contain multiple focal points that the protagonists pass through on their journey. These handfuls of focal points and sublocations allowed Tolkien to differentiate between the peoples and their cultures.

The Scope of *Star Wars*

A long time ago in a galaxy far, far away . . .

The famous opening scrawl of the *Star Wars* establishes the breadth of this imaginary world: it's a galaxy.[8] The *Star Wars* galaxy operates very differently than Tolkien's fictional universe. As we've seen, Tolkien begins his cosmology with the creation of the universe, but he quickly narrows the breadth down to the continent of Middle-earth. What Tolkien sacrifices in the breadth of physical space, however, he makes up for in depth of detail. *Star Wars* is the exact opposite. Instead of going for depth, this world is all about breadth. The allure of the *Star Wars* galaxy has to do with the vast expanse of space and the diversity of worlds, species, and cultures that it contains.

The original three films (released as *Star Wars*, *The Empire Strikes Back*, and *Return of the Jedi*)[9] have surprisingly few focal points. Consider the limited number of locations the characters visit in this seemingly expansive galaxy, and how few sublocations there are in each: 1) the desert planet of Tatooine has the Lars homestead, the palace of Jabba the Hutt, and the spaceport Mos Eisley, the dwelling of Obi-Wan Kenobi and the rolling Sandcrawler of the Jawas; 2) the ice planet of Hoth has the Rebellion's Echo Base, the wampa's cave, and endless snowfields; 3) the world of Dagobah only has Yoda's hut, caves, and unbroken swampland; 4) the gas giant Bespin has the floating metropolis of Cloud City; 5) the moon of Endor has the Ewok village, an imperial base, and forests. Then there are the mobile locations of 6–7) the first and second Death Stars, 8) the spaceships the Millennium Falcon, and 9) Darth Vader's Super Star Destroyer, the *Executor*. None of these focal points or their locations are fleshed out in any great detail and questions about them abound. How exactly do the economies of Tatooine or Cloud City work, for example? How many different Ewok tribes are there on Endor, and do they all get along? The films never address such questions because they reside outside the main thrust of the storyline dealing with the saga of the Skywalkers. Yet despite this seeming shallowness, the original *Star Wars* trilogy still managed to enthrall millions of people worldwide and create the illusion of a sprawling detailed universe. How?

Star Wars succeeded because it worked off the free association of our imaginations. The iconic cantina scene in *Star Wars* provides the clearest example of how a dingy pocket of the galaxy can suddenly expand into limitless possibilities. At the point of this scene, about 45 minutes into the two-hour film, the story has centered on the conflict between the forces of good (the Rebellion) and evil (the Empire) or the Tatooine settlers (Luke's family, Obi-Wan) with the environment (the harsh desert, Tuskan Raiders) without much nuance. The cantina in the spaceport scene explodes these binary oppositions by presenting dozens of new and diverse species drinking, talking, and listening to music. The implication is that all of these creatures originated somewhere other than this desert backwater. In a matter of a few minutes, the audience glimpses a side of the galaxy full of smugglers, bounty hunters, and ne'er-do-wells who have little interest in galactic politics. So while the audience gets little depth of information about the world—no species are identified by name in the cantina, for example— the sheer breadth of possibilities invites us to fill in that void with our own imaginations. In this way, *Star Wars* alludes to breadth and depth of the galaxy without derailing the tightly plotted storyline of the original trilogy of films.

Sequence in *Star Wars*

It is a period of civil war. Rebel spaceships, striking from a hidden base, have won their first victory against the evil Galactic Empire.

During the battle, Rebel spies managed to steal secret plans to the Empire's ultimate weapon, the Death Star, an armored space station with enough power to destroy an entire planet.

Pursued by the Empire's sinister agents, Princess Leia races home aboard her starship, custodian of the stolen plans that can save her people and restore freedom to the galaxy . . .[10]

An enormous spaceship pursues a much smaller one, blasting it into submission with laser fire before overtaking it, boarding it, and subduing the crew. An imposing figure clad in black armor accuses a young princess of being a traitor and part of a rebel alliance, a charge she denies. Two droids carrying top secret plans evacuate the ship in an escape pod, crash land on a desert planet, and come into the possession of a moisture farmer and his nephew. The smaller droid sneaks away from the farmer's settlement, but the nephew tracks him down and, in doing so, meets an old hermit who lives in the hills. The hermit reveals that he was once a member of an ancient order who fought alongside the young man's father and describes times long before the Empire ruled the galaxy.

Of course, that is a very brief overview of the first third of *Star Wars: Episode* IV – *A New Hope*, but even that scant synopsis provides enough detail to sketch out a broad *sequence* of some of the galaxy's most relevant *historical events*. Even the opening scrawl marks some significant events both explicitly (tells the audience of the rebels' first victory) while implying others (there must have been some recent breakdown of a political system in order for a civil war to have erupted). The conversation between Luke Skywalker and Obi-Wan Kenobi brings up several other major historical events as well, such as Kenobi stating he fought in a conflict known as the Clone Wars. A moment later he extends the galaxy's *timeline* even further into the past, explaining that "For over a thousand generations, the Jedi Knights were the guardians of peace and justice in the Old Republic, before the dark times. Before the Empire."

This short conversation a mere 30 minutes into the film gives us most of the information we need to construct a rough timeline that encompasses the majority of stories told in the *Star Wars* universe. A diagram using terminology used for a collaborative worldbuilding project would look like Figure 4.1.

Everything we need to know about the history of the galaxy is bookended by two *termination points*: the Old Republic of the distant past (left termination

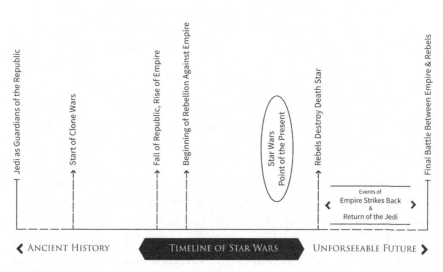

Figure 4.1 Timeline for *Star Wars*

point in the past), and a future that will see an inevitable final showdown between the Rebel Alliances and the Empire (right termination point in the near future). Major historical events include the collapse of the Old Republic, the rise of the Empire, and the beginning of the rebellion. The *point of the present* is around the time the rebels discover the plans for the Death Star.

Moving up or down this timeline allows for adding new details to the history of the *Star Wars* galaxy. Sliding right on the *Star Wars* timeline, we'd be in the historical period of *The Empire Strikes Back* and *Return of the Jedi*; if we push out the right termination point 30 to 40 more years into the future we'd be bumping into the galaxy at the time of *The Force Awakens* and *The Last Jedi*. Sliding left on the timeline we'd encounter the galaxy's history during the time of the prequel trilogy, *The Phantom Menace*, *Attack of the Clones*, and *Revenge of the Sith*. Any point of the timeline can support deep dives in terms of fleshing out the details. For example, all 121 episodes in the *Star Wars: The Clone Wars* animated television series take place in the three-year period between the prequel films *Attack of the Clones* and *Revenge of the Sith*, and the animated series *Star Wars Rebels* was set just after this, between *Revenge of the Sith* and *Star Wars: Episode* IV – *A New Hope*. Dozens of comics, novels, and games have delved into other time periods along the timeline, each adding new characters, planets, technologies, and historical events. It's an example of how a broad timeline can focus on a certain period to begin worldbuilding, but it can also support plenty of other stories that happened in the past or will happen in the future.

Sequence in *A Song of Ice and Fire*

A Game of Thrones, the first novel in George R.R. Martin's *A Song of Ice and Fire* series, is set in a time between a distant mythic past and an impending civil war.[11] The point of the present in *A Game of Thrones* is set 17 years after an earlier civil war, known as both Robert's Rebellion or the War of the Usurper depending upon how people feel about it. It was a coup that put Robert Baratheon on the throne of a continent named Westeros. As king, Baratheon rules over the Seven Kingdoms of the continent, but finds himself constantly embattled and embroiled in political intrigues. Unbeknownst to him and most everyone else, in the northernmost region of the continent, an undead army of White Walkers grows in strength and threatens to move southward and overrun Westeros. Blind to this danger, internal power struggles rage as various political actors plot the downfall of King Baratheon. To further complicate matters, across the sea on another continent, a brother and sister of the ruling family deposed by Baratheon seek to ally themselves with an army of fearsome barbarians in hopes of invading Westeros and winning back the throne.

A simplified timeline of the sequence gleaned from the first half of *A Game of Thrones* might look something like Figure 4.2.

Everything we know about the *A Song of Ice and Fire* series happens between the bookends of the founding of the kingdoms of Westeros and the climactic conclusion with the White Walkers. The point of the present for *A Game of Thrones* is just after event 4, the death of Jon Arryn, which is the catalyst for the subsequent events that shape the novel. The other novels in the series fill in the gap between this point of the present and the right termination point. The encyclopedic book *The World of Ice and Fire* works in the opposite direction, filling in details from the point of the present in *A Game of Thrones* to the left termination point, filling in dozens of milestone events relevant to each of the Seven Kingdoms, as well as providing more information on faraway lands rarely mentioned in the series.[12] As with *Star Wars*, this timeline allows the author to dip into other time periods and tell stories that have the same geographical setting but operate under different political and social conditions, like Martin's collection of novellas *The Hedge Knight*, which tells the stories of Ser Duncan the Tall set nearly a century before the events of *A Game of Thrones*, and the cable network HBO is already planning several spin-off series once the main series concludes.[13]

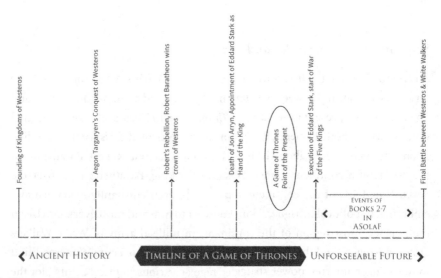

Figure 4.2 Timeline for *A Game of Thrones*

Perspective in Large-Scale Narratives and *Dungeons & Dragons*

Audiences usually learn about imaginary worlds through stories, and this means that information about the world is being filtered through some narrative perspective. This can be a *first-person* account delivered by a character experiencing the action as it happens, or in the *third-person* through a more distant, near-omniscient narrator who has no direct role in the narrative beyond relaying the story. Another option is providing information about the world through several limited third-person viewpoints that rotate between a few primary characters. For audiences who are not used to analyzing narratives, the question of who is narrating the story and how the narrator influences our understanding of a fictional world might be overlooked entirely. Pulling apart the question of narrative perspective can also be surprisingly complex.

For example, it often escapes fans' attention that the texts of *The Silmarillion*, *The Hobbit*, and *The Lord of the Rings* are in fact the handiwork of Bilbo and Frodo Baggins as recorded in the "Red Book of Westmarch."[14] The events in Tolkien's novels are intended to be the products of the hobbits' personal recollections and those of their traveling companions as they reconstruct historical events, penning them in a third-person perspective. This conveniently explains some gaps and omissions in the texts. For example, some stories in *The Silmarillion* receive cursory treatment not because they aren't important, but rather because Bilbo hadn't gotten around to asking the elves in Rivendell about them. It also explains why *The Silmarillion* provides a coherent history of the elves but the origins and details of the other races are less fleshed out. Thus everything we know about Middle-earth in these novels comes from inside the story, filtered through the limited third-person point of view from the hobbits.

Star Wars has no such fictional framing device. In the films, there is no narrator, and the audience learns about the galaxy through the actions of the story's characters in different scenes shown from a distant, impersonal third-person perspective. Even so, the information audiences receive about the world is still highly partisan. The rebels are depicted as the "good guys" and the Empire is unequivocally evil: Darth Vader and Emperor Palpatine are ruthless, the commanders of the Imperial Navy are arrogant and quarrelsome, and stormtroopers carry out immoral commands without hesitation. Since Disney acquired the *Star Wars* property in 2014,[15] the franchise is eager to present the Star Wars galaxy from a variety of different and often competing perspectives. For example, *The Force Awakens* features Finn, a protagonist who is a former Stormtrooper and whose sense of morality causes him to defect to the Resistance.

This theme of moral decision making is continued in books for younger readers such as *Lost Stars* and the *Servants of the Empire*, which depict good-hearted characters who find themselves working for the Empire but grow to question its totalitarian practices. The novel *Dark Disciple* likewise chips away at the moral righteousness of the Jedi Order. The collection *From a Certain Point of View* is an exercise in different perspectives, featuring 40 stories about major events in the original *Star Wars* film as told from the viewpoints of background characters. These new perspectives make the *Star Wars* galaxy a more nuanced and complex fictional world.

A Song of Ice and Fire foregrounds the subjective experience of the world in a more explicit manner, in that the chapters of each novel are told from a different character's perspective. Though the broad narrative paints characters in more or less favorable lights—Eddard Stark is a man committed to high moral values whereas Cersei Lannister is a schemer and backstabber—the narrative perspective of switching viewpoints shows how political intrigues and individual worldviews frame each characters' actions. These rotating perspectives serve to explain, without necessarily justifying, certain decisions. In this manner, Cersei and the other Lannisters are less agents of pure evil, but rather self-interested political actors operating in a ruthless world, where coldblooded murder is often regarded as an understandable act of self-preservation. Even *The World of Ice and Fire*, the encyclopedic history of the Known World, isn't an objective tome but rather written from the subjective viewpoint of the character of Maester Yandel, a scholar writing the manuscript for the benefit of another character, the King Tommen Baratheon. In the world of *A Song of Ice and Fire*, any notion of a singular universal truth is dispelled, replaced by sets of culturally constructed values that change from place to place and from person to person.

However, Tolkien, Lucas, and Martin did not begin their massive worldbuilding projects by creating catalogs meant for public readership. For the purposes of contributors to a collaborative worldbuilding project, a more applicable model is *Dungeons & Dragons*. The game's rulebooks and sourcebooks are not about storytelling as much as they are about providing material for players to create their own storytelling experiences. Players may design their own unique worlds from scratch, or they may use worlds that are part of the publisher's official campaign settings. In either case, information about the fictional worlds of *Dungeons & Dragons* (or any role-playing game) can be relayed via a variety of perspectives.

Consider the three introductions below to the world of Abeir-Toril from the *Forgotten Realms* campaign setting. The first example is an NPOV perspective from a fan-created Wikipedia page that describes the world from outside the fictional world. The second example comes from the official sourcebook *The Sword Coast Adventurer's Guide*, where the description originates from inside the fictional world and is more subjective in tone. Finally, the third example comes from "Volo's Guide to the Forgotten Realms," a booklet included with the book *Dungeonology*, and is comical in its subjective perspective.

First, the Wikipedia page's NPOV perspective is purely factual. It makes no subjective judgments, recognizes Abeir-Toril's fictionality, and gives attribution to its creators, who are not fictional characters but rather game designers who live in our primary world:

> Abeir-Toril (or commonly referred to as Toril) is the name of the fictional planet that makes up the *Forgotten Realms Dungeons & Dragons* campaign setting, as well as the Al-Qadim and Maztica campaign settings and the 1st edition version of the Oriental Adventures campaign setting.
>
> The name is archaic, meaning "cradle of life." It consists of various continents and islands, including Faerûn, Kara-Tur, Zakhara, Maztica, Osse, Anchorome and Katashaka, a sub-Saharan-like continent south of Maztica, where humanity appeared. Toril was originally the name of Jeff Grubb's personal campaign world before it was merged with Ed Greenwood's Forgotten Realms setting.[16]

Next the *Sword Coast Adventurer's Guide* Chapter 1, "Welcome to the Realms," adds some poetic flair and appears to be written by a narrator from inside the world itself. Its style is NPOV with an added literary flourish to prevent it from being too dry. There is no sense that the world is a fictional construct within this description:

> On the world of Toril, between the windswept Sea of Swords to the west and the mysterious lands of Kara-Tur to the east, lies the continent of Faerun. A place of varied cultures and races, Faerun is dominated by human lands, be they kingdoms, city-states, or carefully maintained alliances of rural communities. Interspersed along the lands of humans are old dwarven kingdoms and hidden elven enclaves, assimilated populations of gnomes and halflings, and more exotic folk.[17]

Finally, the third example is from the opening paragraphs of "Volo's Guide" written by a fictional character named Volothamp Geddarm who lives in the world of *Forgotten Realms*. The entry emphasizes his colorful and theatrical personality:

> Welcome, friends, to this bonus volume of mine, "Volo's Guide to the Forgotten Realms." Herein, I give you an overview of this world that we call home: Toril.

Of course, it would be impossible to fit everything about an entire world inside a library, much less a single book. I have dedicated my life to exploring these beloved lands, and I have endeavored to record the most vital, pertinent, and—dare I say—exciting details for the edification of fine people like yourself.[18]

The narrative tone and style of each of these perspectives carry through to descriptions of people, places, and things in the fictional world. Wikipedia and similar fan wikis maintain the NPOV perspective and a keep a clear division between our primary world and the fictional world of Toril. The *Sword Coast Adventurer's Guide* collapses the narrative distance so the information is always coming entirely from inside the world, even if the narrator of the information isn't identified. Finally, "Volo's Guide" is an unapologetically personal description of the world from someone who lives in it. No perspective is inherently better or worse than another. The perspective chosen should be whatever works best for the creative project and its intended audience, and creators should consider the benefits and challenges of these different types of perspectives.

From Framework to Structures

The framework sets up clear boundaries for your worldbuilding project and constrains it to a specific space and time. The scope should put some realistic limits on the size of your world in terms of its *breadth* (its physical size), its *depth* (the level of detail involved), and the number of *focal points* (those locations and sublocations that receive the greatest amount of detail). The *sequence* helps you understand how the world got to be the way it is via significant *historical events*, as well as what it's like now at the *point of the present*, as well as providing some logical trajectories for how it might evolve in the future. The *perspective* should make clear whether an audience is getting information about the world from a *neutral point of view* (NPOV) or from some more opinionated, subjective position. As your worldbuilding project develops, each part of the framework can be adjusted—you can widen the scope, add more focal points, move up or down the timeline, or switch perspectives. The key is that all collaborators understand the framework and agree to work within those guidelines.

The world's structures—how the world operates in the realms of *governance, economics, social relations,* and *cultural influences*—sit entirely within this established framework and are intimately connected to it. A world's structures are fluid and depend on the framework to be rigid. As we've seen in the examples from *Star Wars* and *A Song of Ice and Fire*, moving forward or backward along the timeline will almost always result in different political and social situations. Beyond this, we have ample evidence from the primary world that the cultures of most nations vary from north to south and east to west, and it's common sense to understand that the primary world of 1818 was very different from that of 1918 and different again in 2018. It should be no different in your collaborative worldbuilding project, where the political and social forces will shift when you switch between focal points or move up or down the timeline. A solid, well-established framework will keep your world coherent, consistent, and on track as your group develops the various structures that will add diversity and complexity to your imaginary world.

5

Structures and Substructures of Fictional Worlds

As you read in the last chapter, establishing the *framework* is about setting up boundaries for the worldbuilding project. It is a process of agreeing to build a world within a given space during a specific time span and from a consistent perspective. The next step, developing the *structures*, is the process of describing the different social forces at play in the world. One of the most glaring mistakes beginning writers make is to limit their focus to a single aspect of the world without fully considering all the other interrelated parts. In reality, all strands of the social fabric are connected. We know that precarious economic conditions and extreme stratification of wealth can lay the groundwork for social unrest; state-sanctioned persecution of certain social groups can spark a popular revolution; if the government is run by a religious autocracy, the values outlined in sacred texts would be present in the society's governing documents and would dictate how wealth is distributed. While some social aspects of the world will be more prominent than others, none are irrelevant even if their impact isn't as keenly felt. Most importantly, a change to any one aspect of the society will have a ripple effect through the others. Worlds are always in flux, constantly in a state of becoming something different as they are dragged forward in time.

Collaborative worldbuilding projects use four *structural categories* and fourteen *substructures* within those categories to provide scaffolding for describing the social forces at work within a world. The structures can be used to model a variety of worlds, from ancient Athens to contemporary Tokyo, to an imaginary world like Emerald City from *The Wizard of Oz*. Collaborative worldbuilding relies heavily on working through the intricacies of the world's structures. The key for worldbuilders is taking the time to account for all 14 substructures within the world in a thorough and deliberate way.

Think of each of these substructures as being on a hypothetical scale, where evidence of the substructure in the world can range from being virtually nonexistent at one end of the spectrum and abundant on the other. These substructure values are not intended to be value judgments—for example, a world that has scarce natural resources or is marked by an overwhelming military influence is neither inherently good or bad—but rather reflect the broad, generally accepted truths about the state of a fictional world.

Red Dawn

Governance

Governance includes the political rules that exert some measure of control over members of a society. In order to function as a society, individuals must cede some of their personal freedoms in exchange for greater social good and the protection of other rights. Debating the merits of various tradeoffs between personal freedoms and greater social welfare has kept philosophers and political theorists busy for centuries. However, it must be remembered that all systems of governance are fundamentally human constructs that have taken different forms over different times and different cultures. The three substructures within the governance category are *government presence, rule of law,* and the provision of *social services.*

Government presence describes the role of the government in everyday life. This includes the system by which the society is governed, and to what extent people may choose their leaders. At one theoretical extreme, we have a "state of nature" where no government exists and everyone is responsible for looking after their own personal welfare. At the other extreme is an insistent government presence, where the state has a say in even the most intimate details of a citizen's life.

Rule of law is the government's enforcement of the laws of the land and deals with the administration of justice. A society's rule of law may be dictated orally by a group of elders or by a justice system codified in legal tracts with multiple tiers of courts and officials responsible for enforcing citizens' rights and prosecuting lawbreakers. The powers vested in the police force are a significant component in the rule of law. A society with no rule of law would mean individuals would be responsible for safeguarding their own rights and property with no state support or assistance. An overly aggressive enforcement of the rule of law might result in intimidating the population into obedience via an inflexible, unforgiving justice system.

The substructure of *social services* includes the government's provision of basic healthcare and education for the general population, as well as other services such as transportation, libraries, public parks, social programs, and more. Excellent social services may exist in a world but the government may not be responsible for their equitable distribution. Health care and schooling may be limited or absent for large portions of society while wealthy elites may keep their families and social networks healthy and educated, paying from their own pocketbooks. Widespread social services may not necessarily be positive in nature either, as the government may demand citizens to follow an intense fitness regimen, enforce a strictly monitored diet, or provide mandatory schooling that reinforces the state's propaganda.

Economics

Economics deal with the production, distribution, and consumption of wealth, which includes valuable possessions and material property. This goes beyond hard currency and includes things like real estate, personal property, and cash reserves. There are other types of cultural capital—such as wisdom, reputation, or unique physical attributes—that might not translate directly into money but may operate as a type of currency in a given society. There are also cashless barter economies where people trade goods and services instead of currency. The three economic substructures are *economic strength*, *wealth distribution*, and *agriculture and trade*.

Economic strength is a measure of the production or possession of one or more valuable commodities or resources within the society. A strong economy produces or possesses a surplus of valuable resources, which can then be stockpiled, spent on trading goods and services with other societies, or distributed throughout the society. A weak economy is marked by the lack of valuable commodities and the inability to develop or obtain sufficient wealth to sustain the society. Government policies are often heralded or blamed for the economic strength of a given society, and the desire to increase a state's economic strength has been the root cause of many violent conflicts between nations and cultures.

Wealth distribution is the degree to which the society's wealth is divided among the entire population. Virtually every society will have both rich and poor people, but the size of the economic classes between these poles can be of varying size. In early feudal societies, for example, there was a small ruling class of nobles and a very broad base of serfs and laborers with a narrow band of middle-class merchants. In contrast, the United States after World War II had a very broad, very strong middle class that fueled an expanding economy.

Finally, *agriculture and trade* determines a society's self-sufficiency in terms of natural resources and doing business with foreign powers. A society that produces a surplus of food or other natural resources will often have an advantage over those that struggle to keep their population well fed, however resource-rich societies may also be targeted for pillaging or conquest by foreign invaders. While mutually beneficial trade relationships may reduce the chance for conflicts, members of societies unable to sustain their population by their own means may resort to drastic measures in order to guarantee their survival.

Social Relations

Social relations categories indicate the levels of rights that exist for different social groups. Rights within a society are never granted universally, and the rights we enjoy today (and may take for granted) are neither universal nor eternal, as they change across time periods and cultures. Consider that in the United States, women did not have the right to vote until 1920; that federally enforced child labor laws did not exist until 1938; that racially segregated schools were lawful until 1964; and that bans on same-sex marriage were declared unconstitutional as recently as 2015. Questions pertaining to social relations and rights among different demographic groups tend to be volatile subjects, and often serve as faultlines for tensions within a society. The extremes on the hypothetical scale range from having no rights and outright persecution on one end of the spectrum, to near-perfect equity on the opposite end. The four substructures within the social relations structure are *race and ethnic relations, class relations, gender relations,* and *sexual orientation relations.*

The *race and ethnic relations* substructure focuses on possible inequity within society along racial or ethnic lines. The very concepts of race and ethnicity are human constructions not rooted in scientific data. When we speak about race, we generally refer to physical traits and ancestry, whereas ethnicity has to do with cultures and customs of people. Both are used as a taxonomy, or a way to categorize groups of people, where there exists some marker of difference that distinguishes one group of people from another. Racial groups are often identified by skin color, hair types, or body shapes, whereas ethnicities tend to be defined by language, cuisine, clothing, and cultural practices. Differences across racial and ethnic lines can be recognized, tolerated, or celebrated throughout a society. Of course, intolerance has fueled some of the worst atrocities in human history, where racial and ethnic differences become the rationale for the subjugation and extermination of an entire people. Cases of extreme racial prejudice and state-sanctioned "ethnic cleansing" campaigns are all too common in the twenty-first century, and the lingering anger, distrust, and more subtle forms of discrimination persist for generations and heal slowly, if perhaps never completely.

Class relations deals with hierarchical groupings of members of a society, most often related to their level of economic wealth such as the lower, middle, and upper classes, though the definitions and markers of class boundaries are hotly debated. The lower classes generally include the jobless poor, the working class, and anyone in a perpetually unstable financial position, whereas the markers of the upper classes are accumulation of wealth, financial security, and connections to the most influential members of the society, often politicians or religious figures; the middle class is the group between the lower and upper classes, which can either be large or small. Levels of education and social status can also factor into notions of class, though these factors often correlate to an economic class as well. Caste systems of rigid social stratification also exist, where members of different classes are forbidden to marry or even interact socially. Social mobility, or the ability to climb into a higher class, is also an element of class relations. Tensions along class lines are higher when people are locked into the social class in which they were born with little chance of improving their social station.

Gender relations are the ways in which a culture or society defines the distribution of rights between men and women in relation to one another. Gender is different from biological sex, which is determined by anatomy. Gender is a social construction that includes traits or behaviors that a society has coded as being masculine or feminine. This might include the type of work individuals are expected to do or allowed to do in a society, and whether individuals receive equal recognition for their contributions to society and receive equal pay for their labor. Gender relations also encompass equal access to education, the ability to hold public office or serve in certain professions. People who are transgender or genderqueer can further complicate how a society might recognize gender and gender roles.

Sexual orientation is closely related to gender relations but extends to the rights of individuals who identify as being something other than heterosexual. Homosexuality, bisexuality, and other non-heterosexual preferences are as old as recorded history, but societies have differed in terms of whether they condone, prohibit, or punish the exhibition of such behaviors. These issues converge around a range of political matters, including whether a non-heterosexual partner can be recognized by the state to receive the benefits of the legal rights extended to married couples, and whether polyamorous relationships are outlawed or part of the norm. Non-heterosexual people have a long history of experiencing harassment, discrimination, and being denied entry to schools, public offices, and the military.

Cultural Influences

Cultural influences are the shared values and beliefs of the broader society. Cultural influences are most notable when they become ingrained in social institutions, such as schools and the justice system. Cultural influences vary widely over time, from country to country and region to region. Furthermore, there may be significant cultural differences between people who live in rural areas and those who live in cities. The prominent cultural values of a specific place often give people raised in that environment a sense of home. Indeed, for many people, it's not until they venture outside their hometown that they begin to appreciate the range of diversity in different communities that have different histories and different values. The four substructures of cultural influences are *military influence, religious influence, technology influence,* and the influence of *arts and culture.*

Military influence is the presence of the armed forces throughout society. This is usually associated with the number of currently serving, or former members of, the armed forces and the number of military institutions or facilities in the area. The influence of the military may be prominent in cities with major military bases, a town adjacent to a military outpost in the middle of nowhere, or in regions that live under the threat of an ongoing military conflict, for example along disputed borders. The duties and responsibilities that belong to military personnel versus officers of the law can also cause tension in certain societies.

Religious influence includes the ways religious and spiritual beliefs are woven into the culture and its institutions. Religious doctrine often has explicit instructions on how to conduct oneself properly and to live a morally pure life. Tensions can surface when religious teachings dictate rules for specific members of the society, notably along the lines of race, class, gender, and the prohibition of certain sexual activities. Religious influence also reflects how people outside that faith are received by the community. The culture can be one of inclusivity and the positive exchange of beliefs, or it can be exclusionary and a point of conflict.

Technology influence is the level of importance the development of new tools and knowledge has for the society. History is marked by periods of intense technological innovation, such as the development of China's Four Great Inventions (the compass, gunpowder, papermaking, and printing), the flourishing of mathematics, physics, and engineering during the Islamic Golden Age from around the eighth to thirteenth centuries. The role of technology in society can come into conflict with both organized religion and the arts, depending on how much a society invests in technological development at the expense of other aspects of the culture.

Arts and culture include the society's overall investment in music, literature, performing arts, and the visual and culinary arts. Moments of broad artistic flowering usually occur in response to the politics and social situations of the day. This could mean a system of patronage, where society's elites support the fine arts by sponsoring artists, or it could be a grassroots movement where individuals or collectives resist a totalitarian regime through artistic expression rather than bullets and bombs.

Additional Substructures

Adding a few unique substructures can provide interesting new wrinkles to your world, and some genre-specific considerations can be important enough function to warrant inclusion as substructures of their own. Below are some other examples of substructures that might be added to your world. A word of caution: when it comes to adding substructures to your fictional world, you're creating a significant amount of additional work. While it might seem that you are only adding one new feature, in fact the additional substructure will need to be considered in light of all the other 14 substructures in order for it to be truly ingrained and feel like an organic part of your world. Some substructures you may consider adding include considering *age, ableness, drugs and drug culture,* and the *natural world*.

Age can be a significant substructure that fits within the structure of social relations. In some cultures, the elderly may be looked down upon as nonproductive members of society who have outlived their usefulness. In others, elders may be the most respected members of a community and its de facto leaders. Youths may have few rights and be treated little better than servants or slaves until they reach their age of emancipation or, on the other hand, an entire society may be built on the celebration of children. Certain political positions could only be held by people of a specific age range, or social services may flow disproportionately to elderly or the young. Wealth in a society could likewise be concentrated or denied to people based on their age; a person's age could grant them certain privileges or could be a point of discrimination. The same holds for cultural influences, where military or religious service could be determined by age, as could explorations in technology or the arts.

Ableness is another factor that connects to both social relations and also the social services extended to society as depicted in the governance structure. People who are blind, deaf, or have some other physical impairment or mental illness may be treated with a great deal of respect and even reverence as in the case of oracles, or they may face extreme discrimination or banishment for being viewed as a blight on society. How the differently abled are treated in a society will often be linked to either the role of the government or its wider cultural values. For example, a society where the government provides robust social services and is guided by a benevolent religion may take extra steps to accommodate the differently abled, where an impoverished society driven by military rule may be less forgiving of any perceived weakness among the populous.

Drugs and drug culture is another substructure that can be useful as an additional cultural influence. Certain types of mind-altering herbs, drugs, or alcoholic drinks play a significant role in some societies, particularly if they have religious or ceremonial uses. On the reverse side, other societies ban or limit the consumption of any substance that has a recreational use, such as the prohibition of alcohol and the classification of drugs as controlled substances, which may be declared illegal except in very specific circumstances. Drugs can have a significant impact on the work of law enforcement, and it can also be an important commodity for the economy, especially if neighboring states have stricter or more lax laws regarding drug use.

Attitudes toward the *natural world* can also add an interesting additional aspect to your world, and would potentially fit under the economic or cultural influence structures. A forest or mountain could be cherished by one culture, yet viewed as a natural resource waiting to be harvested by another. Some societies hold specific animals as sacred or keep them as beloved pets, whereas in other societies those same animals may be regarded as a food source or beasts of burden. As with all such cases, there can be deep and acrimonious divisions within a society as well, particularly when it comes to the preservation and consumption of specific natural resources and the treatment of animals.

Example Structures in Fictional Worlds

It's easy to overlook how these structures and substructures influence stories set in large-scale fictional worlds. Plots focus on the circumstances of characters and the decisions they make when confronted with obstacles. These obstacles often take the shape of antagonistic characters or a hostile environment, but a close analysis shows that aspects of governance, economics, social relations, and cultural influences subtly shape the overall narrative in non-trivial ways. The following sections examine the fictional worlds of George R.R. Martin's *A Song of Ice and Fire*, George Lucas's *Star Wars* galaxy, and J.R.R. Tolkien's Middle-earth in terms of the structures and substructures described in this book, and how they help shape the broader narratives that take place in those worlds. As you read, note how each structure operates not as its own discrete unit, but rather as part of a system.

Governance in *A Song of Ice and Fire* and *Lord of the Rings*

Like Shakespeare in his histories, Martin's *A Song of Ice and Fire* examines the question of governance in a pre-democratic world.[1] From the Seven Kingdoms of Westeros to across the sea and the vast continent of Essos, readers view many different types of rulers as the story shifts between different characters' points of view in different focal points in the story. Though all Seven Kingdoms swear fealty to the king of Westeros, each maintains its own internal political structures. In the kingdom of the North, Eddark Stark governs with frankness and honesty, adhering to a strict moral code respected by other clans and houses in the North. That land is depicted as a bleak, inhospitable landscape where the harsh conditions require internal strength and a certain amount of stoicism. The style of governance in the North stands in contrast to the politics of the southern kingdoms, where lies, deceits, and webs of manipulation are the rule. It also contrasts with an even greater difference to the locations across the sea to the east, where the tribal Dothraki society is led by the single warrior who can seize and maintain power through combat. Traditionally, the leader of the Dothraki binds his followers to him through sheer force and maintains it through demonstrations of violence. The collision of these different political organizations drives the first novel in the series, *A Game of Thrones*, as the plot is largely about what happens to a man who embodies the values of the North and finds himself embroiled in the political intrigues of the south.

In terms of the substructures, *government presence* in daily life feels pervasive throughout Martin's world. A lord's subjects have few rights when it comes to privacy or operating without the express permission of their sovereign. The *rule of law*, however, varies greatly. In both the North as well as in Dothraki culture, the ruler serves as judge, jury, and executioner with no policing or formal court system in place; however, the other kingdoms are more beholden to laws, as evidenced in Tyrion Lannister's clever ruse to free himself from imprisonment in the kingdom of the Vail by exerting his legal right to request a trial by combat. Lysa Tully feels compelled to grant his request and each name a champion to fight on their behalf. Such a right applies only to members of the nobility, however, as a commoner could dictate no such terms of their trial. This serves as a good example as to how one of the substructures, in this case the enforcement of the rule of law, may vary wildly in different *focal points* throughout a fictional world, and it can also be applied unevenly based on other factors such as *class*. Another more universal quality of governance, however, pertains to *social services*. Nowhere in Martin's world do we see a ruler making concerted efforts to provide guaranteed healthcare and education to the masses. While Margaery Tyrell may be charitable to poor children in King's Landing and there are numerous examples of families agreeing to foster and educate each other's children, there is no sense that the *governing* institution has an obligation to its citizens to provide basic education or healthcare to the public.

Tolkien's Middle-earth lacks granular details of how governments operate in Middle-earth, which is a point of criticism for many.[2] Even so, *The Silmarillion*, *The Hobbit*, and *Lord of the Rings* do contrast different types of governance that range from the highly hierarchical a much more flat system of governance. Rulers of the major kingdoms in Middle-earth—regardless of whether they are elves, dwarves, or humans—can trace their right to power through royal lineages that span generations and, in many cases, go back thousands of years to the beginning of recorded history. Indeed, one major plot point of *Lord of the Rings* is that, with the victory of Aragorn, there will be a rightful ruler installed on the throne of mankind once more. This divine right to rule goes unquestioned by everyone in the world. Even Denethor, the steward of Gondor, may deny that Aragorn is the true king, but he does not question the system that would place that man on the throne. The peoples of Middle-earth consent to this system of governance and, as far as readers see, believe it to be right and just. In contrast, the armies of darkness marshaled through the ages by Morgoth, Sauron, and Saruman are compelled into obedience in the cruelest ways imaginable. Orcs have no life beyond their enforced servitude to their evil leaders. One last example of a governmental system is that of the Shire, where the hobbits do not draw on esteemed lineage but rather rely on participatory democracy, where the political stakes rarely rise above petty squabbles. In fact, Samwise Gamgee is elected to be Mayor of the Shire for seven consecutive terms.[3]

Tolkien's critics have attacked the simplistic governance structures of Middle-earth as naïve wish fulfillment of an unabashed monarchist.[4] On the whole, the people of Middle-earth tend to be very content in the rigid hierarchical systems of governance under which they live, and the "rightful" leaders rule with no opposition from the populous. We hear almost nothing about petty crime, and the legal and penal systems in these kingdoms are mysteries. The only example of injustice we see would be the occasional unilateral decision of a ruler, such as the attempted arrest of Éomer by King Theoden, who even in this case was under the poisonous influence of the traitorous Grima Wormgtongue at the time of the command. Class tensions are never hinted at, nor are there political rabble-rousers among the working classes. Societies seem to run free from political complications as long as everyone keeps their rightful place. As government figures do not impose themselves on the daily life of the citizens, functional judicial systems are unnecessary. Based on what the audience sees, the populous finds itself clothed, fed, educated, and healthy without any complications. Scarcity, economic disparity, and other social ills don't exist. More generous readers might say that this simplistic view of governing structures is more of a result of the limited narrative perspective of a hobbit than a failure of imagination on Tolkien's part, but even so the portrayal of Middle-earth's social structures feels underdeveloped when compared to the complexity of our primary world.

Economics in *Star Wars* and *A Song of Ice and Fire*

For most readers of vast fictional worlds, economic issues fail to get the heart racing. It comes as no surprise that none of the large-scale worlds used as the primary examples in this book put economics front and center as in books as in Ursula LeGuin's *The Dispossessed* or Isaac Asimov's *Foundation* series. This isn't to say that the question of economic systems aren't important in popular fictional worlds—in fact, they're often what underpins much of the tension that drives characters' actions—but rather that they tend to operate in the background and the characters act within these systems rather than explicitly attempting to strengthen or overthrow them.

Economic issues hardly come to the fore in the original *Star Wars* trilogy. The struggle is cast in political terms, with the plucky rebels against the overwhelming strength of the Empire as they battle for the freedom of the galaxy. Money is hardly mentioned, though the austere, gleaming facilities of the Empire contrast with the dirty and cluttered settings of Tatooine and the rebel base on Yavin IV. The three prequels and several entries in the new Disney canon, however, present the conflict as one driven as much by economics as in politics. In fact, *Episode I – The Phantom Menace* opens with an explanation of an economic dispute between the Trade Federation and the planet Naboo, though critics of the prequels will say that the dispute makes little sense based on the information provided, and the rationale of this maneuver is never explained.

The long-running animated television series *Star Wars: The Clone Wars* provides better explanations for the conflict, wherein the war essentially becomes the pretense for an intergalactic arms race.[5] *Star Wars: The Clone Wars*, which occurs almost in its entirety between Episodes II and III, often revolves around resource allocations. In the war, the Separatists (covertly led by the Sith) stage waves of attacks against planets loyal to the Republic (defended by the Jedi) by deploying an enormous army of mass-produced battle droids. Simple-minded and tactically naïve, individual battle droids were almost comically weak, but they could be deadly in overwhelming numbers. The Republic's defense relied on the Jedi Order and an army of clone soldiers who were literally bred for battle. Clones were far more expensive to produce than battle droids but were capable of complex rational thought, excelled in military stratagems, and exhibited a full range of human emotions. The sheer scope of the war taxed the resources of the Republic, who struggled to keep pace with the nonstop assault of battle droids. The mounting costs caused rifts between different planets in the Galactic Senate who questioned the seemingly never-ending war. Unknown to all but a few, the Republic's Senator Palpatine, head of the Galactic Senate, had orchestrated the war to be both a costly distraction and a justification for eradicating the Jedi Order. Once the Separatists were defeated and the Jedi Order destroyed, Palpatine used existing divisions in the Senate to transform the democratic Republic into the totalitarian Galactic Empire, installing himself at its head as Emperor.

Moviegoers can be excused for not understanding the backdrop to the action since the prequel films do a poor job framing the economic angle to the conflict, as the economic ambitions of the Empire are never made very clear in any of the films. In the new Disney canon, this idea is expressed most explicitly in other forms of media, namely in the novels *A New Dawn, Catalyst: A Rogue One Story,* and the young reader series *Servants of the Empire*.[6] In these books, all of which are set between the events of *Episode III – The Revenge of the Sith* and *Episode IV – A New Hope*, readers see the Empire raze entire worlds, extracting their valuable resources, oppressing the indigenous species, and wreaking ecological havoc. The Empire had no other goal except total domination of the entire galaxy, and in order for this to become a reality, it required a constant expansion of their already massive war machine. Construction of both Death

Stars and countless TIE fighters and Star Destroyers necessitated an enormous amount of resources, including the rare kyber crystals that power the Death Star's terrifying superlaser.

Thus the Death Star is an enormous capital investment for the Empire, both in terms of the materials for its world-destroying power but also in terms of the thousands of workers stationed there, many of whom were among the Empire's best and brightest soldiers and administrators. The young adult novel *Lost Stars* and the *Star Wars: Aftermath* book trilogy describe how the destruction of the Death Star was a serious economic blow as much as a psychological one.[7] As revealed in these novels, the loss of the second Death Star along with the Emperor and Darth Vader was a blow from which the Empire could never recover. Not only did it deepen an already severe leadership gap, but the Empire lost many important ships in their military fleet and, as a result, could no longer dominate enough planets to strip them of their resources.

The Empire's economic collapse is but one aspect of the economic system in a galaxy that is large and diverse. Each focal point location described in the film can be analyzed according to the economic substructures outlined in the collaborative worldbuilding system. Desert planets such as Tatooine and Jakku are considered backwaters with little *economic strength*, as opposed to Core Worlds like Coruscant and Corellia, both of which are at the economic center of the galaxy both figuratively and literally. *Wealth distribution* in the Star Wars galaxy has few prominent examples outside the Empire having sufficient wealth and the Rebellion being cash-strapped, but the brief glimpses we get of tribal communities such as the Wookies of Kashyyyk and Ewoks of Endor suggest communal economies with lower levels of wealth disparity between the richest and poorest. Outside of the films, planets such as Akiva as described in *Star Wars: Aftermath* and Lothal in the *Star Wars Rebels* television series and the *Servants of the Empire* books show a wide gap between the ruling class and the commoners, a tension that eventually boils over into revolution.[8] The city-planet Coruscant's wealth distribution is literally vertical, with the surface city boasting green spaces and glittering skyscrapers while sublevels become seedier and more dangerous lower in the city. Locations differ greatly in terms of their *agriculture and trade*. Planets rich with natural resources such Samovar, which was mined to exhaustion for the minerals doonium and dolovite for the construction of the Death Star as mentioned in *Catalyst: A Rogue One Novel*, become prime targets for the Empire. Planets located along the main hyperspace trade routes enjoyed more trade and economic activity than those in the far-flung reaches of the Outer Rim.[9]

In *A Song of Ice and Fire*, the economy of the Known World plays an important role in the series.[10] Massive wealth inequality describes the entirety of the continent of Westeros, with the commoners known as "small folk" often finding themselves squeezed between rival lords vying for power, and they frequently wind up paying with their lives. Their dire financial straits mean they cannot move away from the war that rolls through the continent and they must weather the storm as best they can, should they be unfortunate enough to find one of the nobility on their doorstep. In addition, Jon Snow learns that the Night's Watch, stationed at The Wall in at the far northern border of Westeros, is not in truth a company of noble volunteers, but rather a ragtag bunch of commoners serving time often for trumped-up crimes they didn't commit, again underscoring the lack of agency small folk have in their own lives. The Night's Watch operates under a constant state of economic duress, never having the resources to defend a wall that is as far from the royals' minds as it is their homes.

King's Landing is an enormous city and one of the most common locations in the series but has few *focal points* that are developed in any depth. The two visited most commonly provide a vivid contrast in the way people live in the city. The Red Keep, which is the seat of power in Westeros, is ornate, clean, and the site of numerous decadent royal affairs. Just down the road, however, the slum of Fleabottom sees filth flow through the streets and human life is worth a pittance. Also, early in the novel *A Game of Thrones*, readers learn that King Robert Baratheon's appetite for feasts has run his kingdom into serious debt with the Iron Bank of Braavos, the financiers of the throne. Their financial dire straits put House Lannister, the wealthiest of all the nobles houses on the continent, in a politically advantageous position as the kingdom relies on their gold, a fact the family regularly uses as leverage. Finally, the fortunes of House Targaryen across the sea face what is at its root an economic problem: how do they retake the throne when they have no finances to fund an army or ships to transport them to Westeros? Daenery struggles to overcome these barriers and also fights for economic freedom for the masses. This includes sacking the cities of Astapor, Yunkai, and Meereen in order to free their slaves and disrupt their local economies that trade in human lives as currency.

Social Relations in *The Lord of the Rings* and *Star Wars*

Examining social relations along the lines of race, class, gender, and sexual orientation in Middle-earth is a complicated task because Tolkien's cosmology is inextricably bound to his deep Catholic faith, which in turn deeply influenced his worldview. Understanding Tolkien as a product of his time helps explain some of the gaps in his world's logic that might seem glaring to many readers today. It also serves as a good reminder that, as authors, we are all susceptible to such oversights due to our own limited experiences of the world, and that building worlds together is one way to ensure against overly simple or dubiously harmonious societies.

Tolkien often receives plaudits for his sophisticated view of *race relations*, or at least as it relates to the interactions between men, elves, and dwarves. One major theme that operates across all of Tolkien's stories is that the peoples of Middle-earth must band together to fight the armies of evil. In *The Silmarillion*, the hero who ushers in the end of the First Age is of mixed blood, and whose genealogy includes elf, man, and the divine. It is no coincidence that both *The Hobbit* and *The Lord of the Rings* require members of these different races to put aside their differences in order to defeat the dark forces that threaten the planet. In the end, the forces of good are rewarded for placing their trust in each other and against all odds win the day—at least for the time being, before the cycles of mistrust begin again and evil once again gains power in the world.

The relations between the races of Middle-earth are complex and believable, as many characters harbor grievances over age-old slights and betrayals between races, and it takes genuine acts of faith for the characters to overcome their own intolerances. Tolkien's depiction of race isn't as positive, however, when we move away from the northwest of Middle-earth. The people known as the Easterlings are described as short, broad, and swarthy—dark skinned and dark haired as opposed to their lighter-skinned and bright-eyed neighbors to the west. The Easterlings are best known for defecting to Morgoth's cause and, ages later, repeating their betrayal by joining with Sauron in the War of the Ring. If one superimposes a map of Middle-earth over Europe, the idyllic Shire occupies roughly the same space as rural England, and Mordor and the land of the Easterlings map onto Turkey, Eastern Europe, and the Middle East. Furthermore, the seat of culture, sophistication, and noble lineage reside in the West. Even if the text only reflects the provincial attitudes of the author Bilbo, it would suggest that perhaps the hobbit isn't as tolerant and worldly as readers might be led to believe.

Class relations are equally problematic, an issue British novelist Michael Moorcock famously addressed in a withering essay on Tolkien entitled "Epic Pooh."[11] Middle-earth is a monarchical system, a world governed by the divine right of kings. In such a system, the ruler is answerable to the moral laws established by the deity and should use their moral authority to provide for the masses. This rigid hierarchical system locks people into strict social classes where they have limited ability to appeal for social change. Their lot in life is to dutifully serve those up the chain of command. Samwise Gamgee, for example, refers to Frodo as "Mr. Frodo" or "Master," always mindful of the difference in their social standing until the very end. The common folk and working class of Middle-earth never receive much attention throughout Tolkien's work, and when they do they are usually described as being simple and honest, and willing to fall into line should a rightful leader emerge among them.

The issue of *gender relations* in Tolkien's work also resists easy generalizations. Tolkien clearly held women in high regard as some of the greatest heroes in his stories are women. Characters like Melian, Lúthien, Elwing, Galadriel, and Éowyn are recognized as some of the wisest and bravest people who walk the earth, usually superior in different ways to their male partners. Women serve a critically necessary function in Tolkien's invented universe, and not just in a traditional sense of fulfilling the role of caretakers of the home. They travel over rough terrain, expose themselves to danger, and deal mortal blows to their enemies. All of this is laudable and Tolkien deserves credit for transcending some of the more traditional views of women's roles in the United Kingdom of his time. However, the main problem with Tolkien's female characters is that there are so few of them. Only 18 percent of Tolkien's named characters are women,[12] and the vast majority of those are only named in passing. The stories of Middle-earth are predominantly those of men, told by men, and many of the stories feature men trying to control or direct women, albeit they are often motivated to keep women safe from harm. The lack of female characters represents a major gap in Middle-earth, and thus it becomes difficult to make definitive statements about the nature of gender relations—there simply is not enough information to draw solid conclusions across the different segments of society, and yet their absence should be disconcerting to the critical reader.

The existence of diverse *sexual orientations* is also absent from the work of Tolkien. Middle-earth is entirely heteronormative without any sense of an alternative. Marriage between male and female is almost always consensual and cast in a positive light; indeed, marriage repeatedly is the salvation of the world and the unions of Beren and Lúthien, of Eärendil and Elwing, of Faramir and Éowyn, of Aragorn and Arwen, and even Samwise Gamgee and Rosie Cotton are symbols of the enduring victory of good over evil. While there's nothing that says a fictional world's range of sexual orientations must accurately reflect the diversity present in our primary world, flattening the world into essentially two options—monogamous heterosexuality or asexuality—is a gross oversimplification of a natural range of attitudes toward sexual relations. In our primary world, the historical record shows a diverse range of sexual relations across time and cultures, where homosexuality, bisexuality and plural marriage have all been prevalent. The closest example of negative relationships would be the incestuous relationship between Túrin and his sister Nïenor, which is the direct result of a curse, and the unnatural lust the elf Maeglin felt for his first cousin Idril. What Tolkien's world lacks, then, is any hint of sexual diversity, though in truth Middle-earth is a rather chaste, sex-starved place to begin with. This in itself is a lack of realism.

The original *Star Wars* trilogy skirted many issues that related to race, class, gender, and sexual orientation as well, but the revamped Disney canon is making a concerted effort to address these issues. Unlike the original trilogy, the humans depicted in the new canon material are from a variety of ethnic and racial backgrounds, though it must be said that same-species racism seems not to be an issue. As is common in many science fiction and fantasy worlds, bigotry exists instead against nonhuman species. In the Empire, few nonhumans serve in any positions of power, a fact made most explicitly in the novel *Thrawn* as the title character faces persistent discrimination based on his species.[13] Nonhumans have second standing in the Empire's social order, which pushes nonhuman species to backwater worlds of the galaxy. This actually explains why there is such a diversity of lifeforms in the cantina in Tatooine in *Star Wars Episode IV – A New Hope*. In contrast, the Rebel Alliance actively recruits anyone who would oppose the Empire and, as a result, they had a much more diverse fighting force.

Broadly speaking, a person's gender does not limit them in the *Star Wars* galaxy. One of the chief enemies represented in non-film media is Ray Sloane, a black woman who rises to the highest command even as the Empire spiraled toward ultimate defeat, as chronicled in the novels *A New Dawn* and the *Star Wars: Aftermath* trilogy. The TV series *Star Wars: The Clone Wars* and *Star Wars Rebels* feature strong female leading characters such as Ahsoka Tano, Sabine Wren, and Hera Syndulla; of course, the main protagonists of the two most recent *Star Wars* films are both women, Rey in *The Force Awakens* and Jyn Erso in *Rogue One*.[14] Furthermore, two of the prime movers of the original Rebel Alliance were both women: Mon Mothma and Princess Leia Organa.

Class relations in the *Star Wars* galaxy were discussed in the previous section on economic structures, where the Empire's strength was described as being measured in both military might and economic dominance, but class tensions play out in other ways as well. Other *Star Wars* media, such as the *Servants of the*

Empire and *Adventures in Wild Space* series and the novels *Lost Stars*, *Tarkin*, and *Thrawn*, suggest that the Core Worlds fancy themselves as far superior to those planets further away from this center, with fringe planets being utterly dismissed as inconsequential.[15] These biases often set up social tensions where those coming from lesser-known worlds must work harder and be better than their peers to prove their worth.

Finally, sexual relationships in the new *Star Wars* canon are also varied and diverse. While romance has never really been at the center of *Star Wars* stories, recent additions to the canon provide plenty of evidence of same-sex relationships. In the novel *Lords of the Sith*, Moff Delian Morrs, who is female, mentions the death of her wife,[16] and in *Aftermath: Empire's End*, the relationship between the men Sinjir Rath Velus and his love interest Conder Kyl is a central plot point.[17] There are even rare interspecies relationships, as the human Kanan Jarrus and the Twi'lek Hera Syndulla, two central characters in *Star Wars Rebels* have an obvious affection for each other, even if the extent of their relationship is only hinted at for much of the series.[18] The plot of the *Princess Leia* comic has to do with interspecies breeding between human Alderaanians and the humanoid Espirions.[19] Such varied configurations of couples and relationships feel unforced and authentic in an expansive and diverse galaxy.

Cultural Influences in *A Song of Ice and Fire*, *The Lord of the Rings*, and *Star Wars*

The cultural influences in the three works being examined are diverse and varied and tend to be tied to specific locations in those worlds. The level of *military influence* in each of these worlds tends to be quite high, which is perhaps to be expected given the fact that a war is always imminent or is currently underway. Everyone is either mired in military conflict or bracing for it to come. Some exceptions to heightened military influence include backwater locations, such as Middle-earth's Shire in the far corner of the map, or in the Outer Rim planets of Tatooine or Jakku in *Star Wars*, which are deemed to be so irrelevant that they're not worth fighting for. In the violent world of Westeros though, an individual's worth is often measured by their martial skill, so the broader story of the *A Song of Ice and Fire* series is largely defined by combat.

Conventional *religious influence* is one of the most interesting aspects of *A Song of Ice and Fire*. Six of the Seven Kingdoms follow the Faith of the Seven, while only the North follows their ancestral religion of the Old Gods. The religious belief system helps define each culture, and audiences see a variety of attitudes about religion, ranging from the dismissive to the devout to the fanatical. In *A Dance with Dragons*, we see a shift as the Faith Militant gain favor with the crown and immediately begin exerting its influence on the wider society.[20] In Middle-earth, however, religion has no formal function. There are no churches or temples of worship in Middle-earth, no religious holidays, and no prayers—although the poetry and snippets of song might be interpreted as types of prayer. Likewise, the *Star Wars* galaxy lacks explicit religious institutions, despite the omnipresent sense of the Force. Even the influence of the Force tends to be centered on specific locations, such as Jedi or Sith temples, or at Force vergences such as Dagobah. These locations hold meaning for those trained to use the Force, but mean little for anyone else. There is no suggestion that the masses prayed at the Jedi temples on Sundays, or that there were other public religious ceremonies associated with the Force.

Technology influence tends to be more the province of science fiction than fantasy, and unsurprisingly technology plays a major role in the *Star Wars* galaxy. From Death Stars to a multitude of droids, to floating cloud cities and starships with unreliable hyperdrives, and of course the iconic lightsaber, much of the delight from *Star Wars* stories comes from the fictional technologies. In fact, in the *Star Wars* galaxy, access to advanced technology correlates with both economic power and military might. Ignored worlds like Tatooine and Jakku are not only economically poor and militarily weak, but they also have low levels of technology. On both planets, being a salvager of high-tech junk is a common career. Tolkien's Middle-earth is on the other end of the spectrum, where technology is rare and usually used to promulgate evil. The major villains in the world—being Morgoth, Sauron, and Saruman—set up literal factories that pump out orcs, siege engines, and other engines of destruction. In chapters in *Return of the King* that were not included in Jackson's adaptation of the novel, Saruman escapes from his tower and finds his way to the Shire, where he begins plundering the countryside with his foul machines. In the world of *A Song of Ice and Fire*, a rudimentary level of technology exists that is roughly equivalent to the Middle Ages in Europe. Sophisticated architecture suggests an advanced understanding of math and science, but travel over land is still challenging and warfare has not advanced past swords and siege weapons. The most impressive uses of technology—being the impossibly tall wall of ice that separates the North from the Wildlings, and Tyrion Lannister's ingenious use of wildfire in the Battle of the Blackwater—are explained via the supernatural rather than the technical. As such, the influence of technology in the Known World is relatively low compared to the supernatural feats of the Night King to resurrect the dead as his army of White Walkers, or the presence of Daenerys's fearsome dragons.

Finally, the influence of *arts and culture* varies in these worlds, but nowhere is it more important than in Middle-earth, at least for the side of good. Humans, dwarves, and especially elves commit themselves to aesthetics and artistry that includes architecture, food, drink, and song. Only the corrupted forces of evil have no eye for beauty and wish to destroy artistic things. In Westeros, art and culture are the domain of the nobility and a luxury that small folk literally and figuratively cannot afford. Very little is said about arts at all, though the detailed descriptions of culinary delights suggest that the nobility does indeed enjoy the finer things in life. Even for the elites, however, the arts matter little compared to political maneuvering. Similarly, in *Star Wars,* the value of art takes a backseat to the political conflict unfolding across the galaxy, although some of the more memorable moments from the original trilogy include the song playing in the Tatooine cantina and the Max Rebo Band's performance in Jabba's palace. The new canon has one character, Sabine Wren of *Star Wars Rebels,* who is an artist in addition to being a demolitions expert.[21] Sabine uses explosive spray paint to tag Empire property with her unique designs and then detonates the graffiti; she also decorates stolen Imperial ships and armor, and paints her quarters on the ship the Ghost in vibrant colors. Other than one minor character who is a poet and appears in the young adult book *Imperial Justice,* the literary arts are almost completely absent.[22] Opulent cities depicted in the prequel trilogy of films and the *Star Wars: The Clone Wars* show boast sculptures, murals, and other public art, but these serve as a backdrop, with no one ever seeming to comment on them.[23]

From Structures to Catalogs of Fictional Worlds

The structures and substructures described in this chapter are most often intangibles that deal with patterns and relationships between different aspects of a society. How these structures and substructures operate on a daily basis and how they impact life for the people who live in that society are matters for debate. In order to better understand the social forces in the primary world in which we live, we rely on research, public opinion surveys, statistics, demographic data, and more. While people can and do draw many different conclusions about a society based on how they interpret that information, we also understand that societies are comprised of more concrete elements, such as the people, places, and things that define the society and give it its character. The role of the *catalog* of a fictional world is to bring that sense of concrete, tangible characters, spaces, and items that embody the society's structures.

For example, if a world has a high degree of *government presence* and *rule of law*, we would expect to see a number of people employed by the state in judiciary or law-enforcement roles; if instead there were an emphasis on *social services*, in turn, we would expect to see many people in that world employed as teachers or in the medical profession. Worlds with high levels of *economic strength* and *agriculture and trade* would likely have prominent locations, banks, markets, and centers of trade. The nature of the world's *social relations* would dictate what neighborhoods certain people live in, what types of jobs an average citizen might hold, and what kind of income they would earn from their labor based on their *race, class, gender,* and *sexual identity*. A society that is heavily influenced by the *military* or *religion* would likely have many barracks and churches, and soldiers and novices, respectively. Worlds that are influenced by *technology* or *art* might have a high-tech laboratory or performing arts theater on every corner.

The catalog requires you to go one step further by carving out additional details as individual entries to make them concrete and feel real. So it shouldn't be just any high-tech lab on the corner, it should have specifics: it's Eon Intergalactic Transponders, Inc. that employs 1,300 well-paid workers, and they jealously guard their trade secrets by hiring a militarized security force to patrol their campus around the clock; it's not any old church, but Temple to Lady Astara the Wise, refuge for the homeless and secret meeting place of the Sinister Six Assassin's Guild. Detail-rich catalog entries breathe life into the world and must reflect the structures of the fictional world. If 20 percent of your world's inhabitants are a species who have blue skin and a horn protruding from their forehead, then roughly 20 percent of your character entries should be this species. If the society is biased against them, it would make sense that most of this species would be of the lower economic classes and perhaps live in a ghettoized corner of the city.

The next chapter discusses how the catalog functions as part of a fictional world and the different parts of a catalog entry. Designing a good catalog template and distributing catalog entries evenly among your contributors will ensure that your world can grow quickly while remaining consistent and coherent with the social structures which you've developed.

6

Catalogs of Fictional Worlds

The *catalog* is an essential part of the worldbuilding process. The *framework* bounds the world to a specific space and time, and the *structures* provide scaffolding for outlining the broad social forces that are at work in the world, but it's the catalog that provides concrete details about the people, places, and things that exist in the world and gives you the most tangible storytelling materials. If the framework and structures provide a skeleton for a fictional world, populating the catalog gives it flesh and blood.

The collaborative worldbuilding process described in this book is heavily influenced by tabletop role-playing games (RPGs). In an RPG, a group of players each assumes the role of an individual character in a fictional world and, through a combination of decision making and dice rolls, they construct a shared story. Sometimes the story lasts a single session, or sometimes it's part of a campaign, or a series of sessions revolving around some central storyline. RPGs encourage creative thinking and improvisation on part of the players. The rules provide a great deal of latitude so the players can explore the storylines that they wish, and a wealth of supplemental materials is made available in the form of sourcebooks. Sourcebooks are essentially catalogs for different aspects of the world. One sourcebook may focus on the specifics of mountaineering adventures, while another may lay out the rules for seafaring campaigns.

Sourcebooks present this information in different types of catalog entries. Good catalog entries pack in a wealth of information. The more descriptive the individual catalog entry, the richer the story-making material. Catalog entries have two parts: *categorical information*, which helps with the grouping and sorting of entries and also ensures a high level of consistency; and the *descriptive information*, which is full of sensory information and provides a narrative for how the entry fits within the larger world.

The RPG evolved into a flexible storytelling system, where rulebooks and sourcebook entries provide enough structure to keep the world consistent and coherent but also allow for an enormous amount of variation and diversity. It's a useful model helps explain the process for your own worldbuilding projects and helps explain the process laid out in this book. This chapter gives a brief history of how the explosive popularity of RPGs was in part fueled by the desire to build and explore fictional worlds, and how the system the designers made was intended to ensure consistency across a broad and complex system and many different styles of play.[1] The chapter continues by describing the most important features of the catalog and how vibrant details contained within catalog entries contribute to spontaneous storytelling. This ability to spontaneously engage in a shared storytelling experience is very similar to what comes at the conclusion of the collaborative worldbuilding process when contributors draw storytelling material from the catalog.

The following section provides a brief history of the RPG and how information about the world became standardized and systematized. The developmental progression of *Dungeons & Dragons* includes the evolution of catalogs that allowed for a huge range of diversity yet still kept each catalog entry consistent and coherent within the fictional world. Compact catalog entries allow for quick and seamless integration into a narrative, and creating compelling player characters helps drive the game's narrative. We will apply these concepts in the catalog creation stage of the collaborative worldbuilding project. For a more comprehensive history of the RPG, see Jon Peterson's exhaustive study *Playing at the World: A History of Simulating Wars, People, and Fantastic Adventures from Chess to Role-Playing Games*, from which much of the below history was drawn.[2]

A Brief History of RPGs, RPG Worldbuilding, and RPG Catalog Templates

RPGs can trace their ancestry back to a specific type of military game that emerged in the late eighteenth and early nineteenth centuries called a *kriegspiel*, or literally "wargame." Unlike earlier strategy games like chess where war was represented symbolically through pawns, the *kriegspiel* used miniatures of actual military units. The game space consisted of boxes packed with sand or dirt to create rolling hills and different terrains, and players would deploy a variety of strategies to outwit their opponent. The purpose of the game was to simulate different military scenarios as a means of training Prussian officers in strategic planning, and thus the *kriegspiel* was not intended as a game for public consumption. The game pieces were hand carved and expensive, it required both significant space and time to play, and players needed some knowledge of military strategy. Up until the late nineteenth and early twentieth centuries, this type of wargame had a limited audience outside a small group of elite upper-class gentlemen who had a disposable income, who owned a home with a parlor large enough to host play sessions, and who had the benefit of some military education. Perhaps the most famous wargamer was H.G. Wells, British author of classic works of science fiction such as *The War of the Worlds* and *The Time Machine*, who was an avid player and penned two wargame rulebooks of his own, *Little Wars* and *Floor Games*.

After World War II, the cost of manufacturing game pieces decreased and the middle class grew. More people, particularly males, found themselves both with leisure time, money for recreational pursuits, and some first-hand knowledge of military strategy. Wargaming clubs popped up across the United States. Players convened to play games that reenacted famous historical battles, for example from medieval times or the Napoleonic era. In these games, players controlled troop movements as if they were military commanders removed from the battlefield. Some players became interested in developing a set of rules so that combat could be experienced from the perspective of the smallest military unit, the individual soldier. In 1971, wargamers and game designers Gary Gygax and Jeff Perren published a medieval miniatures wargame called *Chainmail* that included rules for man-to-man combat as well as a "fantasy supplement" that included mythical monsters and a handful of magic spells. Over a period of years, these portions of the *Chainmail* rules would evolve into *Dungeons & Dragons*, the world's first tabletop role-playing game.

Whereas classic wargames allowed players to participate in large-scale military combat, this new type of game offered something different. Once you assumed the role of a character, players of the game were participating in an epic story like those found in the pages of fantasy novels. The opening paragraph to *Chainmail's* fantasy supplement, penned by Gygax and Perren, makes this connection explicit:

> Most of the fantastic battles related in novels more closely resemble medieval warfare than they do earlier or later forms of combat. Because of this we are including a brief set of rules which will allow the medieval miniatures wargamer to add a new facet to his hobby, and either refight the epic struggles related by J.R.R. Tolkien, Robert E. Howard, and other fantasy writers; or you can devise your own "world," and conduct fantastic campaigns and conflicts based on it.[3]

The presence of fantastic elements detaches the game from the strict realism of historical military reenactments. Once freed from the rules of the primary world, it opens the door for the exploration of all manner of fictional worlds, including those created by the players.

Building Fictional Worlds for RPG Adventures

Rather than providing a game board and some game pieces, the first edition of *Dungeons & Dragons* was more like a toolkit for creating a game. The original *Dungeons & Dragons* was published as three separate booklets, each responsible for a different aspect of the game. The first volume, *Men & Magic*, described the character-creation process, the types of character archetypes that could be played, and various magical spells. *Monsters & Treasure* (Vol. II) provided a list of monstrous adversaries and an explanation of the treasures they hoarded. Finally, The *Underworld & Wilderness Adventures* (Vol. III) described how to set up and play in a campaign setting.[4]

The campaign, or a continuous game narrative that developed over several gaming sessions, was unique to this new form of game. As Gygax writes in the introduction to the first volume:

> While it is possible to play a single game, unrelated to any other game events past or future, it is the campaign for which these rules are designed. It is relatively simple to set up a fantasy campaign, and better still, it will cost almost nothing. In fact you will not even need miniature figures, although their occasional employment is recommended for real spectacle when battles are fought. A quick glance at the Equipment section of this booklet will reveal just how little is required. The most extensive requirement is time. The campaign referee will have to have sufficient time to meet the demands of his players, he will have to devote a number of hours to laying out the maps of his "dungeons" and upper terrain before the affair begins.[5] (Emphasis in original)

In order to support a campaign setting, extensive worldbuilding became a primary and necessary element of the game. Military games like *Gettysburg* may have allowed players to reenact that famous Civil War battle using different scenarios, but that game's final outcome did not carry over to another gaming session played at a later date, nor was it possible to extend the game's range beyond the borders of the Pennsylvania battleground. Whereas most military wargames were bound to a specific place and time, the world of *Dungeons & Dragons* promised to expand along with the players' imaginations.

Gygax also understood that the flexible rule set could be adapted for virtually any genre, stating that "the scope need not be restricted to the medieval; it can stretch from the prehistoric to the imagined future, but such expansion is recommended only at such time as the possibilities in the medieval aspect have been thoroughly explored."[6] In fact, TSR Hobbies wasted no time in rolling out a series of role-playing games that drew from other genres of popular fiction including the western-themed *Boot Hill* (1975), the spy/espionage game *Top Secret* (1980), and the deep space science fiction *Star Frontiers* (1982), among others. All followed the same premise: the core rulebooks provided a set of game mechanics for resolving challenges and then additional source books allowed players to build out RPG worlds as the setting for their campaigns.

The original *Dungeons & Dragons* rulebooks emphasize the importance of adapting the rules to fit the gaming group's style of play. The rules were not presented as inviolable, but rather as "guidelines" and "the framework around which you will build a game of simplicity or tremendous complexity—your time and imagination are about the only limiting factors"[7] with the implication that more time and more imagination would yield better results. The rules also warn against getting "too bogged down with unfamiliar details at first" and that

> your campaign will build naturally, at the pace best suited to the referee and players, smoothing the way for all concerned. New details can be added and old "laws" altered so as to provide continually new and different situations. In addition, the players themselves will interact in such a way as to make the campaign variable and unique, and this is quite desirable.[8]

Through regularly held play sessions, each gaming group would establish its own unique rhythm that could increase in complexity over time. Basic familiarity with the rules was encouraged, but Gygax recommended keeping the rulebooks on hand for reference because play was designed to be unpredictable. If the players had a good grip on the system, the game could handle any scenario they could dream up. Instead of the rules dictating the entirety of play, the players themselves collaboratively worked to create a story, appealing to the rules only as they needed.

The use of dice injected a high degree of variability into every game session. Players rolled dice to generate their characters' abilities and their starting wealth, and the person running the game (called the referee, dungeon master, or game master) could roll dice to randomly determine the location of monsters in a custom made dungeon. Furthermore, during the campaign, there was a rule for "wandering monsters," where the referee rolled a dice at the end of each turn to see if the adventurers stumbled into a random adversary.[9] This made the game unpredictable for all the players, even for the game master. An unfortunate series of rolls could result in the party facing an unexpected foe far more powerful than they could handle and would often result in the entire group's untimely death.

The sparse rules in three original handbooks were lacking in a number of ways. In the beginning, player-controlled characters (aka player-characters, or PCs) were fairly simple, represented by little more than their archetype (either fighting-men, magic-users, or clerics), their numeric abilities, and their alignment (either Law, Neutrality, or Chaos). The rules do not even call for giving a character a name, though the example character in the text has the name "Xylarthen."[10] There is no mention of the character's sex, age, or personality traits. Weapons and spells appear in multiple tables, giving players a handy reference for seeing how much damage they could inflict during combat. These early characters were meant to be thrown into danger with little regard for their lives but, as the designers soon discovered, players began forming real attachments to their characters, giving them backstories and traits that far exceeded what was actually required by the rules. The approach to PC creation would be overhauled to reflect this in the next edition of the game.

The second rulebook, *Monsters & Treasures*, lacks any kind of narrative framing, including an introduction. After the front matter, it launches straight into a list of monsters. The Monster Reference Table features over 50 different adversaries this way, including the first appearance of iconic *Dungeons & Dragons* monsters like kobolds, basilisks, djinn, and gray ooze.[11] This table runs two pages long and provides only statistical information for each type of monster. The individual monster descriptions follow the table and span 16 pages. For example, under the entry Basilisk it reads:

> Although this creature cannot fly, it has the power of turning to stone those whom it touches and those who meet its glance, but it in turn can be petrified by the reflection of its own eyes if the light is sufficient, and it looks at a good reflector. The Basilisk is not intelligent.[12]

Thus every creature had its own statistical record and an accompanying description that tells the referee how to use the monster in the campaign.

While *Monsters & Treasures* provides all the necessary information for fighting monsters, the layout wasn't very convenient. For one, the table isn't organized in any discernible way, not even alphabetically by monster type. Secondly, a monster's stats were often separated by several pages. For example,

Table 6.1 First five entries in *Monsters & Treasures* in the Monster Reference Table, Hostile & Benign Creatures[13]

Monster Type	Number appearing	Armor class	Move in inches	Hit dice	% in lair	Type or amount of treasure
Men	30–300	All variable	All variable	All variable	15%	Type A
Goblins/ Kobolds	40–400	6/7	6	1–1½	50%	1–6 G.P. ea.
Orcs	30–300	6	9	1	50%	Type D
Hobgoblins/ Gnolls	20–200	5	9	1 + ½	30%	Type D
Ogres	3–18	5	9	4 + 1	30%	1.000 G.P. + Type C

the stats for the basilisk are on page 4, but the monster's description doesn't appear until page 10. Artwork throughout the book is sparse, with only about a dozen crude sketches of monsters featured throughout the volume. If the players didn't know what a basilisk looked like, they would need to invent something up on the spot. Logistically, it took effort to bring a monster into play, disrupting the evolving narrative of the session.

As early as 1976, in the pages of *Dragon Magazine #1*, we see a significant shift in the presentation of a monster's information, compiling it into a single packaged entry. In the first installment of a regular column known as the Creature Feature, a monster—the Bulette—has an image accompanied by its statistical information presented in a block, followed by a detailed description of the monster's appearance, nature, and habits (Figure 6.1). Rather than separating the stats from the monster's description, *Dragon Magazine*'s new layout gave each monster a greater sense of individuality. One of the major changes to the monster record is the length of the monster's description. Whereas most descriptions in *Monsters & Treasure* were 100 words or less, the Creature Feature on the Bulette is far more detailed and descriptive. Compare the above description of the basilisk (a mere 50 words) with this 398-word description of the Bulette:

> Thought to be extinct until just recently, this horrifying apparition was cross-bred from armadillo and snapping turtle stock. It has the vicious disposition of the turtle, with the speed and digging ability of the armadillo. When full grown, they can dwarf a Percheron, being from 9–11 feet tall. They are very stupid, making them all the more dangerous and irascible.

Their nickname, that of the 'Landshark,' is well founded. They have voracious appetites, and will eat nearly anything, alive or dead. They show a marked preference for horses and mules, however, and have been reported recently marauding horse herds, and attacking even the best armed parties for the single purpose of eating the mounts. If hungry enough, they will attack virtually any one or any thing to satiate their ravenous appetite. Indeed, The Bulette seems to exist for the express purpose of feeding. They will not hesitate to attack and eat humans, though they are not overly fond of dwarves. They are loath to come near elves, alive or dead, but prize hobbits second only to horseflesh. They have been known to dig hobbits right out of their burrows.

They can jump up to eight feet with blinding speed, are masters at stalking silently, and nearly impossible (90%) to surprise.

When fighting, their primary method of attack is with their awesome jaws, said to be capable of biting the largest charger in half. Their claws are also formidable weapons, and when cornered or wounded, they can strike with all four feet, though they normally favor the front two.

The Bulette (pronounced boo-lay) has only two semi-vulnerable spots. The eyes are AC 4, but very small compared the overall bulk of the monster. The other is the underside of a hinged portion of their back. The only time this area is exposed is when they raise their crest, something seldom done except in the fiercest of fights. This softer area is AC 6, but only about a foot and a half square. The scales behind their head are highly prized as shields, and their teeth are said to be extremely valuable. They are NEVER found underground. They are very rare, and only mated pairs, if such exist, will share the same territory. No young have ever been sighted. The smallest ever seen are of the six die variety. No one knows how or where the young are born or hatched.

This description is much more evocative and provides many more details for the game master to incorporate. We get specific information on the Bulette: its disposition, its dietary preferences, how it fights, its strengths and weaknesses, and more. There's also a shift in the narrative style. Phrases such as "no young have ever been seen" and "no one knows how or where the young are born or hatched" appear to be relayed from a speaker who occupies space inside the game. The knowledge of the world of *Dungeons & Dragons* is both incomplete and imperfect, which allowed players to fill such gaps of knowledge through their play sessions.

Dragon Magazine continued to add new monsters each issue with variations in the format but used the same basic template: the monster's statistical information, an image, and a full description of its behaviors. In 1977, TSR published the (literally) game-changing *Monster Manual*, the first bound

CREATURE FEATURES

The Bulette (a.k.a. Landshark)

Number appearing — 1(90%)-2(10%)
Armor Class — -2
Move — 14"
Hit Dice — 6-11(8-sided)
Lair — 5%
Treasure — none
Magic Resistance — none
Mouth — 4-48 pts
Feet — 3-18 pts

Thought to be extinct until just recently, this horrifying apparition was cross-bred from armadillo and snapping turtle stock. It has the vicious disposition of the turtle, with the speed and digging ability of the armadillo. When full grown, they can dwarf a Percheron, being from 9-11 feet tall. They are very stupid, making them all the more dangerous and irascible.

Their nickname, that of the 'Landshark,' is well founded. They have voracious appetites, and will eat nearly anything, alive or dead. They show a marked preference for horses and mules, however, and have been reported recently marauding horse herds, and attacking even the best armed parties for the single purpose of eating the mounts. If hungry enough, they will attack virtually any one or any thing to satiate their ravenous appetite. Indeed, The Bulette seems to exist for the express purpose of feeding. They will not hesitate to attack and eat humans, though they are

not overly fond of dwarves. They are loathe to come near elves, alive or dead, but prize hobbits second only to horseflesh. They have been known to dig hobbits right out of their burrows.

They can jump up to eight feet with blinding speed, are masters at stalking silently, and nearly impossible (90%) to surprise.

When fighting, their primary method of attack is with their awesome jaws, said to be capable of biting the largest charger in half. Their claws are also formidable weapons, and when cornered or wounded, they can strike with all four feet, though they normally favor the front two.

The Bulette (pronounced boo-lay), has only two semi-vulnerable spots. The eyes are AC 4, but very small compared to the overall bulk of the monster. The other is the underside of the hinged portion of their back. The only time this area is exposed is when they raise their crest, something seldom done except in the fiercest of fights. This softer area is AC 6, but only about a foot and a half square. The scales behind their head are highly prized as shields, and their teeth are said to be extremely valuable. They are NEVER found underground. They are very rare, and only mated pairs, if such exist, will share the same territory. No young have ever been sighted. The smallest ever seen are of the six die variety. No one knows how or where the young are born or hatched.

19

Figure 6.1 The Bulette. © Wizards of the Coast. Used with permission.

hardcover book for RPGs that kicked off their *Advanced Dungeons & Dragons* line of publications. It featured over 350 unique monsters,[14] a staggering amount of new content. The book's publication marked a significant shift in the nature of the RPG as noted in the book's foreword, written by the editor, Mike Carr:

This present work, as will be apparent from its sheer bulk alone, is the result of a considerable amount of work and preparation by many persons. All this has been undertaken with an eye toward providing a final result which can be regarded as the definitive collection of monsters for ADVANCED DUNGEONS & DRAGONS—an encyclopedic collection of information certain to be of invaluable use to players and Dungeon Masters alike, complete with game specifications, background details and, in many cases, with an illustration in addition! Of course, no work can be truly definitive, for as long as players possess an active imagination, many new and fascinating monsters will continue to arise—and this is only as it should be.[15]

The sheer bulk of the book emphasizes the size and diversity of creatures inhabiting the world(s) of *Dungeons & Dragons*. Secondly, this is a work collaboration. Even if Gygax claims in his preface that the majority of the monsters are his sole creation,[16] an entire team of designers was involved in the construction of the manual. Third, the *Monster Manual* is more of an encyclopedia than a rulebook. It was not meant to be read cover to cover. Rather, it functions as a reference work that may be skimmed or searched for information, or a *catalog* of entries that present information in an organized fashion for ease of use. Finally, there was the acknowledgment that the manual was neither a definitive nor exclusive resource. As Carr says in the quote above, "many new and fascinating monsters will continue to arise" both through the "official" channels of TSR Hobbies publications but also by way of players' own active imaginations. The last line—"this is only as it should be"—underscores the invitation made to players: this is your game to make your way. The official products are only supplements to the players' imaginations.

Expansive Creativity Bounded by Uniformity

The *Monster Manual* was only the first product undergoing the major changes of standardization and professionalization. Hot on the heels of the publication of the *Monster Manual* came the *Player's Handbook* in 1978 and *Dungeon Master's Guide* in 1979. In his preface to the *Player's Handbook*, Gygax notes that people who buy and play the game possess an "unusually active imagination and superior, active intellect" and that "a great majority of readers master their own dungeons and are necessarily creative."[17] Yet amid this explosion of participation and creation, Gygax stresses the need for *consistency* across all iterations of the game, or what he refers to as uniformity:

There is a need for a certain amount of uniformity from campaign to campaign in D&D. This is not to say that conformity or sameness is desirable. Nobody wishes to have stale campaigns where dungeons, monsters, traps, tricks, and goals are much the same as those encountered in any one of a score of other campaigns. Uniformity means that classes are relatively the same in abilities and approach to solving the problems with which the campaign confronts them. Uniformity means that treasure and experience are near a reasonable mean. Uniformity means that the campaign is neither a give-away show nor a killer— that rewards are just that, and great risk will produce commensurate rewards, that intelligent play will give characters a fighting chance of survival.[18]

The end goal, then, is to have a system that allows for infinite diversity of people, places, and things in the world, yet be constrained by a uniform system that keeps everything "near a reasonable mean." Without the thread of consistency running throughout the entire system, the created world would lack coherence. The numerical and categorical information helps enforce this consistency. For example, we learn that a dagger is a one-handed weapon that has a speed factor of 2 and clubs have a factor of 4.[19] We understand, then, that, under normal circumstances, all daggers can be wielded twice as fast as all clubs.

The game actively encourages players to add to or modify the information provided in the trio of core rulebooks. As Gygax writes again in his Preface to the *Player's Handbook*:

> Many readers will want more material. There is a wealth of commercial and fan material available for fulfilling such needs. Similarly, even the most important material herein can be altered and bent to suit the needs of individual campaigns. Where possible, true guidelines have been laid down to provide the barest of frameworks for those areas of the campaign which should be the most unusual and unique.[20]

So, for example, a game master may create a new weapon, a magically enhanced "Swiftclub" that can be swung faster than a dagger. When the players encounter it, the game master announces that the Swiftclub has all the same properties of a normal club, except its speed factor is 1 and thus can be used for multiple attacks in a single turn. The Swiftclub is a unique weapon as it only exists for this one group of players, but because it conforms to all other rules, it could also be easily shared with other gaming groups with little need for explanation. Clever player creations could also be shared through submissions to *Dragon Magazine*, at conventions, or in local game shops.

While it's easy to get lost in the jargon and technical aspects of the RPG, the most important part of this innovation was the recognized need for consistency among entries. The underlying rules mattered less than ensuring the catalog entries all adhered to a specific set of criteria. The rules for *Dungeons & Dragons* were very different from *Boot Hill* and *Star Frontiers*, but each game was internally consistent in regards to its rules and its catalog entries. The same holds true for a collaborative worldbuilding project. Most groups will not use stats the way most RPGs do, but uniformity among entries is essential. If one character has their physical attributes listed, then all characters should have their physical attributes listed using the same criteria. This allows for meaningful one-to-one comparisons between entries, and also adds another layer of coherence to the fictional world.

Player-Character Growth and Development

Another dramatic change comes in the detail of the player-characters. In *Men & Magic*, PCs were little more than a combination of an archetype, a moral alignment, and a collection of stats. In *Advanced Dungeons & Dragons*, the PC becomes a persona:

> As a role player, *you become* Falstaff the fighter. You know how strong, intelligent, wise, healthy, dexterous and, relatively speaking, how commanding a personality you have. Details as to your appearance your body proportions, and your history can be produced by you or the Dungeon Master.[21]

While the abilities (strength, intelligence, etc.) are determined by dice rolls as prescribed in the rules, deciding your character's personality is entirely a player's choice. So too is the character's physical description and personal history, which have no mechanical function in the game but add narrative flavor to the game. If a player describes her character as aggressive, she may choose to have the character act before thinking, but the game doesn't provide rules for playing an "aggressive" character.

The six abilities—strength, intelligence, wisdom, dexterity, constitution, and charisma—get much fuller descriptions as well. In the original booklet, the description of the Strength ability is as follows:

> **Strength** is the prime requisite for fighters. Clerics can use strength on a 3 for 1 basis in their prime requisite area (wisdom), for purposes of gaining experience only. Strength will also aid in opening traps and so on.[22]

In the *Player's Handbook*, the description of Strength is five times longer, going into much greater depth than the casual "and so on":

Strength: Strength is a measure of muscle, endurance, and stamina combined. For purposes of relating this ability to some reality, assume that a character with a strength of 3 is able to lift a maximum of 30 pounds weight above his or her head in a military press, while a character with 18 strength will be able to press 180 pounds in the same manner. Strength is the forte of fighters, for they must be physically powerful in order to wear armor and wield heavy weapons. Therefore, strength is the major characteristic (or prime requisite) of fighters, and those fighters with strength of 16 or more gain a bonus of 10 percent of earned experience (explained later). Furthermore, fighters with an 18 strength are entitled to roll percentile dice in order to generate a random number between 01 and 00 (1 00) to determine exceptional strength; exceptional strength increases hit probability and damage done when attacking, and it also increases the weight the character is able to carry without penalty for encumbrance, as well as increasing the character's ability to force open doors and similar portals. The tables below give complete information regarding the effects of strength. Note that only fighters are permitted to roll on the exceptional strength section of STRENGTH TABLE II: ABILITY ADJUSTMENTS.

Here, an abstract concept (strength) is quantified by a numeric value (3) that in turn relates to something tangible in our primary world (lifting 30 pounds over the head). The detailed description now provides a rationale for why fighters tend to have strength as a primary attribute; it's because they wear heavy armor and wield heavy weapons. The other five abilities receive the same in-depth treatment with similarly involved descriptions. The additional language helped contextualize each ability so players could better understand when it would be relevant in their campaigns.

In another departure from the numbers-heavy original *D&D*, the new Advanced books added many more character customization options for players to develop. For example, the available races (dwarven, elven, gnome, half-elven, halfling, half-orc, and human) received extended descriptions that describe their usual habitats and racial abilities, such as dwarves' ability to see radiation in the infra-red spectrum and thus have limited vision in the dark, or that the slight build of elves gives them a bonus to their initial dexterity and a penalty on their constitution scores. There is also a Racial Preferences Table that notes the general relations between races on a six-category scale for each race. The relations ranged from preferred (relations between members of the same race) to hatred (with half-orcs being the race viewed most negatively by the others). Race relations are not handled mechanically—there are no values assigned to a character's tolerance or bigotry—but the Racial Preferences Table provided some structure for exploring racial tensions within the role-playing story.[23]

The number of character classes grew from three in *Men & Magic* (fighting-men, magic-user, and cleric) to five (adding thief and monk) with additional sub-classes and the opportunity to blend two classes by "multiclassing."[24] The previous linear three-category alignment scale (Law, Neutrality, Chaos) added a new dimension by including three new values (Good, Neutral, and Evil) on a separate axis, thus producing a range of nine broad alignments: Lawful Good, Neutral Good, Chaotic Good; Lawful Neutral, True Neutral, Chaotic Neutral; and so on. The rules briefly describe each of these nine alignments, and the concluding paragraph in the section underscores how alignments should be broadly interpreted and likely to change over time:

> Naturally, there are all variations and shades of tendencies within each alignment. The descriptions are generalizations only. A character can be basically *good* in its "true" neutrality, or tend towards evil. It is probable that your campaign referee will keep a graph of the drift of your character on the alignment chart. This is affected by the actions (and desires) of your character during the course of each adventure, and will be reflected on the graph. You may find that these actions are such as to cause the declared alignment to be shifted towards, or actually to, some other.[25]

This paragraph describing alignment is representative of the shift of focus in how the rules of the game were written. The *Advanced Dungeons & Dragons* books still had plenty of tables and charts, but they also added in language that creates a richer world full of more possibilities for characters that are not strictly bound to rules and dice rolls.

In other words, there are rules and dice rolls to determine if a thief PC succeeds or fails an attempt to poison a victim, but it's entirely up to the player to decide how that thief feels about it. Rather than being disposable faceless archetypes, the PC in *Dungeons & Dragons* begins to develop a personality akin to literary characters. They have backstories, personality traits, and motivations. The player's character had truly become the player-character: a fusion of two personalities, one of which existed in the primary world, the other in the fictional world.

With this first major evolution of the game, TSR created a much more convenient, flexible, expandable, yet uniform system for creating large-scale fictional worlds and populating it with interesting people, places, and things. By 1979, the three core rulebooks for *Advanced Dungeons & Dragons* offered players hundreds of monsters, weapons, types of armor, and equipment to use in their games, all of them unified by a central organization system that described each entry both *categorically* (and often numerically) as well as *descriptively*. This combination of categorical and descriptive elements ensures both consistency and flexibility in each entry in a condensed format, allowing any entry to be brought quickly and seamlessly into the game for both mechanical (e.g., combat) and narrative (e.g., the campaign plot) purposes. The system works so well it's now the basis for most of today's tabletop role-playing games and has been a part of every *Dungeons & Dragons* edition including the most recent edition published in 2014.[26]

The takeaway for collaborative worldbuilding projects is that the catalog entries allowed players to tailor their campaign settings however they wished. They could purchase authorized modules and sourcebooks to add content to the world, or they could flex their creative muscles and write their own. Players only needed to adhere to the basic structure of the catalog entry and their creations could be easily incorporated into the many possible worlds offered by the *Dungeons & Dragons* RPG. A collaborative worldbuilding project is built out in a very similar way, using the structure of catalog entries to expand the world in a consistent fashion.

Analyzing Catalog Templates and Entries

It didn't take long for a slew of competing tabletop RPGs to hit the market in the wake of the success of *Dungeon & Dragons*. Today there are hundreds of RPG systems on the market and the vast majority of rulebooks make use of catalogs that are tailored to that game's specific genre and needs. Some RPGs are heavy on combat rules and their catalog entries predominantly feature numbers and stats. Other games that focus on narrative and storytelling feature few numeric values. Regardless of the game or system, all RPG catalogs rely on *templates* that establish the minimum information required for any individual entry and ensure consistency among entries. A typical catalog template has three main parts: a *stat block* that contains the entry's categorical and statistical information; a *narrative description* that explains how the entry fits into the world; and an *image* that's a visual representation of the entry.

When it comes time to build the catalog for your collaborative worldbuilding project, the first order of business is to design templates for each type of entry, and it's wise to compare different types of catalogs to see what might work well for your world. This analysis will focus on the catalog template used in the fifth edition of *Dungeons & Dragons Monster Manual*, focusing on the different types of *fields* in the stat block and what kind of information each field provides. This level of detail is generally overkill for most worldbuilding projects, but consider the kinds of information you will want to keep consistent for the catalog entries in *your* world.

Stat Blocks

The *Monster Manual* describes the *stat block* as "the essential information you need to run the monster" in your gaming sessions[27] and is notable for its informational density. The stat block occupies only a few square inches on the printed page but it packs in a ton of facts. Think about the stat block functioning like the information found on a driver's license: it doesn't tell a person's life story but provides a quick overview of some essential identifying information, is objective in nature, and is expressed numerically and categorically. What follows is a summary of the required information found in the stat block section as described in the Introduction to the *Monster Manual* and how it may apply to your worldbuilding projects.[28]

The first section of the standard template is the stat block, which is mostly categorical information. Each record begins with its (1) *name or title*, which sometimes draws from mythology (e.g., hippogriff), a primary world animal (e.g., giant spider), or is entirely imaginary (e.g., kuo-toa). Listed below the monster's name is its (2) *size*, a category that must use one of six options: tiny, small, medium, large, huge, or gargantuan. A size chart on page 6 of the *Manual* helps determine the correct size by providing the approximate space the monster might occupy and gives an example (e.g., a goblin takes up roughly 5 by 5 feet of space and is small sized). The (3) *type* describes the creature's "fundamental nature" and provides brief descriptions of the 14 possible options: aberrations, beasts, celestials, constructs, dragons, elementals, fey, fiends, giants, humanoids, monstrosities, oozes, plants, or undead. Finally, (4) *alignment* describes the monster's general disposition on the nine-point alignment scale ranging from lawful good to chaotic evil.[29] Some monsters can be any alignment (i.e., a randomly encountered druid might be good or evil) and unintelligent monsters may be unaligned, meaning they act on instinct rather than being capable of making moral or ethical decisions. The information contained in this first section of the stat block already suggests how the monster would react to encountering adventuring PCs. A Mind Flayer (medium aberration, lawful evil) would immediately be hostile to the group, whereas a Pegasus (large celestial, chaotic good) may be persuaded to assist the group, provided they themselves were of a good alignment. While your worldbuilding project might not use strict alignments, think about how listing a few personal dispositions or attitudes for characters could function in a similar way in terms of how different characters might interact with each other.

The second and third sections of the template are mostly numeric and are most useful as game mechanics, so they may be less applicable to worldbuilding projects. They include the monster's (5) *armor class*, (6) *hit points*, and (7) *speed*. These stats are primarily used in combat situations. Armor class is a number that expresses a damage threshold that an attacker must top before inflicting damage, and hit points indicate how much damage the monster can take before it is defeated. Speed describes the distance the monster can cover in a turn and may provide additional information such as whether it burrows, climbs, flies, or swims, which can present different challenges to players. A flying creature covered in rock-hard scales will present a stiffer challenge than a grounded humanoid dressed in rags.

The template's third section is a mix of numeric values and categorical information. The section lists the monster's (8) *ability scores*: strength, dexterity, constitution, intelligence, wisdom, and charisma. The uniformity of the ability scores allows players quickly to establish relationships between entries. For example, a troll who has a strength of 18 is twice as strong as a PC's sorcerer who has a strength of 9. This means the sorcerer would want to keep her distance and perhaps try to defeat the troll using her wits rather than brute force. The fourth section lists other combat-focused attributes expressed in short descriptions, for example (9) *saving throws* against poisons or magic, any (10) *unique skills* or resistances such as night vision or immunity to cold attacks, as well as the (11) *language(s)* the monster speaks, and finally the (12) *challenge level*, or the level of threat the monster poses. This also indicates how many experience points the adventuring party will receive for defeating it. Generally speaking, players may not know the information contained in sections three and four but may discover a monster's strengths and vulnerabilities during the encounter. While a worldbuilding project likely won't use such specific fields, capturing some sense of characters' physical attributes and special abilities will help you better understand how individual people fit in your fictional world and how they may be able to take advantage of specific opportunities that may arise.

The fifth and sixth sections list (13) *special traits* and (14) *special actions* unique to a specific monster, such as the ability to attack with its tail, or to perform a dive attack. Special traits are usually expressed in a few short sentences along with some numeric information; e.g., Death Burst: When the mephit dies, it explodes in a cloud of steam. Each creature within 5 feet of the mephit must succeed on a DC 10 Dexterity saving throw or take 4 (1d8) fire damage.[30] Legendary monsters such as dragons may have an extensive list of special traits, which can make this section quite long. These special traits also help differentiate between monsters of the same species. For example, there are six variations of mephits and each kind has its own special traits. This all adds to the level of detail that can be brought into any gaming session, enriching the storytelling possibilities through these unique attributes.

The seventh and last section is the only optional one, reserved for monsters who can perform (15) *legendary actions*. As the name suggests, only legendary monsters are capable of legendary actions such as attacking multiple times or committing a number of simultaneous moves per turn. An adventuring party should experience shock and awe when coming up against a monster capable of using legendary actions.

The stat block is flexible and extendable enough to account for every monster in the *Dungeons & Dragons* universe, ranging from the low-level nuisances (baboon, challenge level 0)[31] to the legendary monsters that can devour whole towns (tarrasque, challenge level 25).[32] The stat block also provides a great template for modifying monsters or creating your own from scratch, a process covered in the *Dungeon Master's Guide*[33] that walks you through the creation process in order to ensure the monster is neither overpowered nor underpowered for your game purposes.

Worldbuilding projects will rarely need this level of granular detail in the stat block, and it will often make sense to use descriptive phrases (e.g., "very strong") as opposed to numeric values (e.g., "strength of 5") in your stat blocks. Regardless, this is a demonstration of how much valuable information the stat block can pack in without taking up much space. Scanning a stat block should give someone a very good idea of the nature and traits of that catalog entry. The more fields you add to the stat block, the more detailed of a snapshot you will wind up with.

Narrative Descriptions

The stat block helps game masters see how monsters would stack up against the players and understand the powers in that monster's repertoire, but it's the *narrative description* that gives critical details in terms of how the encounter with the monster may play out in the story of the game. For example, goblins attack in packs and often emerge from labyrinthine lairs;[34] werewolves are savage predators that only emerge at night;[35] iron golems are impervious to fire and mindlessly serve those who animated them;[36] and liches tend to haunt secluded locations and show "no interest in the affairs of the living except where those affairs interfere with their own."[37] A good game master will draw from the narrative description and subtly drop in select details when describing the sights and sounds of the scenery to foreshadow an encounter.

Whereas the numeric quality of the stat block is meant to be a fast reference for game mechanics and dice rolling, the rich language in the narrative descriptions supports evocative storytelling. The writers of the monster descriptions use vivid imagery and strong descriptions rooted in the five senses so players can see, hear, smell, touch, and sometimes even taste their adversaries. Goblins are "black-hearted, selfish humanoids,"[38] a werewolf has a "fiery temper,"[39] iron golems shamble with "clanging steps,"[40] the stinking troglodyte dwells in caverns "smeared with grime, oily secretions, and the debris of their foul feasting,"[41] liches are "scheming and insane,"[42] and the giant elk is "majestic."[43]

Storytellers in any medium should never disregard the importance of using succinct, vibrant language and concrete details. Take, for example, the entry of a monster called the Nightmare. In the plainest terms, the Nightmare is a teleporting horse whose hooves, tail, and mane appear to be on fire. Note the literary flourish in the first paragraph of the description in the *Monster Manual*:

> A nightmare appears in a cloud of roiling smoke, its mane, tail, and hooves wreathed in flame. The creature's unearthly black form moves with supernatural speed, vanishing in a cloud of brimstone as quickly as it appeared.[44]

Roiling smoke. *Wreathed* in flame. *Unearthly* black form. *Supernatural* speed. *Vanishing* in a *cloud of brimstone*. These active verbs and vivid adjectives make the Nightmare seem to leap off the page into your imagination. You can easily imagine the flames licking at this sleek black form that appears out of nowhere and blinks out of existence in a stinking, sulfurous cloud. The carefully crafted language pays enormous dividends in any storytelling enterprise, where specific, concrete details simulate a multisensory experience for the reader.

Images

Images are an important part of the catalog but can also present some challenges. The *Monster Manual* is beautifully designed and the monster illustrations take up a quarter to half of most pages in the book. This is a far cry from the first edition *Dungeons and Dragons*, where the amateurish sketches would look at home on the back of a high school student's notebook. Many commercial role-playing games suffer from a lack of or quality artwork. Most small publishers can't afford to commission talented artists for custom illustrations to depict each catalog entry and must settle for having few or no unique images.

The most important is that the image accompanying a catalog entry should reinforce the message of the text. In the *Monster Manual*, we see evil or aggressive monsters assuming threatening postures and snarling whereas neutral monsters usually appear more static and stoic; the handful of good monsters adopting open and welcoming poses. Colors and tones also send strong messages with evil monsters being represented by dark and muddy colors while the forces of good burst from the page in whites and light colors. An image also need not be an explicit depiction of the entry. It could be some impressionistic artwork, a symbol or design, a sample schematic, or more. Different options for catalog images will be offered in later chapters.

Catalog Entries as Narrative Units

A catalog entry collapses an enormous amount of numeric, categorical, descriptive, and visual information into one tidy package, and catalog templates ensure that each entry has the same minimum amount of required information, though the description can be expanded to include much more. In an RPG, the consistency enforced by the stat block and the details supplied in the narrative description means that any random catalog entry can be selected, quickly skimmed over, and then inserted into the game session in a meaningful way. In a collaborative worldbuilding project, the same holds true but instead of being inserted into a game, any catalog entry should be able to slide into a story.

As a general rule, each catalog entry in a collaborative worldbuilding project should function as an individual narrative unit. In other words, each entry should tell a story. Part of the catalog entry's story will be a physical description of that person, place, or thing, but the other equally important part will be its historical and social context. Imagine you have five character entries, all of which are very different. As individuals, they might come from a variety of races, classes, genders, and sexual orientations. They should also have a wide range of personality traits, motivations, strengths and weaknesses, and so on. Mixing well-crafted catalog entries in a collaborative worldbuilding project should produce interesting points of tension for storytelling explorations, either between characters who view the world differently, between characters and working for or against the social forces of their world, or both.

Case Study: The Kobold

This section examines how a single catalog entry operates as a discrete narrative unit within a fictional world. This example comes from the *Monster Manual*. Figure 6.2 is the full page entry for kobolds, an iconic *Dungeons & Dragons* monster. The entry provides information on two varieties of kobolds, one with wings and one without. We'll look at how the story of the kobold unfolds as we follow the eye's path from the image, to scanning the stat block, to finally reading the entry's narrative description.

The striking *image* of the kobold, positioned on the right side of the page, draws the reader's eye and serves as a visually informative introduction to the entry. We see the horns atop its dragon-like head, its strapping muscular chest, its hands brandishing a dagger and sling, and its swooping tail and taloned feet. Its posture is aggressive, its chin up, the face almost sneering. Its weapons are unsophisticated though, and it wears only a rag loincloth rather than armor. Even from a quick scan of the image, we surmise that kobolds are primitive yet menacing.

Next, we'll jump down to the *stat block*. There are two boxes at the bottom of the page, separating the different types of kobolds. Starting at the top of the stat block and moving down through each of the six sections The first section identifies the winged kobold and the kobold. Beneath in italics, we see that they are small humanoids, or the height of a short human, four or five feet tall. Their alignment is lawful evil, which we know from the *Player's Handbook* means that they will "take what they want, within the limits of a code of tradition, loyalty or order."[45] Everything here confirms the first impression established by the image. The second section shows the winged kobold to be a slightly tougher foe than its grounded brethren, having an extra point in its armor class and more hit points; both kinds can move the same speed (30 ft.) though the winged kobold can also fly at that speed. The third section shows near identical ability scores. The fourth section indicates they have identical senses (darkvision and passive perception, no doubt useful in their subterranean dwelling) and speak the same languages (Common and Draconic), and defeating the tougher winged kobold earns a few more experience points. In the bigger picture though, the challenge rating for both is quite low, which tells us that these monsters pose little threat in individual combat. The fifth section provides some interesting narrative details, revealing that they are at a disadvantage in sunlight but gain a combat advantage when attacking in packs.

Based on what we know from what we've read thus far, we can begin to draw a mental picture of how they behave. They must dwell in dark locations and rely

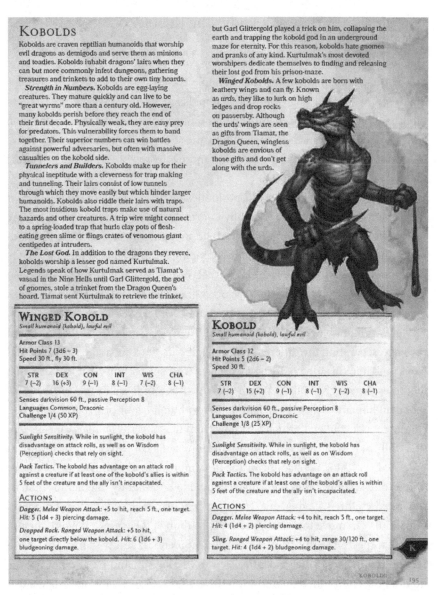

KOBOLDS

Kobolds are craven reptilian humanoids that worship evil dragons as demigods and serve them as minions and toadies. Kobolds inhabit dragons' lairs when they can but more commonly infest dungeons, gathering treasures and trinkets to add to their own tiny hoards.

Strength in Numbers. Kobolds are egg-laying creatures. They mature quickly and can live to be "great wyrms" more than a century old. However, many kobolds perish before they reach the end of their first decade. Physically weak, they are easy prey for predators. This vulnerability forces them to band together. Their superior numbers can win battles against powerful adversaries, but often with massive casualties on the kobold side.

Tunnelers and Builders. Kobolds make up for their physical ineptitude with a cleverness for trap making and tunneling. Their lairs consist of low tunnels through which they move easily but which hinder larger humanoids. Kobolds also riddle their lairs with traps. The most insidious kobold traps make use of natural hazards and other creatures. A trip wire might connect to a spring-loaded trap that hurls clay pots of flesh-eating green slime or flings crates of venomous giant centipedes at intruders.

The Lost God. In addition to the dragons they revere, kobolds worship a lesser god named Kurtulmak. Legends speak of how Kurtulmak served as Tiamat's vassal in the Nine Hells until Garl Glittergold, the god of gnomes, stole a trinket from the Dragon Queen's hoard. Tiamat sent Kurtulmak to retrieve the trinket, but Garl Glittergold played a trick on him, collapsing the earth and trapping the kobold god in an underground maze for eternity. For this reason, kobolds hate gnomes and pranks of any kind. Kurtulmak's most devoted worshipers dedicate themselves to finding and releasing their lost god from his prison-maze.

Winged Kobolds. A few kobolds are born with leathery wings and can fly. Known as *urds*, they like to lurk on high ledges and drop rocks on passersby. Although the urds' wings are seen as gifts from Tiamat, the Dragon Queen, wingless kobolds are envious of those gifts and don't get along with the urds.

WINGED KOBOLD
Small humanoid (kobold), lawful evil

Armor Class 13
Hit Points 7 (3d6 – 3)
Speed 30 ft., fly 30 ft.

STR	DEX	CON	INT	WIS	CHA
7 (–2)	16 (+3)	9 (–1)	8 (–1)	7 (–2)	8 (–1)

Senses darkvision 60 ft., passive Perception 8
Languages Common, Draconic
Challenge 1/4 (50 XP)

Sunlight Sensitivity. While in sunlight, the kobold has disadvantage on attack rolls, as well as on Wisdom (Perception) checks that rely on sight.

Pack Tactics. The kobold has advantage on an attack roll against a creature if at least one of the kobold's allies is within 5 feet of the creature and the ally isn't incapacitated.

ACTIONS

Dagger. Melee Weapon Attack: +5 to hit, reach 5 ft., one target. *Hit:* 5 (1d4 + 3) piercing damage.

Dropped Rock. Ranged Weapon Attack: +5 to hit, one target directly below the kobold. *Hit:* 6 (1d6 + 3) bludgeoning damage.

KOBOLD
Small humanoid (kobold), lawful evil

Armor Class 12
Hit Points 5 (2d6 – 2)
Speed 30 ft.

STR	DEX	CON	INT	WIS	CHA
7 (–2)	15 (+2)	9 (–1)	8 (–1)	7 (–2)	8 (–1)

Senses darkvision 60 ft., passive Perception 8
Languages Common, Draconic
Challenge 1/8 (25 XP)

Sunlight Sensitivity. While in sunlight, the kobold has disadvantage on attack rolls, as well as on Wisdom (Perception) checks that rely on sight.

Pack Tactics. The kobold has advantage on an attack roll against a creature if at least one of the kobold's allies is within 5 feet of the creature and the ally isn't incapacitated.

ACTIONS

Dagger. Melee Weapon Attack: +4 to hit, reach 5 ft., one target. *Hit:* 4 (1d4 + 2) piercing damage.

Sling. Ranged Weapon Attack: +4 to hit, range 30/120 ft., one target. *Hit:* 4 (1d4 + 2) bludgeoning damage.

Figure 6.2 The Kobold. © Wizards of the Coast. Used with permission.

on overwhelming opponents because, individually, they're not very strong. In the final section, we learn that the winged kobold drops rocks on victims from flight, whereas the wingless kobold uses a dagger and sling, as shown in the image. They're more agile than physically strong, and likely choose to attack from a distance. Since both types of kobolds use rocks in their attacks—either dropping them or using them as ammunition for their slings—we can guess that they tend to live in mountains or caves and not in dense forests, plains, or sandy beaches. The combination of the image and stat block, the places where the reader's eye first scans, provide a clear mental picture of the two types of kobolds.

The *narrative description* is five paragraphs and nearly 350 words long. The introductory paragraph reads:

> Kobolds are craven reptilian humanoids that worship evil dragons as demigods and serve them as minions and toadies. Kobolds inhabit dragons' lairs when they can but more commonly infest dungeons, gathering treasures and trinkets to add to their own tiny hoards.[46]

The description here depicts them as cowardly servants to dragons, which suggests that if adventurers encounter them, there could be a much deadlier challenge nearby. Kobolds also are both greedy and petty, given their desire to gather small piles of wealth. The deft use of language in the passage—*craven, minion, toadies, infest*—establishes the tone for the entry, positioning the kobold more as an annoying nuisance than a major threat in their own right.

The second paragraph, "Strength in Numbers," confirms our suspicions that individually they are "physically weak" but that this "vulnerability forces them to band together" and that their "superior numbers can win battles against powerful adversaries, but often with massive casualties on the kobold side."[47] It also relays some interesting facts, such as that they are an egg-laying species (reinforcing their reptilian nature) that can live to be 100 years old, though many die in their first decade due to their inability to fight off predators. This detail might also explain their cowardice.

The third paragraph, "Tunnelers and Builders," explains that kobolds "make up for their physical ineptitude with a cleverness for trap making and tunneling,"[48] creating twisting underground lairs to confuse and confound their enemies. An additional fun detail is that kobolds often rig traps: "a trip wire might connect to a spring-loaded trap that hurls clay pots of flesh-eating green slime or flings crates of venomous giant centipedes at intruders."[49] Green slime and giant centipedes are of course other monsters featured in the *Monster Manual*; were this catalog entry in a wiki instead of in a book, there would be links to those monsters' respective catalog entries. This paragraph also establishes that pursuing a kobold into its lair would be much more dangerous than facing it in the open. The fourth paragraph, "The Lost God," describes the kobold belief system. In addition to their reverence for dragons, they worship the lesser god Kurtulmak and despise his rival, the gnome god Garl Glittergold, which explains kobold's racial hatred of gnomes. The final paragraph, "Winged Kobolds," addresses the few kobolds who can fly, that they are known as urds, and are the envy of the wingless kobolds.[50]

In this short catalog entry for the kobold, we get a detailed picture of this monster and clearly understand how it behaves, its native habitat, its strengths and weaknesses, and most importantly how it might be integrated naturally into the story of a single session or a larger campaign. As a matter of fact, kobolds are a common lower-level foe in the *Tyranny of Dragons* series of *Dungeons & Dragons* modules in the *Hoard of the Dragon Queen* and *Rise of Tiamat*.[51] Kobolds function as a low-level threat and persistent nuisance in these adventures. Though individual kobolds may be anonymous and lacking any distinct personality, the wealth of detail provided about them as a group means they can provide additional twists and turns, as well as storytelling depth, to an RPG campaign narrative.

As robust as the catalog entry for kobolds already is, it can also be expanded. Another source book, *Volo's Guide to Monsters*, provides another eight pages on kobold lore. The section headings include "Expert Tunnelers," "Able Scavengers," "Dragon Servitors," "Arcane Magic Users;" a section on kobold culture entitled "Life and Outlook"; more on the kobold's preferred environment; tips on how to role-play kobolds; notes on kobold names and physical variations, combat tactics, treasures, allies; and a full two pages detailing kobold lairs, including a full-page map of a sample lair.[52] The sourcebook also adds three new types of kobold: the dragonshield, the inventor, and the scale sorcerer.[53] Each of these three new types of kobold has its own unique stat block, image, and description. And the kobold is only one entry in a catalog that features hundreds of monsters. Adventure modules and other sourcebooks like *Volo's Guide* give players an incredible amount of material to adapt when creating their own storytelling scenarios.

Catalogs as Models for Flexible Worldbuilding

Catalogs of many fictional worlds are easy to find on the Internet. Every major media franchise has a wiki that acts as a catalog, linking together people, places, things, and events. Below are examples drawn from fan wikis from Middle-earth, the *Star Wars* galaxy, *A Song of Ice and Fire*, and the digital RPG *Fallout 4*. The discussion of each includes how the wiki creators separate the stat block, or statistical and categorical information, from the entry's narrative description. These are but a few examples among literally hundreds of thousands. Browse around these wikis and click on links to see how the templates operate for the categories used in collaborative worldbuilding projects: *items, locations, characters,* and *historical events*. Check out fan wikis of the large-scale fictional worlds of your choice, such as the world of Harry Potter, the Marvel and D C universes, the world of Pokémon, or other games like *Assassin's Creed, Halo, Gears of War, Final Fantasy,* or a host of others. Find templates that you like the best and adopt something similar for your collaborative worldbuilding project.

Character Entry for John Hancock[54]

John Hancock is a character in *Fallout 4,* a videogame set in the greater post-apocalyptic Boston area. His wiki entry on the Nukapedia: The *Fallout* Wiki can be found at fallout.wikia.com/wiki/John_Hancock. The *image* comes from a screenshot taken from the game and shows Hancock's cracked leathery face of a ghoul, the name of those humans who were disfigured by radiation from the nuclear holocaust. He wears a tricorn hat and garb popular during the American Revolutionary War, playing off the fact he shares his name with a famous figure from United States history.

Below the *image* is his stat block. The biography section provides categorical information including his race (ghoul), sex (male), affiliations (the *location* of Goodneighbor), his roles (mayor), the specific sublocation where he can be found (the Old State House), and family members (the *characters* of his brother, Mayor McDonough, who is at another *location,* Diamond City, and his parents, Martha and Patrick McDonough, both of whom are deceased). The information supplied in each field is also a link to other wiki entries, either for the race of ghouls, the different locations, or the different characters. Hancock's physical traits listed in the stat block include his eye color (dark), hair color (none), and height (1.0, which indicates the same height as the PC). Other categorical information can be found in the Behavior section, which notes he is aggressive, foolhardy, and helps his allies. Statistical information is included for his physical abilities and special perks.

Hancock's *narrative description* is a little over 350 words and it describes his relevant personal history: how he became a ghoul, how he became mayor of the town of Goodneighbor and his style of governance. The remainder of the page describes how Hancock is likely to interact with the player, including how he fits

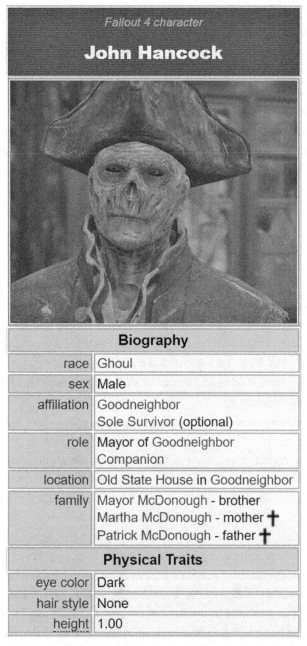

Figure 6.3 John Hancock. Image courtesy of Fallout® 4 © 2014 Bethesda Softworks LLC, a ZeniMax Media company. Bethesda Softworks, Bethesda Game Studios, ZeniMax and related logos are registered trademarks or trademarks of ZeniMax Media Inc. in the U.S. and/or other countries. Fallout and related logos are trademarks or registered trademarks of Bethesda Softworks LLC in the U.S. and/or other countries. All Rights Reserved.

into the wider narrative landscape of *Fallout 4*. The sentence that best sums up his personality reads:

> [Hancock] is exceptionally punitive toward his enemies or those that break Goodneighbor law, but can be a good friend and valuable ally to those who treat him with respect, punish the guilty and protect the innocent.

Although players encounter this character in a game where programming determines the nature of the interaction, Hancock stands on his own as a well-developed character. The entry doesn't provide an exhaustive biography, yet it does enough to capture the spirit of the character. Despite his gruff nature, Hancock can be a powerful friend and is motivated to help those in need. He may quarrel with strong-willed individuals or lend a helping hand if approached in the right manner.

Location Entry for Sullust[55]

Sullust is a planet in the *Star Wars* galaxy that doesn't appear in any of the films (at least not yet) but occurs relatively frequently in other canon media. It's perhaps best known as the home of Nien Nunb, the alien pilot who flew with Lando Calrissian in the Millennium Falcon during the attack on the second Death Star in *Return of the Jedi*.[56] Sullust is also a location in the videogame *Star Wars Battlefront* and is the setting of the last act of the tie-in novel *Battlefront: Twilight Company*. Its wiki entry on Wookieepedia: The *Star Wars* Wiki can be found at starwars.wikia.com/wiki/Sullust.

The *image* for the entry shows us little, except for a portion of a dark blue planet with white, wispy clouds and red blotches and swirls on the planet's surface. The stat block for the entry provides specific geographical data, locating it in the Outer Rim Territories and giving the specific coordinates. Other categorical information includes the physical description climate (hot), terrain (volcanic molten surface), points of interest (six in all, including), and fauna (five entries, also all linked) as well as the societal description that lists a number of fields including the native species (Sullustans), immigrated species (humans), languages (Galactic Basic and Sullustese), the population (at least one billion), its demonym (Sullustan), major cities (Pinyumb), major exports (starfighters and assault shuttles), and affiliations (six in all, including the opposition sides of the Galactic Empire and New Republic).

The *narrative description* of the planet focuses mostly on the period of Imperial occupation and its subsequent status as a site of rebellion. Not including

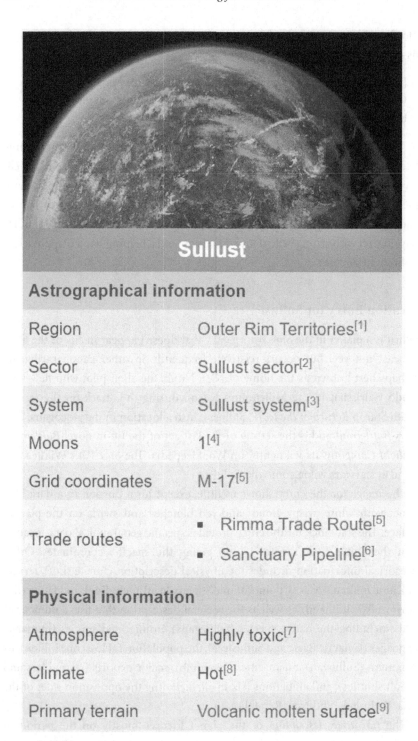

Figure 6.4 Sullust.

the "behind the scenes" information that exists only in our primary world, the entry weighs in around a hefty 750 words. In addition to the importance of Sullust's historical position in relation to galactic politics, it also features a number of links to prominent characters and a number of sublocations on the planet itself, such as the underground city of Pinyumb and the SoroSuub Corporation facilities. The location possesses a past, present, and possible future, but it's also the site of many historical events and is linked to many other significant locations and characters. The inhospitable terrain and subterranean lifestyle would certainly be off-putting to many outsiders, but for many native Sullastans it would be the only home they ever knew.

Item Entry for the Nauglamír[57]

In *The Hobbit* and *The Lord of the Rings*, audiences learn of the long-standing feud between elves and dwarves. Readers of *The Silmarillion* know that much of the enmity can be traced back to a conflict over an exquisitely crafted necklace named the Nauglamír. In short, greed led to a dispute over ownership of the necklace, causing dwarves, elves, and the race of men to spill each other's blood on more than one occasion as the Nauglamír traded hands. Its entry can be found on the fan wiki site Tolkien Gateway at http://tolkiengateway.net/wiki/Nauglamír.

The *image* of the Nauglamír is a piece of artwork by famed Tolkien artist Ted Naismith and his interpretation of what it looks like. The necklace is made up entirely of jewels with the biggest jewel of all, a silmaril, at its center, shining so brightly that the finer details of its handiwork are lost in its glare. It sits inside an ornately decorated wooden case, a work of art itself and consistent with the aesthetics prized by elves.

The *stat block* features no numeric information whatsoever (for example, weight or value is not listed) but instead provides information on its other name (Necklace of the Dwarves), links to the *locations* associated with the Nauglamír (Nargothrond, Doriath, Mouths of Sirion), a listing of its owners (the *characters* of Finrod, Thingol, Lúthien, Dior, and Elwing, all of whom have entries of their own), and its creators (the Dwarves of the Ered Luin). There is also a 15-word description of its appearance.

The *narrative description* is just under 700 words and provides the salient history of the item, including links to all the major players involved in the Nauglamír's story. This entry puts the Nauglamír in its appropriate historical context. For characters in Middle-earth during the First Age, the necklace was

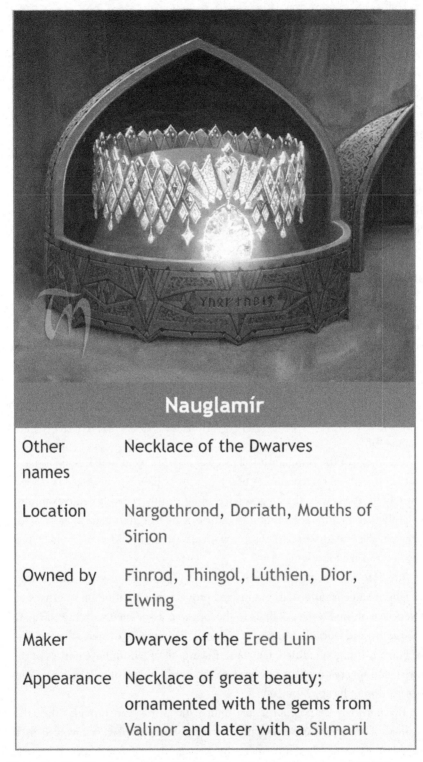

Nauglamír

Other names	Necklace of the Dwarves
Location	Nargothrond, Doriath, Mouths of Sirion
Owned by	Finrod, Thingol, Lúthien, Dior, Elwing
Maker	Dwarves of the Ered Luin
Appearance	Necklace of great beauty; ornamented with the gems from Valinor and later with a Silmaril

Figure 6.5 The Nauglamír. Copyright Ted Nasmith. All rights reserved. Used by permission.

an item of immeasurable beauty but one that brought grave danger to its owner and caused an enormous amount of strife. For later generations, the tale of the Nauglamír serves as an explanation for the frosty relationship between elves and dwarves that carries into the Third Age, the setting for *The Hobbit* and *The Lord of the Rings*, and it is also a cautionary tale about how the forces of evil use vices such as greed and avarice to turn people against each other. Items like the Nauglamír will have a history that is connected to specific locations, and it should spark strong reactions among different characters. For example, mention of the Nauglamír in the Third Age of Middle-earth would rekindle simmering resentment for elves and dwarves, a sense of regret for mankind, and perhaps even cruel mirth for orcs and the forces of evil.

Historical Event for War of the Ninepenny Kings[58]

The War of the Ninepenny Kings occurred about 20 years before Robert's Rebellion, which put Robert Baratheon on the throne, and around 40 years prior to the start of the novel *A Game of Thrones*. Also known as the Fifth Blackfyre Rebellion, this conflict marked the last in a long line of challenges to the rule of House Targaryen over the kingdom of Westeros before the family is deposed in Robert's Rebellion. The entry for this historical event can be found on A Wiki of Ice and Fire here: http://awoiaf.westeros.org/index.php/War_of_the_ Ninepenny_Kings.

The *image* for the event is a beautiful piece of professional artwork taken from *The World of Ice and Fire* that depicts two knights clashing on the field of battle, effectively capturing the violence and confusion of wartime. The caption reveals that this is Barristan Selmy fighting Maelys Blackfyre, where both names link to their individual *character* entries.

The *stat block* for historical event entries on this wiki includes the date (260 AC, or After Aegon's Conquest), location (Stepstones, Free Cities), the result (indicated with the phrase "Band of Nine fall from power End of Blackfyre line"), and a list of the belligerents (more than a dozen different factions on two sides, all linked to their respective entries), as well as the major figures involved (another 14 *characters*), and the losses on either side (three more *characters*, Ser Jason Lannister and Ormund Baratheon from the Seven Kingdoms and Maelys I Blackfyre from the Band of Nine).

The 750-word *narrative description* features dozens of links to historical characters, locations, and events, which explicitly connects this event to the timeline of the kingdom and to individual families. This rebellion, as well as the

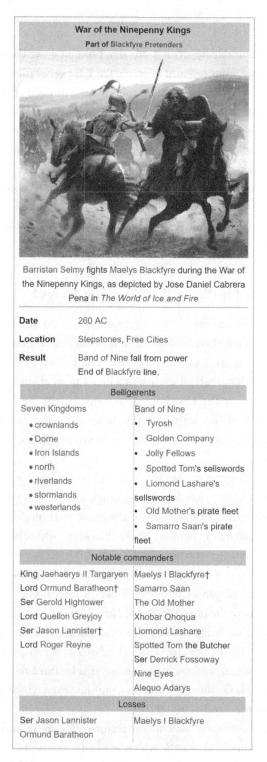

War of the Ninepenny Kings

Part of Blackfyre Pretenders

Barristan Selmy fights Maelys Blackfyre during the War of the Ninepenny Kings, as depicted by Jose Daniel Cabrera Pena in *The World of Ice and Fire*

Date	260 AC
Location	Stepstones, Free Cities
Result	Band of Nine fall from power End of Blackfyre line.

Belligerents	
Seven Kingdoms	Band of Nine
• crownlands	• Tyrosh
• Dorne	• Golden Company
• Iron Islands	• Jolly Fellows
• north	• Spotted Tom's sellswords
• riverlands	• Liomond Lashare's
• stormlands	sellswords
• westerlands	• Old Mother's pirate fleet
	• Samarro Saan's pirate fleet

Notable commanders	
King Jaehaerys II Targaryen	Maelys I Blackfyre†
Lord Ormund Baratheon†	Samarro Saan
Ser Gerold Hightower	The Old Mother
Lord Quellon Greyjoy	Xhobar Qhoqua
Ser Jason Lannister†	Liomond Lashare
Lord Roger Reyne	Spotted Tom the Butcher
	Ser Derrick Fossoway
	Nine Eyes
	Alequo Adarys

Losses	
Ser Jason Lannister Ormund Baratheon	Maelys I Blackfyre

Figure 6.6 War of the Ninepenny Kings

four that preceded it, began over the line of succession for the crown and ends up costing thousands of lives. This foreshadows the events in the *A Song of Ice and Fire* series, where by the end of *A Game of Thrones*, the continent will once again be thrown into yet another bloody civil war. The War of the Ninepenny Kings is recent enough that several significant characters participated in its battles in the days of their youth, including Barristan Selmy, Tywin Lannister, and Brynden "Blackfish" Tully, uncle to Catelyn Tully, who would eventually wed Eddard "Ned" Stark, the primary protagonist of *A Game of Thrones*. While the series never goes into great depth describing the War of the Ninepenny Kings, it establishes a precedent for constant challenges to the throne from within Westeros, and also explains some long-standing friendships and rivalries between prominent members of the noble houses of Westeros. While we often talk about global conflicts like the World Wars as battles between nations, this is an abstraction. Such wars and their outcomes are the results of individual human actions, from the highest-ranking political officials down to the common foot soldier on the front lines and the family members that were left behind. Grounding major historical events in the actions of specific human actors, like this entry for the War of the Ninepenny Kings does, gives the world a more "lived in" feeling and a deep sense of causality. In other words, the world's historical events didn't happen because they were convenient for storytelling, but rather because they are the result of decisions made by specific characters.

Catalogs as Tools for Expanding Fictional Worlds

Building a catalog of a fictional world is something that usually happens retroactively after a worldbuilding project has already expanded to a point where it becomes difficult to manage. Worldbuilding projects tend to be messy by nature. Tolkien literally spent decades working on the languages, myths, and legends of Middle-earth before he wrote *The Hobbit*, which was his attempt to bring some of that work into a tale for children. His son Christopher spent more than a decade parsing his father's notes, and that work now exists as the 12-volume series *The History of Middle-Earth*. There are now numerous fan wikis, including the Encyclopedia of Arda and the Tolkien Gateway, that use wikis as a means for cataloging information about Middle-earth. George R.R. Martin's world has also gotten to an unwieldy size, and he relies on the help from superfans Elio M. Garcia Jr. and Linda Antonsson to keep straight the names, dates, and locations of his massive universe.[59] The duo co-authored *The World of Ice and Fire* companion book for the *A Song of Ice and Fire* series, as well as the website Westeros.org. Other wikis, such as A Wiki of Ice and Fire and Game of Thrones Wiki, are linked encyclopedias of Martin's known world. Another example of a messy worldbuilding project that became wikified can be seen in the nine-part *Fallout Bible*, a series of documents published in 2002 by the creators of the games *Fallout 1* and *Fallout 2*.[60] The bible attempts to gather all of the knowledge about the *Fallout* universe in those games in order to provide fans with a comprehensive resource on details about the fictional world. In 2005, the Nukapedia Wiki site launched, and the material from the *Fallout Bible* became distributed and linked through individual entries.

George Lucas kept journals of ideas about his invented universe, but in truth he knew far fewer details about it than he often let on in later interviews, a fact made clear in both J.W. Rinzler's authoritative *The Making of Star Wars* and Michael Kaminski's *The Secret History of Star Wars*. Lucas had a number of ideas about the story of his space opera but specific details were quite fuzzy. *The Empires Strikes Back* and *Return of the Jedi* revealed more about the galaxy but, in terms of finer points of how the galaxy operated, it remained as sketch work— Lucas had enough information to provide a backdrop for his epic story but, otherwise, it was a galaxy full of holes. Surprisingly, much of the details we know about the fictional *Star Wars* galaxy today comes not from Lucas himself, but from a tabletop RPG and its voluminous catalog of entries.

Though it may be hard to comprehend today, the *Star Wars* franchise had gone dormant in the years following the release of *Return of the Jedi*. As Chris Baker explains in his article "How a Pen and Paper RPG Brought 'Star Wars' Back From the Dead,"

> There was a time when Star Wars was completely moribund. In the late Eighties, the original film trilogy was a distant memory, the kid-friendly TV specials were done, the Saturday morning cartoons had petered out, and there were no new novels or toys on the horizon.[61]

Equally implausible, however, is the fact that the resurrection of the *Star Wars* franchise has a great deal to do with the licensed role-playing game published by West End Games. Tabletop RPGs had grown throughout the 1980s and West End bought the rights to the intellectual property and published their first *Star Wars* rulebook in 1987.[62] In order for players to explore the vast galaxy of *Star Wars*, however, they needed much more information about what existed in the universe. On top of that they needed to understand how those newly discovered pieces of the galaxy worked within the rule system. As described on Wookieepedia,

> In order for players of the roleplaying game to create new adventures, West End Games needed to provide supplemental material describing the Star Wars universe in previously unknown detail and to make it *self-consistent* and *coherent*. As an example, the Aurebesh alphabet was originally a random piece of set dressing used in Return of the Jedi. Stephen Crane copied those symbols and turned them into a complete and workable alphabet which would later be used in the prequel trilogy. Developing and extrapolating from details like this in a consistent fashion turned West End Games' Star Wars products into a de facto reference library for other developers of the EU.[63] (Emphasis added)

What we see in these accounts is very similar to the collaborative worldbuilding process described in the book. The original three films provided a broad framework for the fictional world, but the role-playing game catalog provided a way to expand the galaxy in a consistent and coherent fashion, and even minor details included in catalog entries could branch off and become a new narrative arc. The Star Wars Expanded Universe truly took off with Timothy Zahn's trilogy that began with *Heir to the Empire* in 1991 and he was provided with the West End Games RPG catalog to incorporate into the novel; it would become the default reference guide for subsequent material in the Star Wars Expanded Universe as well.[64]

The massive expansion of the *Star Wars* galaxy is perhaps the best model for a twenty-first-century collaborative worldbuilding project. In a sense, George Lucas and a small team of writers built the framework and structures of the galaxy, established a few focal points, and told a trilogy of connected stories set in that fictional world. The rule system designed by West End Games' tabletop RPG gave a second team of writers some catalog entry templates to further develop the galaxy, and they added all manner of new named characters, species, locations, items, and historical events to further deepen the fictional world in concrete detail. On the heels of this, the Dark Horse comics series and other novels in the new Star Wars Expanded Universe added to this already substantial catalog. Lucas himself drew from the Expanded Universe material when writing the prequel trilogy, and details from the West End Games RPG still show up today in *The Clone Wars*, *Star Wars Rebels*, and in other parts of the new Disney-sanctioned canon materials.

This is all to demonstrate that a well-designed catalog is a powerful engine for driving collaborative worldbuilding projects. As we will see, details included in one entry can spawn five other entries as the world expands organically outward from the core of the metanarrative. The West End Games RPG provides a perfect example for how a well-designed catalog can quickly populate a fictional world in a consistent and coherent fashion, producing all kinds of quirks and details that can spin off into other entries or stories of their own.

Part Two

Collaborative Worldbuilding Projects

7

Collaborative Worldbuilding Resources

A collaborative worldbuilding project is complex and can grow out quickly. This chapter covers some resources that can help you organize your group through the various stages of the project. The companion website for this book collaborativeworldbuilding.com features content to support your collaborative worldbuilding endeavors, including a print-and-play worldbuilding card deck, several downloadable forms, guides for educators using the book in classrooms, and other worldbuilding books, games, and resources. The site also links to many examples of collaborative worldbuilding projects.

As the most efficient way to build your fictional world is to do it online, this chapter also describes a variety of online tools that keep things simplified and organized. Because tools and features change quickly, this chapter provides some general guidelines for different kinds of digital tools you should consider using, as well as pointing you to some specific pieces of online software that will prove useful in your project.

Worldbuilding Card Decks

On collaborativeworldbuilding.com you will find a deck of cards designed to be used in conjunction with the phase of the project where you develop the *structures* of your fictional world. A basic print-and-play set can be downloaded for free, or you can order a color deck with professional artwork from the site. The deck has three kinds of cards: category cards, numeric cards ranging from 1 to 5, and trending/stable cards. You start by arranging the category cards in four columns. Each category card represents one of the 14 substructures. To build a world, you shuffle the numeric cards and deal one out beside each category card. You repeat this process with the trending cards. At the end of the process, you should have four columns of cards, with each category having a numeric and trending/stable card next to it. You now have a model of a fictional world, but it needs some interpreting.

To interpret the world, have your group consider the numeric value for each category. A low number card (1) means that there is *little* of that category in the world, whereas a high number (5) means that there is an *abundance* of that category. The trending/stable cards indicate which categories are experiencing some sort of change and are trending toward a higher or a lower value. For example, a trending card next to a 4 means the category could be trending downward toward a 3 (meaning that aspect of the world is decreasing) or it could be trending upward to a 5 (meaning that aspect of the world is becoming more prominent). A trending card on a 1 or a 5 can be interpreted to mean an intensification of an already extreme value, toward a hypothetical value of 0 or 6, respectively. You should also consider the speed at which the societal change is happening. If an aspect of the world is gradually changing over a long period of time, such as a few decades, the impact on daily life might be relatively low. If the transformation occurs rapidly over a matter of days and turns the world upside down—for example, a military coup or a natural disaster—the people in the society are more likely to be alarmed and react much differently to the sudden change in their world.

Figure 7.1 provides us with an example of how we might interpret the values of a randomly generated world. The first step is to look at the low and high values, which will provide the greatest points of tension in the world. The second step is to look at which categories are trending and decide whether they might be increasing or decreasing in the world, given the points of tension. In Figure 7.1,

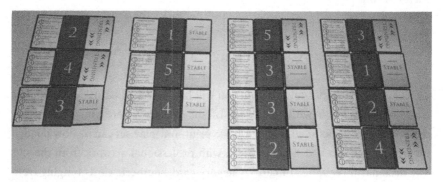

Figure 7.1 Collaborative worldbuilding deck.

The Values are: Government presence (2 trending); Rule of law (4 trending); Social services (3); Economic strength (1); Wealth distribution (5); Agriculture and trade (4); Race relations (5 trending); Class relations (3); Gender relations (3); Sexual orientation relations (2); Military influence (3 trending); Religious influence (1); Technology influence, Arts and culture influence (4 trending).

the categories of *economic strength* and *religious influence* are the lowest values while *wealth distribution* and *race relations* are very high; *government presence* and *technology influence* are both low (value of 2), and *rule of law* and *arts and culture* are relatively high (value of 4). The categories of *government presence, rule of law, race relations, military influence,* and *arts and culture* are all trending values, meaning each is changing in some way, either toward a higher or lower value. Low government and low economic strength suggest a post-apocalyptic world, and high values in the equal distribution of wealth and race relations might indicate a commune-type environment, where the people of the world are making an effort to eliminate a rigid class structure and social divisions along racial lines. A value of 2 for *government presence* indicates a relatively low level of government presence in daily life, which isn't surprising in a post-apocalypse, but what the term "government involvement" means for this world, or how a value of 2 would be different than either values of a 1 or 3, must be worked out through group discussion. The category is also trending. It could mean that what little government the group has established is being resisted and is disappearing (a 2 value trending down to 1), or it could be that a fragile government is finding its feet and slowly but surely developing more governing structures (a 2 value trending up to a 3). *Agriculture and trade* is stable and strong (4), so one possibility is that this is a newly formed society coming together for the first time after the societal collapse and they are just beginning to form the foundations of a democratic government. But that is just one possibility, and only a brief analysis of the categories and their values. Other people may read the cards differently and see another kind of world coming into view. Chapter 10 provides a much more thorough example of how one world's numeric structures are analyzed by a group of four people working on a collaborative worldbuilding project.

The deck also includes extra cards for adding optional categories, as well as additional numeric cards that can be deployed in different ways. The default numeric deck is designed to produce balanced worlds with clear points of tension among a few high and low values, but you can add or remove cards as you wish. For example, removing a few 3s from the numeric deck and replacing them with 1s and 5s will produce a more volatile world. That can be fun to play with but it can also lead to greater difficulty in interpreting the numbers in a logical fashion. You can also create cards for any additional categories your group wants in their world.

Download the deck and practice generating a new world and interpreting the results. Avoid manually changing any of the value or trending cards after you deal them out. The system is designed to have a few curveballs thrown in. If you don't understand how a world might make sense with the values that were dealt, don't reshuffle or swap out cards that you initially see as being inconvenient. Instead, think harder. Flex the muscles of your imagination.

Worldbuilding Worksheets

The collaborativeworldbuilding.com website also has three different worksheets you can download to help you manage your worldbuilding project, which are also included in the appendices in the back of this book. It's good practice to go to the website to print out one worksheet for each contributor so everyone can record the world's values and take their own notes during your brainstorming sessions. The Worldbuilding Structures Worksheet (Appendix A) allows you to record the values for each of the 14 substructures, including whether those values are stable or trending up and down. The Framework Worksheet (Appendix B) aids you in noting the scope, sequence, and perspective your group has decided on. This worksheet gives you room to hash out the starting timeline of major historical events in relation to the world's point of the present as well. Finally, the Scope and Schedule Worksheet (Appendix C) helps keep track of who in the group is responsible for writing what parts of the metanarrative, as well as divvying up the different types of entries for the catalog. Writing the metanarrative will generate the need for several entries to cover the major people, places, things, and historical events in the world. This worksheet facilitates assigning the creation of these entries to individual contributors, and also sets guidelines for the quantity, type, and delivery date of additional wiki entries, and who is responsible for making them.

The worksheets, like the card deck, aren't *required* for collaborative worldbuilding projects, but they work with the concepts of this book and should make the process smoother. They provide an additional level of structure and assist you in keeping the project moving forward at a consistent pace and within the group's agreed upon scope. As with all of these resources, feel free to modify them or develop your own tools that will work best for your group.

Online Resources

One of the most important parts of the worldbuilding process is making all the work transparent to all the contributors at any time. Anyone should be able to add, revise, or comment on the content whenever they have time, or whenever inspiration strikes. It also means that people should be able to scan the world quickly to make sure that what they're adding won't be incoherent or inconsistent with the rest of the world, and that any problems that creep in can be addressed quickly as they crop up. The best way to keep everyone on the same page is to use free online software that will update all the group's changes in real time. While some groups I have worked with have chosen to incorporate collaborative project management software like Slack or Trello, most projects do fine using three pieces of software: some form of online document sharing, a wiki, and online mapping software.

Document Sharing

The earliest stages of collaborative worldbuilding involve a lot of brainstorming a series of diverse, and many incompatible, ideas. Whether you jot down ideas on paper or type them out, it's a good idea to collect them all in a shared online document in Google Docs and share editing privileges with all the collaborators. Google Docs (and similar software) allow users to revise the document and track changes, so it's clear what was recently added or deleted, and you can easily revert the document to an earlier version if later you decide to back out of certain changes. Wiki sites, while important during the catalog creation phase, aren't well equipped to handle simultaneous editing, for example if there are several users editing a single wiki page. In the early stages of writing the metanarrative, and while working through the framework and structures, it's easier to use a shared document first. You can paste it into a wiki page when it's closer to being finished and is undergoing fewer major revisions.

Wikis

A wiki is an online database that can be edited online by anyone, with Wikipedia being the most prevalent example. Wikis become an essential tool when it comes to building entries for the catalog of your fictional world. The main page of the wiki is often the metanarrative that describes the features of the world, similar to how Wikipedia pages describe any given country or large city. The greatest advantage to using a wiki for a collaborative worldbuilding project is the creation of catalog templates, which enforce consistency and clarity of individual entries for the world's people, places, and things. Most wiki sites have discussion areas for each page, where every entry is its own page and there are additional features like tags that help to keep pages organized. These are all concepts discussed in greater detail in Chapter 12.

As with shared documents, wikis allow you to track page edits, allow people to embed comments on pages, and many fee-based wikis allow you to assign specific permissions to groups or individual users. Most free wikis allow you some basic permissions functionality, such as setting public viewing for certain pages on the site and restrict viewing and editing of other parts to authorized users. There are a number of free and paid wiki services you may use. You can see a list of possible wiki sites for your project under the Resources page at collaborativeworldbuilding.com.

Mapping

Marking the locations of the people, places, and things and linking them to their corresponding wiki entries is an important part of the worldbuilding process. It helps the contributors, as well as a wider audience, visualize the distances between locations and situate them within certain regions. Many fantasy and science fiction books have a map in their opening pages for exactly this reason.

Unfortunately, despite the number of free mapping tools available online, creating maps for your collaborative worldbuilding project is not as easy as it should be, particularly if you're using an imaginary geography. Most mapping software is intended for real-world uses rather than fictional ones, and uploading a custom image as your base map is frustratingly difficult. There are only three basic requirements for an online mapping service: 1) the map should be able to be edited by multiple users; 2) the users must be able to drop markers on the map; and 3) those markers should include links to the specific wiki entries. As easy as this sounds, it can be time consuming and frustrating to get the online map to function exactly as you wish without a lot of fiddling with scripts and code.

The easiest option is using a *primary world location* as your base map. This works well for any fictional genres that tend to use real-world locations, such as post-apocalyptic fiction, steampunk, cyberpunk, dystopian fiction, urban fantasy, and others. For these types of worlds, Google Maps is a fairly flexible and user-friendly solution, though it's irritating in its lack of some simple customization options. For example, there is no easy way to remove select map labels, such as street names. There are other options that provide extremely granular controls over map data such as Mapbox, the Google Maps APIs Styling Wizard, or ArcGIS, but these solutions introduce other challenges, such as struggles in granting privileges to simultaneous users, requiring users to host the maps on their own websites, or are fee-based services. The features of these tools change rapidly though, and with luck, a good solution will present itself in the near future.

At the time of writing, there remains no perfect option for uploading maps of fictional lands. While it can be done, it requires a nontrivial knowledge of image tiling and web programming that goes beyond the scope of this book. You might ask a computer-savvy friend to help you out, or you can experiment yourself if you have the patience for trial and error. Look to collaborativeworldbuilding.com for mapping advice and some examples of online maps of fictional worlds.

Analog Alternatives

If your group doesn't have reliable access to the Internet, or if you just prefer a non-digital approach, you can still engage in collaborative worldbuilding the old-fashioned way: with pencil and paper. After all, Tolkien, Lucas, Martin, and Gygax and Co. all built out their massive fictional universes before the Internet became part of daily life. Though it's possible to run a collaborative worldbuilding project offline, the analog approach comes with a number of challenges, the most serious of which deal with version control and managing the catalog.

Someone in the group must be responsible for holding the master document for the fictional world. One approach is to keep two notebooks, one for brainstorming and the other to commit the final agreed-upon ideas to paper. As the metanarrative of the world becomes solidified, that document could be copied and provided to all the contributors. As far as the catalog goes, multicolored notecards are an ideal solution. Choose card colors to represent certain entry types. For example, all yellow notecards should be characters, green notecards are locations, and so forth. The color gives a visual cue for separating out the different categories at a glance and helps keep the catalog ordered, much like a library's card catalog system. As long as contributors agree to use the correct template for each category of entry, using notecards can be an easy and flexible way of building out the catalog.

Analog mapping is likewise easy. All you need is a corkboard and a representation of your fictional map. Numbered stickers or thumbtacks can refer to the list of locations in the catalog. In many ways, using a physical map is far easier than monkeying with a digital one, though you do lose the robust tagging options and the contributors have no easy way to bring a copy of the map home with them.

Future Developments and Additional Resources

It's my hope that in the near future I will be able to develop online collaborative worldbuilding software that streamlines this process, where each contributor has their own login to a centralized site that allows a group of collaborators to write the metanarrative, select a map, design catalog templates, and build out the entries. Until that project becomes a reality, worldbuilders will have to make do with the tools at their disposal. See the collaborativeworldbuilding.com website for links to recommended resources and updates on future developments.

8

Before You Begin Your Project

Part Two turns from theoretical issues to practical considerations for beginning your collaborative worldbuilding project. No two projects will be the same, and different groups will work in different ways. The advice that follows is the result of dozens of collaborative worldbuilding projects conducted over many years of trial and error, and that were conducted in many different environments— in classrooms, at conferences, and among friends. While your mileage may vary on individual suggestions, as a whole this chapter identifies a number of broad things to consider as you embark on your collaborative worldbuilding project.

Number of Collaborators and What It Means to Collaborate

How many people should be involved in collaborative worldbuilding project? It depends on your purposes. Theoretically, there is no limit to the maximum number of contributors, but it's wise to start small the first few times until you get comfortable with the process. Generally, the ideal number of contributors is four to six people. A group of four seems to be minimum to produce sufficiently diverse viewpoints, while a group of six tends to be the upper limit for being able to gain consensus without the process bogging down. There are plenty of other variations that can work, however. One model includes a core of four to six contributors who write the metanarrative and then opening up the catalog creation stage to a wider group of eight to ten collaborators. Another model suitable for large groups of twenty or more is to have a core group of writers develop a high-level concept for a worldbuilding project, but allow smaller groups of four to six to develop their own separate worlds within the world. This could be each group working on different neighborhoods of a single, vast metropolis; or each group could create distinct nations on a continent, or each group could create separate planets that exist in the same galaxy.

In order for your project to be truly collaborative, everyone needs to be equally invested in each stage of the project. One tendency for beginning worldbuilders is to have each collaborator carve out their own space in the world to develop and then try to merge the separate pieces at a later point. As a strategy, this almost never works. When working in isolation, writers tend to get very attached to their ideas and this attachment deepens over time. This means people are very reluctant to revise or rework parts of their ideas in order to make them fit well with other's ideas about the world. This often leads to arguments or a number of glaring inconsistencies in the world's logic. If your group wants to work on a collaborative worldbuilding project, everyone should be able to see their ideas braided through every aspect of the world. For example, if you have a group of four, don't have each writer develop one of the four structural categories (governance, economics, social relations, and cultural influences). Instead, pair off. Have two people work on governance and two on economics. Then switch the up the pairs for social relations and cultural influences. The same holds for populating the catalog. Distribute the work so each contributor has a roughly equal number of items, locations, characters, and historical events to work on. This helps a great deal in ensuring consistency and coherence, and it also increases the likelihood that all the contributors will remain invested throughout the entire worldbuilding project.

Working with Preexisting Worlds

Come to the collaborative worldbuilding project with a completely open mind. Often, someone will come to the group project with a very specific idea about the kind of world they want to build. Unless everyone has signed up for this type of project ahead of time, this gets things off on the wrong foot. For starters, the control of the project has a de facto leader, being the person who brought forward the concept. The leader then feels authorized to reject any idea that doesn't fit with their conception of the world, which quickly drains the creative energy from most contributors. Beginning with a single person's preexisting world can work, but only if that person is genuinely interested in adding fresh eyes and diverse new ideas to what has already been developed. If you do start your project with a contributor's preexisting world, make sure to run through all the steps in each stage of the project as described in this book, paying close attention to the establishment of the framework and development of the structures. By methodically moving through these steps, the group will be able to fill gaps in the world's timeline, patch any holes in its internal consistency, and gain a sense of co-ownership of that preexisting world.

This advice also holds true if your group's project is a work of fanfiction that extends a portion of a preexisting world from popular culture. For example, if your group is interested in creating a new region set in Stephen King's world of *The Dark Tower* series, run through the entire worldbuilding process from the beginning to guarantee that all the contributors share the same understanding of the world and how it operates. This not only avoids misunderstandings that can crop up in later stages, but it also helps identify some aspects in the world that are open to multiple interpretations, which in turn can be the most fun parts to develop in new and unique ways.

Building from Simple to Complex

The collaborative worldbuilding process starts very broadly and becomes increasingly complex as the project advances. This is an intentional strategy, as it allows for the greatest range of ideas to be vetted by the group from the start and develop naturally toward more specificity. For example, don't start the project with the singular goal of creating a world where magic is powered by the sacrifice of animals. That might be an idea that you, as an individual contributor, are interested in and wish to work toward. Instead of insisting on this detail from the onset, follow the process and work it in more organically as the world evolves.

Following the process in this book, the idea of sacrificial magic would come into play during the phase of developing the *structures*. This way, instead of being a lone idea that the world revolves around, sacrificial magic would become enmeshed with other political, economic, social, and cultural forces at play in the world. This is a much more nuanced representation of how the world operates and allows for plenty of other types of storytelling opportunities to emerge that have little to do with this single aspect. If you start with broad concepts and follow the outlined steps—determine the genre and audience, establish the framework, and develop the structures—your world will become increasingly complex with lots of intriguing details in no time.

Boundaries and No-Go Zones

Collaboration requires trust among the contributors. The collaborative worldbuilding process requires the group to discuss some potentially hot-button topics such as politics, religion, racism, sexism, and more. While the system described is intended to spark meaningful conversations among contributors, each member should also be able to set boundaries for how the group handles certain topics and feel comfortable requesting that the group refrains from delving into certain topics altogether. For example, if a contributor has suffered a trauma, such as during military service or as a victim of a violent crime, they may wish to steer clear of those aspects of the worldbuilding project. This isn't to say that uncomfortable content should be entirely off limits to discussion, but rather that the project shouldn't be an exercise in probing painful memories or issues that are likely to spark hostilities between contributors.

On the other hand, some people are committed to using fiction to interrogate issues of injustice and inequality in their fiction while others may look to creative work as a release from matters they confront on a daily basis. Chapter 10 provides strategies for "fixing" certain substructures, a process that sets the values in place for certain categories and redirects points of tension elsewhere. For example, fixing values to ensure that a world is more egalitarian along race and gender lines necessarily means that there will be greater frictions when it comes to issues of governance, economic stratification, and other competing cultural influences. While in theory most of us would wish to live in a world that is ruled by a just government, where wealth is abundant and widely distributed, and the culture operates on mutual respect and understanding, such an idyllic world is a poor setting for great storytelling. Good stories put characters under different types of stresses and strains, and the authors and audiences alike want to see them fight for what they believe in. While you want to respect the wishes of each contributor and make the worldbuilding space safe for everyone, you also don't want to sanitize the world to the point where you lose all productive points of tension. Thorny, difficult, and morally ambiguous worlds give us far more story-making potential.

Clarity of Scope and Schedule

When we encounter sprawling universes like the ones discussed earlier in this book, a natural impulse is to think that bigger is necessarily better. One of the greatest benefits of collaborative worldbuilding is that it accelerates the speed at which a group of writers can create a large-scale fictional world, but don't mistake quantity for quality. Breadth is only half of the equation when it comes to the scope of the world. The other half is depth. Starting out with a too ambitious plan, also known as *overscoping*, can undermine your project before you even begin.

Using the Scope and Schedule Worksheet (Appendix C) can help prevent your project spiraling out of control by establishing the amount of work required and the due dates for different portions of the project. For example, if each person is expected to write 200 words to the metanarrative, you may decide to give everyone five days to make their contribution. While you don't want to lose momentum, contributors can get discouraged if they can't keep up with an aggressive plan. With open communication, most groups quickly find a pace that works for them. Ambitious groups might be more bold with their schedule, while other groups who have other competing demands for their time (work, school, children, and myriad other obligations) may negotiate a slower pace. The worksheet communicates the speed at which the group's project intends to proceed. Problems can arise if one or two people begin to produce far more worldbuilding material than other members of the group, and writers begin dropping out of the project if they feel as though they can't keep up with the work being produced.

Overproducing contributors can unintentionally overwhelm over a collaborative worldbuilding project, so the best strategy is to channel their motivation into productive outlets that don't diminish the work of others. One solution is for those eager to add more to the world to focus on adding *depth* across entries. For example, a motivated writer could read through other people's entries and flesh out smaller details or create explicit connections between entries or resolve any emerging contradictions. Another strategy is to redirect their energy to adding detail to a series of important *historical events*. The stories of the past are essentially infinite, and adding more concrete details deepens the reservoir of story material from which others may draw. For example, a minor detail from an expanded historical event may crystallize the motivations for a specific character, or explain why a certain location has the qualities that it does.

Using the "Yes, and . . ." Approach

Collaboration between multiple parties often works like merging onto a busy highway. When someone is coming up to highway speed on the onramp, drivers already on the highway might have to speed up, slow down, or change lanes to make space. If everyone refuses to budge the result is anything from road rage to a multi-car pileup. Open and honest communication is critical to keeping the project moving forward and making it fun for everyone, and the "yes, and ..." approach reduces the chances of such high-speed collisions. "Yes, and ..." is a concept borrowed from improvisational comedy. The gist is that it's best to accept what others have said and try to expand upon it rather than resisting or rejecting it. In practice, this means saying "good idea, and let's add to this ..." as opposed to saying "no, that's not going to work."

Sometimes a contributor will have an idea that just doesn't fit well with the rest of the group's vision for the world. For example, let's say a few people in the group have established a delicate balance of power between two rival political groups in a city that they think will be interesting to explore. Another contributor wants to add a new character who is a wealthy, boorish drunk and inserts him as a major figure in one of the factions. The other contributors see this as disrupting the balance of power since this doltish new character couldn't help but cause a major altercation, collapsing what was supposed to be a productive tension into some inevitable outcome. Instead of merely removing this character, the "yes, and ..." approach would work to find an alternative. Perhaps the character's previous actions have stripped him of any decision-making powers and he is regarded as a joke by both sides of the conflict, or it could be that there is some other quality that makes the character untouchable, or maybe his sense of importance is fabricated. Or what if this character was the root cause of the conflict to begin with? In any case, the group should openly and honestly explain why the character as conceived doesn't seem to fit as-is and provide some productive alternatives. *Yes,* this character can exist in our world, *and* ... here are some suggestions as to how he may add greater narrative value. This approach not only keeps all the contributors happy but can also add some new twists. Maybe that rivalry between the two factions was a little *too* well-balanced and this bombastic new character injects a legitimate sense of danger into their relationship.

Surprises, Secrets, and Need-to-Know Information

Because collaborative worldbuilding projects grow out quickly, it can be hard to keep tabs on all the moving parts. One of the best parts of participating in such projects is coming across something new and exciting created by another contributor. It might be a fascinating object, an interesting historical twist, a compelling character, or some other unexpected bit that adds immeasurable value to the world. It's equally gratifying when someone riffs off one of your ideas. These sorts of surprises happen naturally as people add to the world over time, and one of the great pleasures of the project comes with making these unexpected discoveries.

This sense of discovery can't happen when people try to keep certain parts of the world secret in order to later spring the surprise on the other writers. This usually takes the form of creating a character who has a mysterious untold secret, or a location where "no one knows what's inside" with the intent to reveal this information later in the storytelling phase of the project. For example, a writer's character might have a secret. She's built a cyborg army that she keeps hidden in a warehouse on the outskirts of town, waiting for the right moment to release them to cause mayhem. Sometimes contributors will write in an entry for a character that leaves the mystery unexplained, i.e., "She has a secret that she will tell no one, not even her closest friends." Unfortunately, the other contributors are in the dark too. This kind of impulse confuses the question of *audience*. The writer who created the character with a secret is essentially running a story nested within the collaborative worldbuilding process, ready to spring the surprise on the other contributors.

To be blunt, this *never* works out well. Other writers feel cheated rather than pleasantly surprised when this happens, namely because secretive information runs contrary to the spirit of collaboration. If only one person knows the secret, then it prevents others from expanding on it or connecting to it. It works much better if all known information is provided to the *collaborators* even if it is not widely known to *characters* within the fictional world. To use the example above, the problem is solved by modifying the entries to read that the character "has built a *secret* cyborg army" and that "*no one* knows that this warehouse holds the cyborgs." With this revision, the contributors know the secret, but characters who live in the fictional world are still in the dark. This allows another writer to connect to this storyline. For example, someone might be inspired to create a location entry for the manufacturing plant that is unwittingly producing the microprocessors for the cyborg units, while another contributor might create a character entry for the landlord of the warehouse who suspects his tenant is up to some shady business. By revealing the secret to the other contributors, it allows them to branch off the idea and add some new wrinkles of their own.

As a general rule, everyone working on the world should have access to *all* the information about the world. The exception is groups that are building a campaign setting for a role-playing game. In this case, the person acting as the game master has good reason to keep secrets from the players. For example, if a vampire lord holds a prince captive in his labyrinthine lair, it makes sense that the game master doesn't want to share the map or give detailed descriptions of the rooms and their treasures. Likewise, if the king who sends the party on the rescue mission has ulterior motives, that shouldn't be public knowledge for the players either. This is why the first step in the collaborative worldbuilding project is to clarify the issue of *audience*. If everyone understands that the group's contributions will be public knowledge for both the writers building the world as well as for the fictional characters who live in it, the game master has plenty of room to flesh out the details for discovery in gaming sessions without interfering with the larger worldbuilding project.

The Dangers of Essentialism

One of the basic tenets of collaborative worldbuilding is that worlds are messy, complex, diverse places full of messy, complex, diverse people. However, both speculative fiction and role-playing games are often guilty of *essentialism*, or the belief that there are a certain set of attributes that are inherent to any given people. Essentialist beliefs usually collapse into negative stereotypes applied to specific groups of people that are intended to describe some "natural" state of the world; in other words, that the descriptors are essential qualities of a given gender, race, or ethnicity. Essentialist statements are in fact often intended as compliments. For example, take this news article reporting on former NFL football player Reggie White's remarks in a speech to the Wisconsin State Assembly:

> In his effort to promote racial harmony, the Packer player, who is black, said that each racial and ethnic group has its own "gifts," that, when taken together, form "a complete image of God."
>
> But in describing those gifts, White said that blacks "like to sing and dance," while whites "know how to tap into money." He said that Hispanic people "are gifted at family structure. You can see a Hispanic person and he can put 20 or 30 people in one home."
>
> Asians, he said, know how to "turn a television into a watch." American Indians, he said, "have been very gifted" in "spirituality."[1]

White intended his comments to be positive, with each race possessing a "gift," but instead drew sharp criticism for promoting essentialist claims about whole races and ethnicities. White's comments ignore any economic, social, or cultural factors that play into these stereotypes and they also fail to recognize how they might be damaging to the people who belong to these populations.

Essentialist beliefs often creep into speculative fiction and role-playing games. In fantasy worlds, for example, wood elves can move through the forest with ease, are expert shots with a bow and arrow, and can see in the dark. In an RPG, characters of this race may receive stat bonuses in skills related to stealth and archery and be given the special ability of night vision. The danger here is presenting this information as though these are all *essential qualities* rather than learned skills. Imagine in this hypothetical world that an infant wood elf was kidnapped and raised underground by dwarves until adulthood. It would stand to reason that this elf would *not* naturally know how to navigate a forest quietly or be an automatic expert shot with a bow, as these are learned *skills* ingrained in the culture of the forest elves due to their environment. The kidnapped elf would, however, still have night vision because that is a biological fact for this race of elves.

Is it essentialist to say all dwarves are squat and strong, and all elves are lithe and acrobatic? These are, after all, common traits that help define these fantasy races. Tread carefully when approaching such questions. Think through the ramifications of the question and do your best to distinguish between cultural and social norms and biological differences between species. Examine your contributions, as well as the contributions, of others spot-checking for potential essentialist claims. Far from being mere political correctness, the way you handle such questions becomes highly relevant when it comes to characters' creation. For example, imagine a character who is a pacifist but belongs to a warlike culture. Opposing violence as a means of resolving disputes would produce interesting dilemmas and problems for this character. Or to use the previous example of the wood elves, imagine an elf who had been born without the trait of night vision. This could be seen by the rest of the tribe as a disability and put that character at a disadvantage in her community. This steers thinking away from groups who possess certain essential traits and toward individual characters who have to deal with very specific problems, given who they are and the world in which they live.

Dispute Resolution and Being a Good Collaborator

Make no mistake, disputes between creators *will* happen. It helps to keep in mind that this is a feature of collaborative worldbuilding, not a flaw. Trying to capture a diverse, realistic world in written language is a complicated, often conflicted task, and reasonable people can disagree on matters of substance. However, you can go too far in the other direction, where quick consensus results in a clean and frictionless world because the participants are too worried about possibly offending each other. A well-made world ought to possess tensions, societal fault lines, and even contradictions that the group will work through by talking and, whenever possible, making a good faith effort to find solutions that accommodate divergent viewpoints without choosing a moral high ground. After all, our primary world has plenty of warts and unseemly bits; it stands to reason that a realistically drawn fictional one should too.

During the worldbuilding process, issues pertaining to the audience, genre, and the framework rarely cause disagreements. Developing the structures, however, often inspires contributors to voice stronger opinions. It's also common for individual writers to shy away from suggesting creating worlds that are unjust and oppressive. Good solutions, as mentioned earlier, are to use the worldbuilding cards to generate the social structures and to fix certain values to account for any hot-button, non-productive topics. That way the collaborators can concentrate on interpreting the points of tension that emerge from the randomly generated world rather than fixating on disagreements within the group.

Another easy way to avoid bruised feelings during the process is to break deadlocks quickly by appealing to dice rolls or flipping coins. For example, if after five minutes of debating, no one can agree whether your world should be the size of a nation, a region, or a city, roll a six-sided die and let that make your decision for you. Say the number rolled corresponds to the size, with 1 being a small city and 6 being a large nation. Let fate decide. Don't be afraid to revert to such deciders early and often. It's much more interesting (not to mention efficient) to spend time debating how to work with the random material you've been given rather than becoming entrenched on what idea is better than another. Relying on the "Yes, and . . ." approach can also assist you avoiding and resolving disagreements. Instead of choosing one idea over another, the group can work to incorporate both ideas.

Collaboratively built worlds are intended to make space for many different ideas and worldviews. If you're not legitimately enjoying yourself during the process, then there's something wrong. If the group finds itself continually squabbling over key points of the world, it might be possible that you moved too quickly through (or skipped over) part of the process. If you find that your ideas are always the ones being voted down, consider shifting your attention away from the big questions and focus more on working with what the rest of the group seems enthusiastic about. Finding your own space within someone else's concept can be even more interesting than if people choose to adopt your idea.

You might also tactfully point out that you would appreciate it if the group made an effort to incorporate more of your ideas.

A final conflict to address is the bossy worldbuilder who only wants things his or her way. First off, don't be this person. Secondly, the whole point of collaborative worldbuilding is that the contributions of different perspectives create a richer, more interesting fictional world. Use these above resolution tactics to keep things from coming to a head, and remember that keeping open lines of communication is important. If someone is dominating the project, don't be afraid to raise this point. Quite often, people who are bubbling over with ideas are simply excited about the project and don't realize that they're crowding others out. In these cases, a friendly reminder is all it takes to redirect them into more productive channels.

The Lure of Endless Worldbuilding

The previous sections covered how to keep the project moving forward in a positive fashion and staying within your agreed upon scope until you reach your desired completion point. This last point covers the opposite case, in which the group is so busy happily worldbuilding you can't seem to stop. Collaborative worldbuilding projects can be like a snowball running downhill in that it can take time for it to come together but, once it hits critical mass, there becomes an enormous amount of momentum carrying it forward.

Is this actually a problem? Yes, in many cases it can be. Unless the world was intended to be an unending creative experiment unto itself, most worldbuilding projects are intended to be the setting for some kind of storytelling output. There needs to be a specific point at which the group agrees to stop worldbuilding and begin storytelling.

The longer you work on a world, the more invested you become in it. This investment means you know lots about the world, and in turn it means that you're constantly discovering and inventing new things about it. For every character you create, you could add that character's parents, their siblings, their close friends, their rivals. One location begets three sublocations and a half-dozen items that can be found within. The possibilities for continuing to develop the world are endless. To keep your worldbuilding under control, use the Scope and Schedule Worksheet to determine your stopping point for each stage. For example, a group of five could agree that the worldbuilding project will consist of a metanarrative of approximately 5000 words and seventy-five wiki entries made up of twenty-five people, twenty-five places, and twenty-five things to be completed over a period of two weeks. At the end of that timeframe, the group should agree to take stock of the world. They may decide they want a bigger world and repeat the process for another two weeks, and they'd wind up with twice as much story-making material, or they can decide to add some finishing touches and move on to the storytelling phase. Committing to a scope will prevent the project from losing shape. Of course, you can keep extending the worldbuilding phase for as long as you wish, but this should be a deliberate group decision. Otherwise, you run the risk of the worldbuilding project fizzling out with you never reaching the storytelling phase.

Planned Returns

The sprawling worlds discussed in this book—those of Tolkien's Middle-earth, Lucas's *Star Wars* galaxy, and Martin's Known World—did not spring into being fully formed. They literally evolved over decades, growing from a germ of core ideas to a network of linked storytelling pieces. You and your group shouldn't strive to do it all at once either. With a committed group of writers, the world will get plenty big quickly enough to provide a solid foundation for storytelling. You might even have everyone commit to not doing any more with the world for some period of time, perhaps a few months, to allow the contributors to tell some stories set in the world without having to worry about the fictional earth shifting beneath their characters' feet. It's a sure bet that if you're writing a short story in this world you'll create characters, locations, and items that don't exist on the wiki. You can always add entries for those elements so they become a tangible part of the world's catalog.

The group also might wish to return for another significant round of worldbuilding. You might shift to a new set of focal points as the primary setting to develop, or you could use your timeline and move the point of present ahead 50 years, where the protagonists of your stories will be much older, or even dead, and you follow the stories of the next generation. Or you can go in the opposite direction, moving the point of the present 50 years in the past, and go into greater detail about the era of your protagonist's parents and grandparents.

You've already read a lot about worldbuilding and have developed a keen understanding of the *framework* and *structures* of fictional worlds, the role of the *catalog* in the process, and best practices for working with others on a collaborative worldbuilding project. In the next chapter, you'll finally get down to business and start building your world!

9

Building the Foundation and Establishing the Framework

The first stage in a collaborative worldbuilding project is building the *foundation* for your fictional world. The first two steps in building the foundation are (1) picking a *genre* and (2) discussing the project's *audience*; then you move on to establishing the *framework*, which involves (3) determining the *scope* in terms of the *breadth* and *depth* of the world, (4) arranging the world's history into a *sequence* of events, and (5) choosing a *perspective* from which you will describe the world. The last steps are (6) defining the *map*'s borders and (7) drafting a *metanarrative lead*, or the short narrative that describes the world's framework.

Alternative Approach: Beginning with Randomized Structures

Another approach is to start the entire worldbuilding process by determining the *structures* first and letting that determine the genre. This is a more challenging route (and not necessarily recommended for novice worldbuilders) but it can be an extremely rewarding imaginative exercise as it requires flexible thinking about different genres. In this alternative approach, the group skips ahead to generating the random values for the fictional world's structures using the worldbuilding card deck as described in Chapter 10. Once the values of the world's structures have been generated, the group chooses the genre based on how they're interpreting those values. For example, the values may lead the group to interpreting them as a classic cyberpunk or high fantasy type of world. Once the group settles on their chosen genre, they would continue building the foundation as described in this chapter, starting with Step One and determining their audience, then moving through the remaining steps as usual.

Building a solid foundation ensures that everyone understands the goal of the worldbuilding project so there's no confusion down the line. Usually, the discussion of genre and audience can be resolved very quickly and the framework often falls into place rather quickly as well. A good framework should center your worldbuilding efforts from the start, but it should also be easily and intuitively extendable. All the contributors should understand how the group might widen the world's scope or further develop different time periods of the world without having to think too hard about it. Establishing a solid framework is extremely important but, if you follow the steps below, it generally comes together very quickly and without a lot of fuss. Move through these steps in chronological order without skipping any, but understand that you will frequently return to previous steps in order to refine details and add new information about the world as you discover it. For example, you might find that you might need to widen or narrow your scope. Continual revision is not only acceptable, it is in fact necessary.

This chapter also provides extended examples of a group of four people building a fictional world called Tal-Vaz. These examples are intended to illustrate the rhythms of the process in progress. While this is not a transcription of an actual worldbuilding project, the people working on the project and the world they developed are composites drawn from years of managing actual worldbuilding projects. The Tal-Vaz examples carry through to the chapters on developing structures and populating the catalog as well. Refer to them if you get confused about what you're supposed to be doing at any stage, or what the product of a certain stage might look like.

After you work through the process once, you'll see it's more of a system of loosely contained brainstorming than an orderly, by-the-numbers system. This too is by design. You will want to set aside an hour or so for your to group to meet in person to begin building the foundation. Before you meet, choose a wiki, create a new site, and share it with your collaborators so you'll have it when you need it. You should also start a Google Drive folder and share that with all the contributors too. Then direct the group to go to collaborativeworldbuilding. com and download the Framework Worksheet (Appendix B). Then it's time to get to work!

Step One: Audience and Genre

The group needs to understand the intended audience(s) who will be reading their work as well as what genre of fiction they're working in. To keep the issue of audience simple, a worldbuilding project is either *closed*, meaning only the contributors will ever see the raw material of the worldbuilding project, or *open*, which is where the worldbuilding materials are viewable to anyone. For more information on these audience models, refer back to Chapter 3.

With the issue of audience resolved, move on to the genre (or genres if you're genre-blending) of the worldbuilding project. To facilitate the discussion, it helps to refer to existing fictional worlds as examples. For example, are you talking about a fantasy world more similar to *The Lord of the Rings* or *Conan the Barbarian*? Or a post-apocalypse like the *Mad Max* films or Cormac McCarthy's *The Road*? Specific examples give the group a starting point for the concrete details of the genres under discussion. Draw comparisons and contrasts with worlds the other contributors are likely to be familiar with and feel free to use worlds represented in literature, film, games, comics, or whatever other form of media that illustrates your point. This can be especially useful when genre blending. For example, the videogame *Dishonored* might be described as a post-apocalyptic steampunk world where magic exists. Be specific as you toss around ideas. Is your deep space world going to be more strictly science fiction like *Star Trek*, or a looser science fantasy like *Star Wars*? If you have a computer or tablet available, share images, videos, snippets of texts to illustrate aspects of the genre you like. At this stage, think very broadly about the genre and its prominent features. Don't get ahead of yourself. Grittier details about the world will come later when you begin developing structures. Right now, it's only about the big picture.

Building Tal-Vaz, Step One: Audience and Genre

A group of four people—Aaron, Bryan, Cassandra, and Karly—want to build a world together. Their plan is to spend the months of September and October developing a world to be ready for November's National Novel Writing Month (NaNoWriMo) where they will write their novels set in the same world. They've decided ahead of time that the worldbuilding project will be openly visible to anyone who happens across it and they have started a new wiki site. Aaron also set up a Google Drive and shared access to all of its contents with the other three contributors. The group agrees to meet in person at a coffee shop for a few hours to build the foundation for their fictional world.

The first step for the group is picking a *genre*. Karly has an idea for a world that's in the Renaissance era, only infused with steampunk technology. She's thinking of Leonardo da Vinci flying machines and crazy steam-powered contraptions. Bryan recently took a course on the Renaissance and loves the idea, saying they could draw on that historical period for some of the social tensions, for example enormous wealth inequality, feuding noble families, inventors scrabbling to find patrons who will support their work and more. Neither Aaron nor Cassandra know much about the time period but they agree that it sounds like a fun concept. Cassandra says she was hoping to incorporate magic into this world. Karly says she reads a webcomic called *Shadowbinders* that blends steampunk and magic, and Bryan says he knows the role-playing game *Victoriana* mixes magic and steam, so it's not unheard of. No one has strong opinions on it, so they agree that there can be some magic in this world, which roughly corresponds to a fifteenth- or sixteenth-century setting with elements of steampunk.

Step Two: Determine the Scope

With the audience and genre decided, it's on to establishing the *framework*, the first step of which is determining the *scope* of the world. One of the biggest mistakes beginning worldbuilders make is *overscoping*, or creating a larger world than they can develop well. A world's scope has *breadth* (which relates to its physical size), *depth* (which relates to the amount of detail), and a handful of *focal points* (the "worlds within worlds" and places where the action generally happens). Symptoms of an overscoped world include too much breadth without any depth, overwhelming depth that lacks any meaningful context, or too many focal points lacking enough development to differentiate between them. The goal of this step is to establish a manageable scope that strikes a balance between the breadth, depth, and the number of sufficiently fleshed out focal points. Remember, you can always expand the scope later by widening the breadth or adding new focal points. Starting with a small, coherent core of a world and expanding outward is always a better option than beginning with an unrealistically large world that can't be easily managed.

The initial scope should be determined by 1) the size of your group and 2) the amount of writing the contributors want to commit to the project. If you have 30 people in a fiction-writing club who want to build a collaborative world as a year-long project, the scope might be very large. Creating a galaxy with a dozen detailed planets would be reasonable. However, if you're working in a more typical group of four to six people, you'll want to start with a much tighter scope and expand outward from there.

When determining the breadth, think about it in spatial terms. Are you talking about a fictional world that's the size of a large city? Or something bigger, like a region, a nation, or a world? Or are you talking about many worlds, galaxies, or dimensions? Consider the kinds of stories you want to tell in this world. If you want characters traveling long distances and encountering new things, increase the breadth and spread out the focal points; if you want them to dig deeper into the diverse experiences, narrow the breadth and go for depth by working on a single city. Begin with a modest number of focal points that provide some sense of contrast between them. Each focal point operates as its own self-contained world, though focal points in close geographic proximity will share many key characteristics.

A good starting point for a group of four to six contributors is to have around six to ten focal points. Remember from Chapter 4 that *The Hobbit*, *Star Wars*, and *A Game of Thrones* are all very rich stories, yet they each only needed a handful of focal points that were developed in any significant way. At this point, your focal points can be abstract concepts along the lines of "the desert planet" or "the orc lair in the mountains." They will be developed in greater detail later. Right now, you simply want to mark the main locations on which you wish to focus the group's attention.

Building Tal-Vaz, Step Two: Determining the Scope

Next up for the group is determining the *scope*. Bryan suggests a compressed space, the size of a medieval city like Florence, or maybe a bit larger like London or Paris. The world could be about the different warring families, each who live in different districts within the city. Cassandra thinks it should be slightly larger, perhaps a region that has a few major cities, each ruled by a different family. Karly suggests they split the difference between these two ideas by creating a region with two major urban areas, maybe a few hundred miles apart that aren't exactly at war with each other but aren't chummy either. That way they can create tensions within the cities as well as have a rivalry between them. Aaron says that they could also add a few towns or villages between them too that might get caught in the crossfire, but most of the work could be concentrated on the urban centers. They like this for a starting scope and focal points: a region with two major urban areas a few hundred miles apart with a few districts in each and some smaller villages further out in the desert. They want to come up with a name for the region and Cassandra laughs and suggests "talvez," the Spanish word for "maybe," based on how often they're saying it. Aaron actually likes it and jots all of this down on his Framework Worksheet but tweaks it to give it a name with a fictional feel: the region of Tal-Vaz.

Step Three: Arrange the Sequence

The key parts of arranging the *sequence* during the initial framework stage are establishing the *termination points* on a *timeline*, having a few *historical events* to work around, and establishing the *point of the present* for the worldbuilding project. As you develop the history of the world, significant historical events naturally begin snapping into place. Don't rush it. This is still the big picture phase. Consider too that worlds tend to be most interesting at moments of dramatic change: a major enemy threatens a border; some groundbreaking technological discovery has been made; the natural world is being torn asunder; the worlds of two cultures collide; an old political system has been toppled, or society is undergoing a volatile transformation. These are only a few possibilities, but each one provides multiple points of tension for the people living in those worlds.

Take out the Framework Worksheet (Appendix B) and look at the timeline box. The *point of the present*, or the "now" of the worldbuilding project, is usually near the right termination point, or the future. For now, don't worry about what might happen in the future. The left termination point, the one that establishes the past, should only extend as far back as is useful for making sense of the world you're building. Jot down what the left termination point signifies, and then put vertical slashes on the timeline for a few world-altering historical events. Write a descriptive phrase for each event that captures its significance.

Avoid overloading the timeline with historical events at this stage. A few of the most significant ones will suffice for now and plenty more will emerge as you continue the process. Don't worry about long gaps in the timeline and, for the moment, don't spend time calculating precise dates between milestones. Rough estimates are fine.

Building Tal-Vaz, Step Three: Arranging the Sequence

Next up is the *sequence,* and the group is stumped because they know almost nothing about the world. Karly says that the world should be on the verge of some change, and Aaron suggests that the wealth of the cities could be a relatively recent phenomenon and that the sudden development of new technologies could mean that one city could finally gain control of the region. Karly points out that if the wealth is new then it means that there was a previous time in which the region was poor, or at least not prosperous. Aaron says the left termination point can be a dimly remembered distant past and the first milestone is some breakthrough that marks the beginning of Tal-Vaz's rise in wealth. Cassandra suggests that the breakthrough is the rediscovery of the wisdom of the ancient path. Or maybe, she offers, a rediscovery of ancient magic that leads to the sudden bump in prosperity? Karly says she was hoping to focus more on crazy technology than magic—like a Da Vinci flying machine that ran on steam power rather than a spell but that magic could factor in somehow. The group continues to think it over.

Cassandra thinks they can have both. What if one city leans toward magic and the other toward technology? That gives them another point of tension between the cities and even for the factions within them. Bryan sketches out a timeline on his Framework Worksheet. He marks the left termination point in the timeline as a distant, ancient time that no one in the world knows much about. Many centuries later, he puts a vertical slash as the first milestone, which is the discovery of ancient texts, some of which describe mathematics and science, and some of which describe magical rites. He adds another slash representing a milestone that's only a few decades after the discovery, where there have been a number of technological and magical advancements, and that's their point of the present. These innovations have triggered a power struggle between the two cities over the region of Tal-Vaz. Just past this second milestone, he adds the right termination point for the unknown future—no one knows whether the cities descend into all-out war or something else happens. The worldbuilding project will focus on the point of the present between the second milestone and the right termination point. He takes a picture of his crude timeline and uploads the image to the Google Drive.

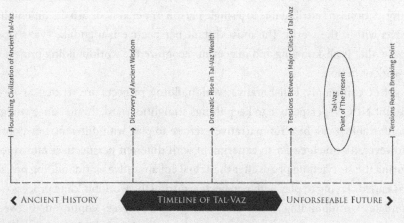

Figure 9.1 Tal-Vaz Timeline

Step Four: Choosing a Perspective

Perspective is best kept simple, especially if you're new to collaborative worldbuilding. Using Wikipedia's NPOV style is the easiest model to follow, but even that might require some clarification among your group. You can choose other perspectives, but the most important thing is that everyone understands and agrees to keep the perspective consistent across the worldbuilding project.

For example, you may wish to discuss among the group the issue of what it means to have a neutral point of view. Wikipedia's NPOV style attempts to stick to the facts—or at least provide multiple perspectives on the facts—and let readers draw their own conclusions. Fictional worlds may operate differently though. If you're building a world that's besieged by brain-sucking demons from an alternate dimension, you might find it appropriate to describe them as categorically evil. It's easy to slip from an NPOV into making value judgments, so contributors should at least be on guard and spot check each other to ensure the perspective is consistent across the project.

Another discussion point would be the distance of the narrative voice used for the worldbuilding project. The closest perspective is a "view from the ground," something like *Volo's Guide to Monsters* or Maester Yandel's *The World of Ice and Fire*, where the worldbuilding project is a product that exists in the fictional world, written by someone who lives in that world and has less than complete knowledge. Further removed would be a "view from the clouds," something like the *Monster Manual* where the descriptions are written from within the fictional world and acknowledges gaps in knowledge, but the information isn't attributable to a single person or persons, or to a document that exists within the world. The most distant perspective is a godlike "view from space" that is all-knowing and may even recognize the worldbuilding project as a work of fiction.

Most commonly, collaborative worldbuilding projects are written as from distant NPOV perspective to keep things straightforward, though once you get comfortable it can be a fun narrative exercise to play with different viewpoints. However, it's much easier to experiment with different perspectives and voices during the storytelling phase after the actual collaborative worldbuilding project has ended. Trying to play with perspective during the worldbuilding process can conflate worldbuilding with storytelling and causes confusion between contributors, so it's strongly recommended to keep it simple the first few times you try a worldbuilding project.

Building Tal-Vaz, Step Four: Choosing a Perspective

Aaron floats a tentative idea of writing the world as a series of journal entries from the perspective of cloistered monks, but that idea is quickly shot down. The group unanimously agrees to keep things simple and use a distant NPOV perspective when writing the metanarrative and catalog entries, using Wikipedia as their general model. This means neither of the cities in Tal-Vaz is inherently good or evil or that using magic is right or wrong for the contributors. Rather these are all points up for debate within the world and, obviously, people in the world will have varying, and often strong, opinions on these matters. When describing historical events, the group agrees to think through as many different viewpoints as possible and reflect the diversity of views in the narrative. For example, if someone adds a significant moment in the history of magic, they should be sure to show the reaction of both the pro- and anti-magic crowds.

Step Five: Define the Map Borders and Focal Points

When defining the boundaries of your world's map, center it so the majority of focal points are within the map's borders. There will sometimes be a few named locations beyond the borders of your map that are mentioned though never fully developed, but the map should include all the places where the majority of the action will be happening. Think about the scope of your fictional world and compare that to some places in our primary world that have a similar population, climate, and topography. For example, if your world is an urban cyberpunk environment, the downtown area of any contemporary global city would suffice as your map. If you're working on a medieval fantasy world, sparsely populated deserts, jungles, mountains, and coastlines could work for your online base map.

Building Tal-Vaz, Step Five: Determining Map Borders and Focal Points

Cassandra says they should pick a primary world location as a base map. They quickly agree that the cities should be inland and that neither one should have a distinct economic advantage based on their geography, such as being on a river or sea. Karly suggests an arid climate, maybe a desert and suggest using the cities of Phoenix and Tucson in Arizona as their model. The cities are a little over 100 miles apart, so the lower half of the state of Arizona can be analogous to the region of Tal-Vaz.

Step Six: Draft the Metanarrative Lead

The metanarrative lead is a short paragraph that provides a concise summary of your world. In these early stages of the project, the lead serves as a reference point so everyone is on the same page regarding their understanding of the world and the project going forward. The metanarrative lead describes the framework as decided by the group without much detail. As you continue to develop the structures and populate the catalog, you will revise the metanarrative lead many times, it will grow to be about 300 to 500 words, and it will highlight the essential people, places, and things that describe your world. But for now, this first draft of the lead should be limited to giving a clear sense of your world's intended *scope* and *sequence*, and exemplify the narrative *perspective* you will use for the project. To get a sense of what a completed metanarrative leads looks like, search Wikipedia for any city, state, region, or nation and read the opening paragraphs above the table of contents. The lead is usually a handful of paragraphs long and provides an overview of the subject of the entry.

As seen in the examples, it's never too early to start naming parts of the world and adding some more specifics details, as long as everyone is on board with the ideas. Moving forward, it's easier to refer to "Chicago" than "the big city by the big lake." Everything is very much in draft stage at this point, and future ideas will require you to revise many of these elements, but assigning names to people, places, and things makes them feel much more real and bestows a sense of permanence to the worldbuilding process.

Building Tal-Vaz, Step Six: Writing the Metanarrative Lead

With the framework established and a base map defined, the group starts drafting the metanarrative lead. Bryan reads from his notes recapping what they've decided so far. They decide the cities need names and, after discussion and some eye-rolling at silly suggestions, they settle on Varoja as the northern city (Phoenix) and Sal-Kala (Tucson) to the south, separated by about 100 miles of desert. Each city is a focal point that will be developed and will have several sublocations within them to designate different districts within the cities. Varoja and Sal-Kala are undergoing a type of renaissance thanks to the discovery of ancient knowledge, where advanced technologies and a little magic have created new wealth for the previously impoverished region. This has caused escalating conflicts between the major noble families in the two cities. Aaron opens a Google doc, titles it *Tal-Vaz Metanarrative* and shares it with the others, and begins writing:

> *A long portion of the three-thousand-mile Cassius Trade Route runs through a desert region known as Tal-Vaz, marked by two major cities: Varoja on the northern end and the smaller Sal-Kala, which lies to the southeast. After centuries of stagnation, Tal-Vaz is experiencing a cultural renaissance thanks to the unexpected discovery of ancient texts that unlocked secrets of mathematics, physics, biology, chemistry, alchemy, and more. Over the span of a few short decades, the cities have transformed from sleepy oases for weary travelers to becoming important destinations in and of themselves as word of Varoja's amazing steam-powered flying machines and the mystical mysteries of Sal-Kala carried up and down the Route. But with wealth comes power, and with power comes conflict. The region is on the brink of outright war as the noble families of the two cities vie for political control over Tal-Vaz.*

Karly says the lead is a bit more flowery than what you'd find on a Wikipedia page, but she likes it. She says they should decide if they want that kind of literary flourish throughout the project or whether they should stick to providing just the facts from a more neutral perspective, and the group decides they prefer the flavor in the language over more dry descriptions. They also talk a bit about some of the details they'll need to flesh out more, like what other cities are along the trade route as well as figuring out just what these different types of technologies are. They hold off on going into any further details and agree to mull it over for a few days, as their agreed-upon time is up. Bryan invites everyone to his place over the weekend so they can work a bit longer, and reminds them to bring a computer or tablet if they have one.

Transitioning from Framework to Structures

A good framework sets the boundaries of your worldbuilding project and concentrates the forthcoming world on a specific place and time. The framework should capture the broad information including the genre of fiction, the size of the world, handful of key locations, and a series of historical events of major importance. A base map that incorporates the focal points should provide information about the climate and topography of the setting(s) if the scope covers a wide physical space. All of this should be captured in broad strokes in the metanarrative lead, which also begins establishing the style and tone of the worldbuilding project. Building the framework can usually be completed in a single session of an hour or two. If it takes longer than that, it often means that you're getting ahead of yourselves and delving too deeply into details about the world. Remember to keep concepts broad at this point. If your group has the energy and the time, there's nothing stopping you from finishing the framework and continuing on without a break. If you do so, it's important everyone commits to following the steps described and not view everything after building the framework as a free-for-all.

The next stage, developing the *structures*, pins down specific aspects of the world in much greater detail. It's a far more complex process that takes much longer and should take place over a few sessions so the group's ideas can stew a bit. The nature of the world may shift and change multiple times throughout the process, but all that shifting and changing should happen within the *framework* you just built. If ideas start emerging that are outside the framework—for example, the addition of new focal points that fall outside your *scope*, or historical events that will throw a wrench in the logic of your *sequence*—the group needs to decide whether to adjust the framework to accommodate them. If aspects of your framework don't match with contributors' ideas about the world, inconsistencies will soon crop up and the whole project will spiral toward incoherence. Take a moment after you've built the framework to review and check that everyone is satisfied with the project's direction.

10

Developing the Structures and Substructures

Developing the *structures* of your fictional world is the most important step in the worldbuilding project. It's also the most complex. There are many moving, interrelated parts in this stage where each decision impacts other aspects of the project, and the amount of detail about the world increases substantially. In order for contributors to discuss how they see social structures operating in the fictional world, they also need to discuss how social forces work in our *primary world*. This entails sharing personal opinions about potentially touchy subjects such as the proper role of government in society, the level of gender equality or racial tensions in society, the influence of the military or religion on society, and so forth. Disagreements about how our primary world "actually works" are common, and everyone has a responsibility for keeping things civil and respectful. This step also raises the issue of how best to illustrate examples of these social structures in a fictional world without relying on assumptions, stereotypes, and clichés. This chapter helps you navigate the complexity in a balanced way that make differences of opinion as productive points of dialogue rather than personal attacks and keeps the overall worldbuilding project moving forward. Developing the structures is a rigorous intellectual challenge and open-minded contributors gain valuable insights about how other people think, interpret, and feel about their own notions regarding how different worlds "work."

At this point, you should only be developing the structures that describe your world's scope as you established in the framework. In most projects, you will need to adjust some, if not all, of the substructures for each focal point. Focal points usually inherit many of the structures of the broader culture, but some specific aspects of the focal point might be quite unique. To use Tolkien as an example, within Middle-earth there are multiple focal points—the Shire, Rivendell, Lothlórien, Rohan, Gondor—that are each unique and distinct from one another. Each location reflects some of the broader structures of Middle-earth, but each is also unique in its own way. Whatever general statements that could be made about the social structures of Middle-earth would need to be detailed in more specifics; for example, the fact that Rohan is a warrior culture whereas the Shire very much is not. Each focal point functions as its own "world within the world" of Middle-earth and the social structures would be different in important ways.

Preparation and Brainstorming

Developing the structures is a fluid process of constant brainstorming and recording of ideas. Notes should be bullet points, phrases, short sentences, and questions. Don't worry about writing a narrative yet—this stage is for throwing out ideas to see what sticks. Notetakers should strive to capture the gist of ideas and key details. At this point, all ideas should be welcomed and encouraged, even if they don't end up being incorporated. Everyone in the group has an obligation to ensure that all contributors are granted an equal chance to forward their ideas. It's easy for eager extroverted people to interrupt or talk over people who are more reserved, or for men to speak over women.[1] Be mindful of this and don't hesitate to tactfully hush others if you see another contributor having difficulty getting an idea out. Stop every so often and go around the table, asking if anyone has anything to add. This is more than just being considerate. It is crucial to guaranteeing all contributors feel invested in the worldbuilding project and will stick with it through completion.

The group can appoint a notetaker or everyone can take individual notes, either in their own notebook or, better yet, aggregated in an online document. If your group has more than five people, appointing a moderator to regulate the flow of ideas and establishing a speaking order is strongly recommended to make sure that the notetaker doesn't miss anything crucial. You may wish to flag any ideas that will need resolving later, but many times contradictions resolve themselves by working through the process. If possible, use a projector or widescreen television to share live edits with the group. Other low-tech strategies include using a poster pad and marker, whiteboard, or chalkboard if they're available.

The goal for note-taking and frequent recapping is 1) visibility and 2) providing equal chance for input. If you don't have the ability to project the notes on a screen, break every ten minutes to recap what's been said, and read aloud to ensure the language being used reflects the contributors' intentions behind those ideas. Visibility for the notes allows contributors to correct, clarify, or revise something they had said. Given the subtleties of the social structures, people may be particular about using precise language to capture the exact meanings and connotations they wished to impart.

Generating Social Structures

Before you begin, download a set of the worldbuilding card deck from collaborativeworldbuilding.com and have it on hand, ready to go. Refer back to Chapter 7 if you need a refresher on how to use the worldbuilding deck. Download and print copies of the Worldbuilding Structures Worksheet (Appendix A) for each contributor as well. To set up the structures of your world, place the category cards in four columns: *governance, economics, social relations,* and *cultural influence.* If you choose to add other categories, such as the influence of *magic* or the social relations with *non-humans,* add them to their appropriate columns, and remember to include an equal quantity of numeric and trending cards for each category you added. Each category card lists one of the 14 substructures and will have a numeric value (1 to 5) placed next to it, as well as a card indicating whether that substructure is stable or trending. There are three different approaches to determining numeric values for the social structures: 1) generating the structures randomly; 2) fixing values for certain substructures and randomizing the rest; and 3) setting values for all the substructures.

Adding Random Substructures and Other Numeric Values

All worldbuilding projects should use the 14 substructures that fit under the main four categories of *governance, economics, social relations,* and *cultural influences.* However, the worldbuilding deck also includes six additional substructures in *age, ableness,* and *non-human* (all under social relations) and *drugs and drug culture, natural world, magic* (all cultural influences). For added difficulty, shuffle these six cards and without looking randomly select one. Add that substructure to the appropriate column and remember to include an additional numeric and trending card to each of those decks.

Another strategy to generate more polarized worlds is to add one or two extra high and low numeric cards into that deck. In this case, you might have 14 category and trending cards but sixteen numeric cards. Shuffle the numeric cards well and deal them out as usual, one per category, knowing that you will have two extras left over. This increases the odds of the world having more extreme social forces, so only add one or two extras or you run the risk of having a highly imbalanced world.

Regardless of which strategy you adopt, the meaning behind the substructure descriptions and numeric values are intended to be interpreted broadly among the collaborators. To use just one example, what defines *class relations* may be different in your fictional world than the way we think about it in our primary world, and what the number 4 actually signifies in terms of class relations should be a point of debate for the group. Rather than being objective, inarguable truths about the world, think about the categories and values as being more fluid and open to interpretation, but still being broadly representative of what most people would say about the world. Remember too that the trending card signifies a point of change, where the category could be shifting higher or lower. It's up to the group to decide what makes the most sense. The categories and numbers are far less important than the way they are first collectively interpreted and then translated into the *metanarrative*, or the story of your world. Here are more detailed descriptions of each of the three strategies followed by an extended example of the group working through the interpretations of their generated world, Tal-Vaz.

Strategy 1: Generating the Structures Randomly

Randomly generating all the structures tends to be the most popular approach for collaboratively worldbuilding projects for a number of reasons. First off, it cuts through lengthy and sometimes heated debates about the kind of world the group wants to create. Instead of arguing over who has the better ideas, you can let the deck decide where the tensions reside in the society. That simplifies things as the group's job becomes one of interpretation rather than judging competing ideas. Another major benefit of randomization is that people are often hesitant to create a world that is plagued by terrible racism or sexism, even though ugly worlds tend to be great settings for storytelling. Randomly generating the structures solves this problem as the deck is designed to generate worlds with easily identifiable points of tension.

The unpredictable results of the values also serve as fantastic thought exercises. It requires a good deal of critical thinking to interpret the values in a way that makes logical sense, and it takes additional deep thought to put that interpretation into a metanarrative that tells a story about the world. There are no correct or incorrect ways to read the values, though some interpretations are often stronger than others. Interpretations require people to articulate how they see social forces connecting as a system of interrelated parts. Furthermore, the deck can generate hundreds upon hundreds of variations of possible worlds. The categories and values might be interpreted very differently based on the genre your group has chosen as well. For example, the values for *governance* or the *economy* will likely mean different things if you're building an epic fantasy world or a post-apocalyptic world.

If you choose to generate the world's structures randomly, resist the urge to switch out any numeric or trending cards after they have been dealt. While you might think this will make the world more coherent, it usually only serves to make it more predictable. Instead, embrace some of the values you see as contradictions and work as a group to find an explanation for how it makes sense in the context of that world. It may require you to redefine how the group is thinking about what substructures like *government presence* or *race relations* mean. Let your imagination and group discussion make sense of the numbers, even if at first they resist an easy interpretation.

Strategy 2: Fixing Values for Certain Substructures and Randomizing the Rest

In certain circumstances, you may want your world to have certain defining features due to the genre of fiction with which you're working. For example, post-apocalyptic worlds tend to have few resources, enormous wealth stratification, and limited or no government presence. Steampunk worlds have exotic technologies but tend to highlight social division across race, class, and gender representative of the Victorian era; cyberpunk worlds, on the other hand, also incorporate incredibly sophisticated technologies but often feature corrupt governments or massive corporations that hoard wealth and oppress the masses. Other genres, like a high fantasy world, tend to be more open, but maybe you already have an idea for your world, for example that you want it to be ruled by a religious order, or that the world has devised a way to enforce gender and racial harmony. These are good cases for "fixing" values for a few of the substructures that are the world's defining features and then randomizing the rest. This allows you some control over the kind of world you're creating but also leaves some of it up to chance.

In Chapter 8, the topic of boundaries and "no-go zones" was also discussed. For a variety of reasons, group members may not enjoy a world that features certain kinds of tensions, most commonly ones that are highly racist or sexist. While building worlds with these social ills can be a fantastic exercise in critical thinking and providing an outlet for creative critiques of our primary world, it can also be that contributors simply don't wish to delve into these often stressful topics in their worldbuilding project. In these cases, it's appropriate to fix a few categories, either with middling values or with numbers in categories that suggest a highly equitable society. Remember too that by using the deck, fixing a few categories in social relations will necessarily mean points of tension will emerge in governance, economics, or cultural influences.

Finally, don't feel that your choice of genre requires you to fix certain values in place. It can often be more interesting to build worlds that run contrary to genre expectations. For example, what if you created a post-apocalyptic setting that had abundant resources? Or a cyberpunk world where the culture despised technology? Trying to square the randomized values with your understanding of genre conventions can lead you to exciting new conclusions, so don't let genre expectations hem you in.

Strategy 3: Setting Values for All Substructures

Based on what you decided as the group as you built the foundation, it's often possible to sketch out some structural values of the world from the onset. Read through the list of 14 substructures and after each one ask if anyone sees it as one of the defining features of your fictional world. For each one the group identifies as being a defining feature, jot down a phrase or a short sentence that captures why the substructure is noteworthy. For example, if your group wants to build a *Mad Max*-inspired post-apocalypse world, your initial notes might look something like this:

- Governance: Government involvement – no government presence, anarchy
- Economics: Wealth – little to no wealth in the world; fuel and weapons act as wealth
- Economics: Distribution – highly stratified, no method to redistribute wealth
- Social Relations: Class – high class tensions, warfare between haves and have-nots
- Cultural Influences: Technology – motorized machinery defines the culture

Set up the worldbuilding card deck in four columns as usual, and then place the appropriate numeric and trending card next to each of these categories. With these defining features identified, you look at the remaining cards in your hand and start placing them next to categories, fleshing out the relationships between the substructures. Using the deck this way safeguards you from overloading the world with too many high or low values resulting in an incoherent world of extremes. It also gives you the greatest control over the points of tension in the world. This strategy is also the one most commonly used when creating a worldbuilding project that's attached to a preexisting world. For example, in the *Star Wars* galaxy, the planet Coruscant is one giant city that extends thousands of levels downward beneath the planet's surface. If your worldbuilding group is intending to develop a cross-section of levels of the city-planet, it might make sense to work through what the group already knows about Coruscant based on canonical *Star Wars* material and methodically fill in the categories with appropriate values.

It might also be the case that you begin with this strategy but then realize that your group doesn't really know (or perhaps care) what the numeric value might be for one or more categories, or may not know whether the values are trending or stable. If this happens, simply shuffle the remaining cards and deal them out randomly.

Interpreting Values of Structures and Substructures

The structures and substructures provide an outline for the story of your world. Each structural category receives its own section in the world's metanarrative description, and each category's narrative description should at least touch on each of its substructures. It's crucial that the group must account for each and every one of the 14 substructures within the categories, giving them all serious consideration and skipping none of them. Undoubtedly, some of the substructures will be more prominent in the world than others, but in order for the world to grow organically, all of the substructures need to be discussed and understood by all the contributors. The below sections are intended to offer a possible range of interpretations for, and connections between, the substructures. This is not a definitive list by any means. Interpretations will vary based on the values you generated or selected, how the group defines those categories and values, and the fictional genre of your world.

Interpreting Governance Structures

Governance structures (with the substructures of *government presence, rule of law*, and *social services*) describe the way a society is governed on a day to day basis. High values (5) for *government presence* indicate that the government is heavily involved in virtually every aspect of a citizen's public, professional, and personal life; for *rule of law*, that law enforcement is rigorous and ever-present;

and for *social services*, that citizens are provided with robust levels of healthcare, education, transportation, and other services. The low values (1) for these substructures respectively indicate a near-absence of government figures or administrative structures, virtually no law enforcement or courts of law, and no provision of social services of any kind for members of the society.

Societies are often, but not always, governed by legal documents that outline the rights of individual citizens in relation to the powers of the government. Different nations have different laws and justice systems, and they grant and protect citizens' rights in different ways. One nation may have a complex legal system where people accused of crimes must be granted a fair trial by impartial proceedings, whereas another society may grant its law enforcement officials the ability to serve as judge, jury, and executioner with no due process for the accused. In other cases, governance systems are not codified in written law. Tribal elders may dictate rules for the society. The leadership of the society could be determined via democratic processes, or they could be passed down through hereditary lines or formal appointments, or leadership could be claimed through power grabs, coups, or other methods.

A formal system of government might not exist at all, where it's purely survival of the fittest for individuals. On the other end of the spectrum, the government could be heavily involved in every detail of a person's life, determining their career roles and who they marry. The rule of law may be enforced by a zealous police force, through ad hoc vigilante justice, or through community self-policing; punishments for transgressors could be execution, imprisonment, banishment, monetary fines, or communal shame. Social services, such as education and healthcare, could be provided through schools and public health offices, or knowledge could be passed generationally through oral traditions or rites. Appointed healers or caregivers could be responsible for the health of the society, or there may be no healthcare or education provided by the government at all, where each family unit must provide for themselves.

Privileges and biases in a society often appear in their governance structures. For example, leadership positions might be restricted by gender, class, race, or religion; the justice system may be more or less forgiving based on the accused's position within society. Quality education and healthcare services may be available to elites but denied to the masses. A society with a high level of government involvement could be a utopian commune that strictly enforces equality and punishes any kind of discrimination, or it could be a totalitarian dictatorship that persecutes anyone deemed to be a malcontent. A government that provides robust education for all its citizens could be teaching them advanced literacy, science, and math skills to better their society, or it could be indoctrinating them with state propaganda from an early age.

Governance substructures intersect with *economic substructures* in that governing requires resources, and that the governing system usually has the power to control the distribution of wealth throughout the society through taxation and courts of law. Governance intersects with *social relations substructures* in that the government is responsible for bestowing rights upon its citizens, but enforcing those rights can vary along the lines of race, class, gender, and sexual orientation. A government may also deny participation in the political process to specific groups within the society. Governance substructures intersect with *cultural influences substructures* in that a culture's values are often encoded in its laws and systems of governance. For example, laws might be founded on core religious beliefs, or these cultural influences can determine who is allowed to serve in public offices, or dictate the level of spending on the military, technology, or the arts.

Interpreting Economic Structures

Economic substructures (with the substructures of *economic strength, economic distribution,* and *agriculture and trade*) have to do with the amount of wealth and its allocation within a society. A high value (5) for *economic strength* denotes an enormous amount of wealth in the society. For *economic distribution*, it indicates that the society's wealth is evenly distributed, with very little stratification from the top of society down to the bottom. For *agriculture and trade*, it means that the society produces a surplus of goods or services in relation to its needs and enjoys brisk trade both within and outside the society. Low values (1) suggest a society with painfully little wealth or resources, that ownership of wealth in the society is highly stratified, and that the society has little means of generating wealth or involved in active trade, either domestically or with other societies.

We commonly think of wealth as hard currency—coins, bills, notes, etc.—but it also includes property, real estate, or other types of commodities, such as the control over natural resources. There are also non-monetary barter economies where individuals exchange a wide variety of material goods, such as livestock, crops, or minerals. There are also service economies where people perform tasks in exchange for goods or services; information economies where knowledge has a value, sharing economies where private property is uncommon as people lend or rent goods instead of purchasing them, and gift economies where people do each other favors in exchange for future considerations. Multiple economies can operate simultaneously, including those not regulated by the government. While wealth is rarely distributed evenly among a population, the gap between the wealthiest and poorest members of a society might be small, such as in communal setting, or extreme, like in a feudal system. Natural resources and connections to other societies can play an important role in a society's economy. Societies often find it advantageous to trade with outsiders, but trade agreements can often become points of tension depending on the two governments' priorities. In addition, a poorly defended society that is rich in natural resources can be an open invitation to foreign invaders.

Economic substructures are greatly affected by *governing substructures* as they often have to do with how wealth is distributed through a society, most notably through systems of taxation. Depending on the society, the government is often responsible for issuing and regulating currency and managing trade with foreign nations. Economic substructures intersect with *social relations* in that wealth often relates to how societies think about class distinctions, and wealth stratification often runs along the lines of race, gender, and sexual orientation. Certain social groups might be denied employment in lucrative professions, and high levels of income inequality are often a root cause of social unrest. Economic substructures also have to do with *cultural influences*, as societies often demonstrate their cultural priorities through the kinds of programs funded by the state. The amount of the society's wealth that is allocated for religious, military, technological, or artistic advancement can be a cause for rejoicing or consternation, depending on one's individual viewpoint.

Interpreting Social Relations Structures

Social relations structures (and the substructures of *race/ethnicity, class, gender, sexual orientation*) deal with levels of equal access to resources and enforcement of rights within the society. High values (5) indicate a near-perfect state of equity along the lines of race, class, gender, and sexual orientation, where every member of the society can expect to receive the identical level of benefits as anyone else. Low values (1) are indicators of massive inequalities in society, where the oppressed classes have virtually no rights and face continual harassment, persecution, and subjugation from the dominant society.

Racial and *ethnic* discrimination typically occurs when members of a majority group oppress or have distinct advantages over members of a minority group. The roles can also be reversed, where the members of the minority group seize control wealth and power and oppress the native majority, such as in the case of imperial powers colonizing a native population. *Gender* and *sexual orientation* operate in a similar way, where rights can be bound to rigid definitions of gender and sexual identities that may deliberately exclude certain groups of people. A society can be male dominated (patriarchy) or female dominated (matriarchy) or ruled by those who do not fall into gender binaries. In these cases, a certain gender or genders may be treated as second-class citizens, or worse.

Class most often refers to differences in income across the population, where the poorer classes are routinely disenfranchised. However, class can be defined in other ways too. For example, a society may define classes by the possession of knowledge or specific skills, such as being part of the hunter class, warrior class, or clergy, where these revered classes of people enjoy privileges over others. Social privileges and discriminations can be compounded as well. For example, in our primary world, a wealthy white male would enjoy a number of advantages in society, whereas a poor woman of color will face multiple levels of discrimination due to her race, class, and gender.

Social relations substructures connect to *governing substructures* in many important ways, most notably that agents of the government tend to be responsible for guaranteeing equality—or in the negative sense, ignoring inequality—for members of the society through the many mechanisms of the legal system. They connect to *economic substructures* in that unequal distributions of wealth, power, social mobility, and equal rights within a society often correlate with a person's individual race, class, gender, and sexual identity. *Cultural influence substructures* reflect the values of the society and will be ingrained in social substructures. For example, specific genders, races, or people of a certain sexual orientation can be denied from serving in a religious order, a branch of the military, or holding powerful political offices. A class of "untouchables" may be denied basic rights or services, such as healthcare or education.

Interpreting Cultural Influences Structures

Cultural influences structures (with the substructures of *military influence*, *religious influence*, *technology influence*, and the *arts influence*) tend to be deeply ingrained in the fabric of society, and are often more apparent to an outsider than to someone raised in that community who sees these influences as "normal." High values (5) mean that these categories have a very strong grip on the wider society, where most aspects of daily life would be infused with aspects of these cultural influences; for example, where every street corner has a military post, a church, a laboratory, or a museum. Low values (1) indicate that these substructures are either virtually absent or hold no sway in the society at all. They could often be disparaged or actively persecuted by the dominant culture, where members of the military might be harassed, religious figures scorned, advancements in technology feared, and practitioners of the arts ridiculed.

Strong influences may manifest themselves in many ways, such as compulsory military service or attending to mandatory religious rites. It could also include a fetishization of technology or the arts. It could also be the reverse, where technology is shunned and artistic expression is banned. Cultural influences can mix in interesting ways too. For example, religious art may have enormous value, or leaps in technological advancement could be achieved through military research. They can also fuse in other ways, where the military is powered by religious fervor, or every piece of technology is infused with a deeply artistic aesthetic. Cultural influences are often visible as physical locations. This could mean places of worship or holy sites for pilgrimages, the presence of military training centers, bases, or outposts, or the prevalence of technological universities, research parks, and laboratories, or cultural institutions such as museums, performing arts centers, and displays of public art such as murals and sculptures.

Cultural influences substructures are often reinforced through the *governance substructures*; for example, laws being prescribed by religious texts or a militarized police force that establishes its own rule of law. The society's cultural values are often reflected in their *economic substructures* as well, dictating whether they provide resources for religious institutions, investments in weapons and military training, if they fund learning and technology advancements, or if there is widespread public support for artists. They also often shape attitudes regarding *social relations substructures*, such as whether the society is eager to adopt knowledge and art from all segments of society, or whether a privileged group defines cultural values and respects tradition over more avant-garde forms of creative expression that celebrate cultural diversity.

Other Structures and Substructures

As discussed in previous chapters, some worlds have additional structures or substructures that you may wish to consider. In certain speculative fiction genres, you will want to consider social relations with *non-human species* (which includes robots or other artificial intelligence) and the influence of *magic*. There are also non-genre specific substructures for social relations that include *ageism* and *ableism*, and for cultural influences there are the substructures of *drugs and drug culture* and the attitude toward the *natural world*. Each additional substructure needs to be fully ingrained in the world and part of the metanarrative, so each one creates a significant level of work. A new substructure must be connected to *each* of the other 14 substructures. For example, if your group creates a science fiction world where robots walk among humans, the group would need to work through issues of *governance* (Are robots allowed to vote? Must they follow laws? Do public funds help pay for their programming and maintenance?), *economics* (Are robots paid for their labor? Are they allowed to own property or currency? Can robots be bought and sold?), *social relations* (Do robots have more or fewer rights than humans? Are there levels of discrimination against certain models of robots? Are robots allowed to reproduce, marry, or have sexual relations with humans?), and *cultural influences* (Do robots worship or have souls? Can they serve in the military? Are they regarded as autonomous beings or pieces of technology? Can they write plays or perform ballet?).

Remember too that any of these issues (and of course many others you might imagine) will bubble to the surface naturally without needing to add another substructure. For example, if you develop a world that prizes high levels of physical productivity, it would be reasonable to assume that the elderly are seen as less valuable. Ageism would come to the fore as a logical result of the world's mechanics rather than choosing from the start as an additional substructure. Only add substructures if your group wants to make a concerted effort to deal with the tensions that substructure will raise. If your group is very interested in generating a world that features potential conflict among different age groups, go ahead and add it.

Building Tal-Vaz: Developing the Structures

The four contributors regroup a few days later at Bryan's house to begin developing the social structures. Bryan printed out four Worldbuilding Structures Worksheets, one for each person. He also purchased a Worldbuilding Card Deck that he has on his table. Aaron hooks up his laptop to Bryan's 42-inch HDTV and mirrors the display so everyone can see it. He opens up a Google doc entitled "Tal-Vaz Structures" and shares it with everyone via email. He creates four headings in bold for the structures—politics, economics, social relations, and cultural influences—and adds each of the substructures beneath them, counting to make sure he listed all 14. Karly reminds him to add another substructure for *magic* under cultural influences bringing the total to 15.

Bryan suggests they use the strategy where they fix some of the values and randomize the rest using the worldbuilding deck. Aaron begins writing in the broad facts they'd agreed to in their first session, creating bullets next to the corresponding substructure and puts a value next to it, mostly just to get people talking.

- *Economic strength* – suddenly very wealthy (4 or 5)
- *Economic distribution* – highly stratified between ruling families and the rest (1 or 2)
- *Technology influence* – profound influence thanks to ancient discovery (4 or 5)
- *Magic influence* – present in the world but not prominent (1)

They all agree that these are the defining features of the world. They scan through the other 11 substructures and none of them jump out as being more prominent than the others.

Bryan says that he doesn't think the *economic distribution* should be a 1, which means it can't get much worse. He also thinks that it might be a stretch for these cities to reach the highest possible *economic strength* of 5. He suggests they fix those substructures at 2 and 4 and no one argues against it. Karly says the same thing about the category of *magic influence*, where a 1 would mean that it has virtually no influence at all or is outright shunned. Cassandra says she mostly agrees but reminds Karly that they're developing the structure for the entire region of Tal-Vaz. Magic could be unpopular and hold very little influence outside Sal-Kala, but in that focal point, magic will definitely have much more influence. Karly isn't entirely convinced by that but, after a little debate, she relents and the group resolves to switch it to a 2 as well.

Karly takes the numeric deck places the 4 card next to *economic strength* and a 5 next to *technology influence*; she puts a 2 card by *economic distribution* and *magic influence*. Because they added a substructure, they need to add one additional numeric and one trending card too. She slides them into their respective decks and shuffles them. She then begins dealing the cards out, assigning one number card and one trending card per category with the following results with (T) representing the trending categories:

The group begins combing over the results and offering interpretations. Cassandra notes that the Governance structure isn't that interesting, beyond the trending *government presence*. The rest of the values suggest that the political situation is stable and the citizens of Tal-Vaz have a good level of social services, probably funded by their newfound wealth. She wonders if the government presence is trending up to a 4, meaning the government is becoming more involved—possibly with more taxation, or a more robust election process. Karly suggests that if the noble families are gaining power, perhaps it's trending down

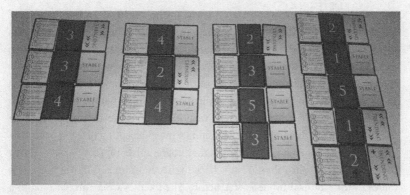

Figure 10.1 Tal-Vaz Structures

to a 2, suggesting they'd want less government oversight so they could control more of the power. They all like that idea but want to wait before committing to it. Aaron types as fast as he can, taking notes and asking people to repeat what they'd said to make sure he caught everything. He puts a question mark in parentheses next to ideas they want to return to.

The group moves to the Economic structure. The high level of *economic strength* and poor *economic distribution* were fixed values, but the 4 in *agriculture and trade* was randomly dealt. Since Tal-Vaz used to be a desert backwater and not good for agriculture, they unanimously agree that it must be increased trade. The other curveball for this column is that the *economic distribution* is trending, so the big question is whether it's trending up toward a more equal distribution (3), or trending down indicating worsening economic stratification (1). Bryan votes for the latter, connecting it to the idea that the government is shrinking, not growing. He argues that the strongest members of society could be extracting the most wealth and destabilizing any existing governance structures that would prevent them from doing so. People warm to that idea, but don't want to commit to it just yet. Aaron records it in the notes with a question mark in parentheses beside it. Karly points out that this would give them a few different levels of conflict to play with: there would be tension between the classes and between the members of the government and the nobility.

Looking at the Social Relations structures gives them pause. *Class relations* aren't too bad as they have a value of a 3, meaning the high degree of wealth stratification in Tal-Vaz isn't a cause of major strife. But why? Aaron suggests because the people aren't used to money so they don't understand the amount of riches being passed around, and, besides, the newly wealthy are pacifying the masses by providing a high level of *social services*. He also notes that the society operates with near complete *gender equity* (5), so there's no substantial difference between how men and women are treated in the world. He notes that *sexual orientation* isn't a hot-button issue in this world. The glaring issue for this world's social relations, Karly says, is *race relations*. At a 2 that means it's pretty poor, and it's trending—is it getting even worse or better? After they mull this over for a few minutes, Aaron says this makes sense. If trade to the cities has increased, Tal-Vaz is seeing more races and ethnicities than ever before, and many are probably taking advantage of the new wealth. But does this increased exposure to outsiders mean that Tal-Vaz is becoming a more accepting or a less accepting society? The group again goes silent as they contemplate this.

Cassandra says they should come back to this question and moves to the low values in the Cultural Influences structure. She likens Varoja and Sal-Kala to a pair of liberal arts college towns in the middle of nowhere, highly secular with a *religious influence* of a 1, and they're generally opposed to warfare with *military influence* being a 2 that's trending. Bryan picks up on that idea: what if the cities were sites of ancient and long forgotten universities? And the major breakthrough that changed the cities' fortunes was the accidental discovery of a massive university library full of ancient knowledge? The region never needed a military because there was nothing to take; there was no *art* scene (value of 1) because no one's coming to that harsh desert climate to make art. The others nod, feeling like pieces are starting to fit into place. Aaron says that doesn't quite make sense because whichever city had the library would be the one to grow—there's no reason the neighboring one would. Bryan counters with the idea that instead of one big library, they discover several smaller ones clustered around each of the cities.

Cassandra attempts to connect these ideas back to the political structure by presenting another problem: why would there be feuding noble houses in the middle of nowhere? Maybe because of Varoja, the larger city of the two, had two main families who traded off ruling the city based on a popular vote—sort of like conservatives and liberals. Sal-Kala was smaller and has always been ruled by one enormous ruling family. Cassandra continues her brainstorm. They could now have five ruling families—two in Varoja and one in Sal-Kala, with the remaining two coming from outside the region. They could be powerful scholars and business people who brought their expertise to the excavation project. Karly warms to that idea, adding that they could be the outsiders pushing for some of these changes like getting rid of government structures. That adds yet another level of tension—the outsiders who come to Tal-Vaz helped unlock the region's hidden potential. That would annoy the locals because they've been sitting on a treasure trove without knowing it, but some would appreciate the fact that they turned from a backwater into a pair of thriving cities with plenty of wealth to support the community. Bryan points to the *race relations* and says the outsiders could be multiracial groups too, which would give the people of Tal-Vaz another reason to dislike the outsiders. The ideas are coming thick and fast and Aaron is begging people to slow down so he can get everything recorded. Cassandra starts jotting the ideas in her notebook as a backup, just so they don't lose any.

They begin recapping to make sure they've hit all the substructures. Aaron notices they skipped over the military's trending status, but that's easily explainable: now that they have resources others will want, they need a way to defend themselves from potential invaders. The military influence is still low at 2 but is trending upward to a 3, and probably in a hurry. The outsiders could also be agitating for that change.

Aaron also wants to return to the timeline and add some historical events. The *point of the present* is at this moment in history, where tensions between the families threaten to boil over, but how long has it been since the discovery of the ancient libraries to the point of the present? They debate this, weighing the plusses and minuses—anything less than 20 years seems unreasonably fast given the society's stage of development, but more than 50 years is too long in that it doesn't make sense that they wouldn't have been conquered already. Cassandra votes for adding a milestone marking the discovery of the first site 30 years earlier from the point of the present. At the point of the present, a good number of natives of Tal-Vaz are just beginning to understand that they are not entirely in control over what's happening to their society.

It's been a few hours of work and the group's brains are getting tapped out. They agree to pull the notes into a short narrative describing the region of Tal-Vaz and its two major cities. Aaron dictates the narrative as he types it out, stopping and starting to incorporate the other's suggestions. After several stops and starts, he has an expanded description of their metanarrative lead. The paragraphs read:

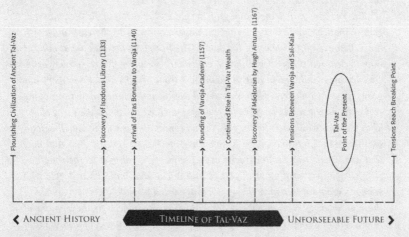

Figure 10.2 Tal-Vaz Revised Timeline

The cities of Varoja and Sal-Kala were villages, hardly anything more than rest stops for travelers crossing the harsh desert on the Cassius Trade Route. For years the region was controlled by nomadic clans. Family A and Family B held control of the city of Varoja, while Family C governed uncontested in Sal-Kala. Periodic squabbles aside, the clans had little reason for conflict over the meager resources as traders spent only enough time to replenish their water and food supplies, enjoy a hot bath, and sleep for a night or two away from the blowing sand. This changed in year XXXX with the accidental discovery of the Major Library beneath the streets of Varoja. This attracted little attention until scholars of Family D got wind of the library and came to Tal-Vaz to see what ancient wisdom the library held. Using sophisticated excavation techniques, they soon uncovered even larger libraries and began deciphering the trove of books and scrolls within. Keeping their discovery quiet from the people of the city, Family D sent word back east along the route beseeching others in their clan to establish Tal-Vaz as their new home. The secret could not be contained, however, and Family E began their own secret excavations south in Sal-Kala in the year XXXX, exhuming the Magic Library and gaining their own foothold in the region. In the subsequent years, dozens of new sites, both small and large, were uncovered throughout the region.

With the wonders and inventions emerging from Tal-Vaz, brisk trade has brought prosperity to the region. While much of the wealth has flowed to the five noble families, they have invested in the health of the cities, providing enviable levels of education and medicine for the citizenry even as their populations rapidly grew. The outsiders to Tal-Vaz were amazed at the equality of the sexes, where women could be fearsome warriors and men could tend to domestic duties without shame. This ran contrary to the customs elsewhere on the continent, as was the abolition of any established religion. They also were bewildered at the lack of a standing army, knowing that even a modest military force could roll through the region and claim both of the cities with little effort, but the desert shields them from such attacks—for now.

Tal-Vaz is experiencing major growing pains. The riches of Tal-Vaz have not gone unnoticed and rumors swirl that imperial powers to the east and north have their eye on this jewel of the desert. The five noble families are at odds at how to deal with this alleged threat, either through proactive diplomacy or by establishing a military to defend themselves from attack. Also, resentment has grown in some quarters of Tal-Vaz, as some of the indigenous inhabitants of the region resent the sudden influx of foreigners who have disrupted their way of life. They blame the outsiders for the growth and commotion of the city and the cloud of anxiety that hangs over the region. They mock their style of dress and how they treat their women like fragile pets. The feeling of disgust is often mutual, with newcomers scoffing at the crude and uncultured indigenous people who were too ignorant to realize the wealth that existed beneath their feet. To add to these simmering tensions, there are Varojans who object to the rumors of mysticism and arcana emanating from Sal-Kala, which smacks of dealings that are either religious or unnatural in nature.

The group is satisfied with that for the expanded metanarrative lead. A quick review shows that they're covering all of the 14 substructures plus the added substructure for *magic*. They still have lots of questions and fleshing out to do, most notably to better define the families and what these "wonders and inventions" bringing prosperity actually are, but the combination of framework and structures give them a solid scaffolding for the next step, writing the metanarrative. They are creatively spent and agree to wrap up for the evening. They find a day and time for the following week that works for everyone and Cassandra offers to host them at her apartment.

11

Writing the Metanarrative

Once the group has a grip on the structures and the substructures, it's time to break down the metanarrative into chunks and starting parceling them out to the contributors. The Scope and Schedule Worksheet (Appendix C) assists you in distributing the work as evenly as possible and setting guidelines on how much each contributor should write. You want to avoid having a single person contributing 5000 words while everyone else writes 500, or a situation where one of the four structures becomes three times longer than any of the others.

Your group should have an online document of shared notes and each contributor should have the Worldbuilding Structures Worksheet (Appendix A) showing the values for each substructure in the world. Create five new Google Docs or, alternatively, five new pages on your wiki, for each of the four *structures* and one for *historical events*. This is where everyone will write their metanarrative chunks and, near the end of the process, you will copy them into one long metanarrative. For now, it's easiest to keep them separate. Block off an hour or two where the contributors can write in close proximity of one another. During the early stage of writing the metanarrative, the group needs to be able to ask each other clarifying questions and get fast answers so they can keep writing. Since all of the structures and substructures are connected, any major changes or new developments to one substructure will ripple through many, if not all, of the others. As time goes on, the world's details will become more concrete and the number of significant questions about the world will dwindle.

Writing the metanarrative has three separate *check-in periods*. The writers need to complete a certain amount of writing for each check-in, the purpose of which is to ensure consistency and coherence in the metanarrative as it grows. The speed at which the group moves through the check-ins will depend on the group's ambition and availability. There are a number of ways to divide out the writing tasks. Volunteering usually works best, provided each structural category receives sufficient attention. The Scope and Schedule Worksheet helps establish a clear timeframe for this portion of the project.

Everyone should work on each of the structural categories and every substructure must be addressed in the metanarrative in some fashion, even if it's only a few sentences. Some different strategies to guarantee diverse coverage include:

- Having two or more contributors assigned to each structural category
- Assigning each contributor two or more substructures in different structural categories
- Requiring contributors to switch structural categories after each check-in
- Work out a system of checks and balances where a contributor is responsible for writing in two structural categories and providing feedback and commentary on the two others
- Require every contributor to create one or more historical milestones
- Add any other system you can come up with where writers are responsible for multiple structural categories

The key is dividing the writing responsibilities thoroughly and evenly, mixing different contributors' perspectives on the world. Do whatever you can to discourage contributors from developing a strong sense of ownership over any single part of the world. While it's natural for people to be drawn to their areas of interest, the fundamental principle should be the sharing and blending of concepts and inviting others to add their own ideas.

Check-in #1: Staying on the Same Page

Check-in #1 should happen in a compressed timeframe of an hour or two and ideally the contributors are in close proximity or can hold a conversation across a table in real time. Check-in #1 converts the bullet point phrases from the brainstorming list for each structural category into sentences that become part of the longer metanarrative. For example, a bullet that reads "invasive policing, no privacy" should turn into an actual sentence: "The police force has few limits on their power and citizens have no expectation of privacy." That sentence can then be worked into a paragraph describing the *governance* structure.

For check-in #1, assign everyone a small amount to write, 250 to 500 words as an upper limit. A little more or less is fine, but when it starts pushing 1000 words that's too much before the first check-in. Check-in #1 is primarily for questions of clarification and declaring new connections for the metanarrative. Keeping the time short also means the group can quickly review what everyone else has done and correct any misunderstandings.

After an hour or so, stop typing and start talking. The writers responsible for each category might give a quick verbal report on what they came up with, focusing on new ideas and asking clarifying questions about the direction in which they plan to head. It could take longer if the different ideas aren't cohering into a narrative that makes sense. It's better to spend the time now to work out the kinks than hoping they will somehow work themselves out. Generally speaking, they don't. Faulty assumptions almost always wind up in a nonsensical snarl that requires some significant backtracking and deleting of work. When everyone—and that does mean everyone—feels good about the direction the metanarrative is heading, it's on to check-in #2.

Building Tal-Vaz: Check-In #1

The group meets at Cassandra's apartment late Saturday morning, laptops in hand. They quickly hash out some responsibilities and they agree to work in pairs. *Historical events, governance structure*, and the *economic structure* will be started by Bryan and Karly; Aaron and Cassandra will begin with the *social relations* and *cultural influences* structures. Bryan says that everyone should begin nailing down names for the families, locations, and anything else that needs a name. If it's something major, like one of the ruling houses, shout it out so everyone hears. Cassandra sets her phone's alarm for an hour at which point they'll stop writing and review what they came up with.

The hour passes quickly. Bryan and Karly start their recap with the ideas that they came up with and the names they used. This is some of what they decided:

- Bryan established the year 1133 as the year the first archaeological site was discovered. He arrived at that year by looking at the clock at 11:33 am.
- Karly named the Varojan two indigenous families the Gallegos and Cuevases. She got the names from an online name generator. Karly also determined that a fellow named Eras Bonneau of the Bonneau clan is the outsider who came to Varoja to investigate the library site in the year 1140. Karly names the site the Isodorus Library after a prominent ancient scholar, and she renames Magic Library outside Sal-Kala "the Máolorian." They guess the point of the present is around 1175.
- Bryan named the cities at the ends of the Cassius Trade Route, with the western one named Paulstra, which roughly resembles Barcelona in Spain from our primary world, the eastern one is Trammelore-by-the-sea, which has some things in common with Marseilles in the south of France. He also names the continent Arvalon.

- Bryan and Karly spent most of the hour working on the names and dates and didn't write much at all for the *governance structure*, beyond a few sentences of what everyone already agreed to, namely that there is little formalized government structure due to the fact that the people were nomadic tribes. The Gallego and Cuevas families controlled Varoja for the last several decades, though the arrival of Eras Bonneau has strained that relationship, which was never too friendly to begin with.

- For the *economic structure*, Bryan determined that the Cassius Trade Route links Paulstra to Trammelore with Tal-Vaz as the desert region between them. The cape to the south of Tal-Vaz has treacherous weather and is prone to pirate attacks, so well-guarded caravans along the Trade Route were a much safer, albeit much slower, option for trade between the two traditional economic powerhouses. Now Varoja and Sal-Kala are worthy trading cities in their own right due to the riches being unearthed in those locations. Both Trammelore and Paulstra have large appetites for the knowledge and wares coming from Tal-Vaz.

- Cassandra and Aaron spent their time digging into the indigenous nomadic society that's rapidly changing. The harsh conditions of the Tal-Vaz shaped both the *social relations* and the *cultural influences*. In short, they believe any kind of discrimination leads to inefficiencies that can be fatal in the desert, and thus they trust each member of the tribe to do what they do best. They do not understand the notion of traditional gender roles, as it's common for nurturing men to take care of family issues and for athletic women to hunt, herd, and gather water for the tribe.

- Historically the people of Tal-Vaz never needed to worry about race relations because no outsiders stuck around long enough to force them to deal with the question. They tend to view same-sex relationships with suspicion as such relations do not result in repopulating the tribe with new members but tends to be a "don't ask, don't tell" situation. Class distinctions are also something new to them. Since there were so few resources to go around, no one begrudged the hardest-working members of the tribe a larger share of the hunt or harvest. Their social system now is coming under serious strain as more people than ever before are coming to Tal-Vaz and staying, and the sudden inequalities in wealth couldn't be more apparent.

- Culturally, they are nothing if not pragmatic. They scoff at both religion and artistic expression as wasteful extravagances that have no place in the desert. They are also deeply suspicious of standing armies, knowing that the desert would wipe out a large unit of soldiers faster than any enemy force ever could. They appreciate any kind of invention that simplifies their lives or improves their health and have welcomed many of the technological discoveries made in recent years. However, they are highly suspicious of claims of magic, with most people feeling it occupies a gray area between religion and some kind of illusory performance art. Personal opinions on magic range from tolerant skepticism to outright hatred.

Overall, the group is really excited about how Tal-Vaz is coming together. Cassandra hits the online name generator for the tribe that controlled Sal-Kala and the outsiders who are into magic. They generate ten names and pick out their two favorites: Laquino for the indigenous tribe and Antuma for the outsider clan. Karly thinks they need to have schools in both cities to formalize the study of the ancient sites. They name them Varoja Academy and the Máolorian.

They agree that they need to be more concrete about what's coming out of these ancient sites. On the *Scope and Schedule* worksheet, each of the four contributors agrees to add at least 250 words to the narrative for each of the four structural categories over the next six days. They plan to meet again on Friday for check-in #2. Bryan asks everyone to review the Google Doc for each section every couple of days and add questions to the top of the document. If it's an emergency question, they all agree to email or text message. Otherwise, check-in #2 is on for that coming Friday.

Check-in #2: Fleshing Out the Metanarrative

At this point, your group should feel confident in their ability to expand the metanarrative in a consistent fashion. The final metanarrative should weigh in around 4000 to 7000 words, though those words won't be evenly distributed across all the structural categories. If the world is fraught with deep-seated social problems, the *social relations* category alone might take up half of the metanarrative. If the issues of *governance* are straightforward and unremarkable, that section could be much shorter, perhaps less than 1000 words. You never want filler text to reach some arbitrary word count, but addressing the complexity built into each of the substructures should put you somewhere in that range. If the metanarrative hits 7000 words, your group should think about branching out sections into their own pages, a process described in check-in #3. These are just general guidelines, but they represent a good range to shoot for when fleshing out the metanarrative.

The function of check-in #2 is to resolve any outstanding issues and determine how much metanarrative work remains. A good rule of thumb is to reconvene for check-in #2 when each of the four structural categories has reached about 1000 words. That will bring your total metanarrative to about 4000 words plus the *historical events*. For many worldbuilding projects, the metanarrative might be nearly complete at this point. For others, it could only be partially done.

Between check-in #1 and check-in #2, the contributors should be working across several different structural categories and adding details to each as they flesh out the story of the world. Everyone should be thinking about connections between structures and historical events, between substructures, and being on the lookout for any growing inconsistencies or incoherencies that need to be addressed. Touch base often to clarify with the other contributors that everyone still sees the narrative evolving in the same way. There should be full disclosure of concepts among contributors with no surprises. An email to the group or a post to a discussion board goes a long way in preventing wasted work and hard feelings.

Ideally, check-in #2 happens in a face-to-face meeting after every contributor has finished writing and has read the entire metanarrative beginning to end. The main features of the world should be pronounced at this stage, and all of the substructures should be well fleshed out. One good way to check the consistency and detail of your work is to compare it to one or more Wikipedia pages of cities or regions of a similar size to your world. Look for gaps in your metanarrative and see what kind of information is included in a typical Wikipedia entry for our primary world. Another smart option is to invite outside readers to read the metanarrative and see what they have to say. A fresh set of eyes can often detect any glaring holes or weaknesses in the narrative.

Once you've scheduled a time to meet for check-in #2, come prepared with a list of notes, questions, and observations about the metanarrative. This should be an open and honest conversation about the state of the project, where each contributor is given time to speak freely. If you have questions or problems, state them tactfully and provide some possible solutions. It's equally important to compliment other contributors on parts of the metanarrative that you truly appreciated and felt added value to the world. Check-in #2 is not a time for groundbreaking new ideas. At this point, the foundation of the world is settling fast and any major changes will require a significant amount of review and rewriting. Having said that, serious problems need to be addressed even if it means undoing work that's already been done. There's no point in growing out an obviously flawed world. It's good practice to go back through the steps of the collaborative worldbuilding process to identify where the core problem began. Have a notetaker draw up a list of clarifications, revisions, and problems to be resolved. A bulleted list works well to identify the work to be done and, if necessary, assign a contributor to resolve each bullet. If the list is long, you may wish to do this work and run through check-in #2 again to review the edits.

If the structural categories and historical events exist in separate documents or on their own wiki pages, you should combine them into a single document before check-in #3. The metanarrative page should begin with the *metanarrative lead*, revised to reflect the new information you've learned about the world. Below that, paste the section describing *historical events* in its own section, followed by the *governance, economics, social relations*, and *cultural influences*. Reading from the top of the page to the bottom, it should tell a story of the world that begins with a broad overview that describes the scope of this world, continues with major historical events that shaped its timeline, and then provides a detailed description of how the social structures operate on a day-to-day basis in the *point of the present*.

Another important step between check-in #2 and check-in #3 is to identify important people, places, things, and historical events in the metanarrative that will need to be expanded on in catalog entries. Underline them in the metanarrative to visually draw attention to them. It's very helpful for these identified catalog entries to be assembled into a single list before check-in #3 as it speeds up the process of distributing the work of creating entries and gives the contributors an idea of how many entries will need to be created.

Building Tal-Vaz: Check-in #2

A few days before the group agreed to meet, Cassandra emails everyone to point out that they lack an explanation for where the ancient Tal-Vaz civilization went and why no one ever went looking for it. She suggests that the civilization is like an Atlantis swallowed by sand, a place that everyone has heard of but people assumed was more folklore than reality. She suggests that now, in the point of the present, the people of Tal-Vaz have proof this ancient society actually existed and there are a growing and vocal minority who blame magic for bringing disaster down upon them. The rest of the group thinks that idea works, and everyone agrees to comb over the metanarrative looking for places to insert those details and to smooth over any obvious inconsistencies.

The group meets on Friday as planned, with everyone having reviewed the metanarrative. They each found a few minor inconsistencies that need to be worked out regarding dates and the founding of the Varoja Academy and the

Máolorian. They also have a growing cast of characters from the different ruling families that they want to connect. Aaron likes the idea of marriages complicating some of the family rivalries. Cassandra is getting more interested in the cultures of Trammelore and Palustra but is mindful of working on the framework and not getting too far out on the fringes. Bryan and Aaron spend time working on the inventions coming out of Varoja, and Karly and Cassandra develop more of the magical side, blending sleight-of-hand tricks with more powerful spells. Aaron reminds them not to get ahead of themselves and that they should focus on finishing up the metanarrative so they can move on to the catalog and develop some of their ideas. Everyone agrees to finalize all the metanarrative changes and underline all the people, places, things, and historical events that will need catalog entries. Karly volunteers to copy everything into one page and pull out everything that's underlined and put it on a list. They schedule check-in #3 for that Tuesday, in three days' time.

Check-in #3: Narrative Branches and Transitioning to Catalog Creation

By the time you reach check-in #3, the world's metanarrative should be between 4000 and 7000 words compiled into a single document as the front page of your wiki. Once the metanarrative provides a solid trunk for the world, the rest of the worldbuilding project needs to spread outward in direction rather than simply getting thicker through the middle. If some portion of the metanarrative—whether that's a detailed recounting of a historical event or the actions of a specific person in the world—gets too long to fit comfortably within the metanarrative, you should consider creating a separate page in the catalog. Splitting off longer portions of the metanarrative into different catalog entries, a process called *narrative branching*, keeps the metanarrative tight and focused, and allows for readers to move between the metanarrative and the catalog entries in a nonlinear, freeform fashion as they learn about the world.

Before check-in #3, contributors should read the completed metanarrative and continue to refine it to add depth, strengthen connections, smooth out rough edges, resolve contradictions, and begin identifying potential narrative branches and catalog entries. There are no hard and fast rules for when something must branch into its own catalog entry, but remember that the function of the metanarrative is to give a broad overview of aspects of the world, not delve into every gritty detail. If we look at a Wikipedia page for a long and complex event in the primary world such as World War II,[1] under each section we see links to other pages, such as the link to *Timeline of World War II* under the "Chronology" heading, and *Causes of World War II* under "Background." This strategy helps keep the main page concise, while pages that branch from the main page can offer more details and competing perspectives.

Begin check-in #3 with outstanding questions and clarifications. If someone has made a change that they weren't sure about, now is the time to ask. In the best-case scenario, these edits are made live so everyone can see the new finalized language. As the group reviews the metanarrative, continue underlining the people, places, and things that contributors feel could use their own catalog entries. By doing so, you can start to get a sense of the number catalog entries the group will need to create and whether you're remaining within the *scope* you determined in the framework. If it seems like a daunting list of entries, scale back. Maybe some of those locations or characters don't need to be fully fleshed out in entries, or at least not at this stage.

Check-in #3 ends the process of writing the metanarrative and begins the process of catalog creation. While the metanarrative will continue to undergo slight tweaks and revisions, it should be a solid story that tells the history and workings of your world right up to the point of the present. The catalog creation stage adds most of the volume to the world, so you want to be absolutely sure that no major discrepancies exist or inconsistencies will spread throughout the catalog entries. If you have questions, let them be heard and answered. The process becomes much more individualized after this, so it's worth spending time as a group to make sure everyone is clear before transitioning to the next stage of catalog creation.

Building Tal-Vaz: The Metanarrative

The group meets once more to wind up the metanarrative and begin working on the catalog. Aaron isn't entirely happy with the metanarrative as he thinks the *cultural influences* section is too long and *governance, economics,* and *social relations* are too short. Karly agrees that the culture section almost becomes a narrative itself, but she doesn't mind because it tells a compelling story about the history of the people of Tal-Vaz. Karly says that she sees Aaron's point but that they don't want to tinker with the metanarrative forever. She's excited about creating the entries and then getting on with the storytelling as she already has an idea to write a story about star-crossed lovers from opposing families. Bryan shrugs and says it could go either way. Aaron relents and says he will go with the majority on this one. The group spends time reading through the metanarrative on their laptops and tablets. Cassandra volunteers to be the one to make the final edits. Everyone finds one or two small tweaks in language and identifies some catalog entries. They read it over one last time before declaring it done.

The final draft of the metanarrative weighs in at around 4400 words. It appears in its entirety below.

Tal-Vaz

(Metanarrative lead)

Tal-Vaz is a rugged desert region in the southwest corner of the continent Arvalon. Due to the harshness of conditions, for most of its recorded history Tal-Vaz was only populated by a few nomadic tribes of cattle herders, some of whom tended small farms near the few reliable water sources. Two villages formed around these water sources, the northernmost named Varoja and the southern village named Sal-Kala. With the rise of mercantilism in Arvalon, a passageway through Tal-Vaz developed and became known as the Cassius Trade Route, linking the metropolises of Palustra in the east to Trammelore on the western sea. Over time, the villages grew into small towns. Varoja grew at a faster rate than Sal-Kala but both became frequent rest stops for traders on the route.

History *(about 1100 words)*

After a ferocious sandstorm in the year 1133, on the outskirts of Varoja a goatherd fell through the roof of a small home that had belonged to some older civilization. The dwelling was assumed to be a workshop full of ancient hand tools and a few strange mechanical devices that no longer functioned. Some believed the devices were children's toys while others guessed that they could be pieces of larger contraptions. By 1136, four other sites had been discovered around Varoja and one near Sal-Kala, though they attracted little attention from anyone outside the occasional curious traveler.

This changed dramatically in 1140 with the arrival of Eras Bonneau, an antiquities scholar from Palustra who specialized in excavation techniques. Over a two year period, Bonneau plotted the discovered sites on a map of the region and used mathematical equations to hypothesize where the center of the ancient city might have been. Exhausting the last of the funds from his family's estate, Bonneau purchased a shabby property on the southern side of Varoja that had an unusually deep cellar. Keeping his theory to himself, Bonneau dug several branching tunnels over a period of 50 days when, on the brink of despair, he finally made his breakthrough and discovered the Isodorus Library, a site which remains the single largest intact structure of ancient Tal-Vaz. Cautious to the point of being paranoid, Bonneau immediately understood the importance of what he had found. He kept his discovery secret but immediately sent for his blood relatives and a handful of trusted colleagues to join him in Varoja.

The secret would not last long, however, and by 1145 word had spread along the Cassius Trade Route about the mysterious things being unearthed in Varoja. During this period, Bonneau began experiencing his first run-ins with the Gallego and Cuevas families. The two were mild political rivals that had swapped control over Varoja a number of times over the preceding century. Though they lacked the strength to overwhelm Bonneau and his growing clan of Palustranians, they were savvy enough to exert themselves on the local economy, with the matriarch Darija Gallegos imposing taxes and tariffs on citizens and traders. The Cuevas Clan cornered the market on services such as inns, taverns, and hired security. The income derived from these activities was modest at first but would grow proportionally with the dramatic rise in Varoja's stature that was well underway. Only Eras Bonneau and the Bonneau clan were allowed access to the scrolls and leather-bound texts that lined the shelves of the Isodorus Library, all of which were written in an ancient language that needed painstaking deciphering. The first rebuilt artifact the public was allowed to see was the Bone Dragon (also known as the Scroll Dragon) kite in 1150, though the scholars had not yet discovered how to make it glide.

Under Eras Bonneau's leadership, by 1154 there were 40 scholars researching in the library, all of whom had significant ties to Bonneau or his clan. By 1157, Bonneau began referring to the cluster of buildings around the library as the Varoja Academy, which was now a gated and well-guarded facility that included its own sleeping quarters and a private dining hall. That same year the Academy formally began accepting applications and they courted controversy by accepting Ando Cuevas of Clan Cuevas in 1158. Intended as a sign of good will, it angered the Gallegos who saw it as a slight. Tensions were high until the point Ando completed his studies in 1163. However, by 1170, enrollment in the academy more than doubled in size and had 100 scholars, a majority of whom were not related to Bonneau, though the scholars paid astronomical tuition fees as well as heavy royalty fees for any inventions they derived from Isodorus materials. Relations between the Gallegos, Cuevases, and Bonneaus generally remained cordial but strained, though individual members of the families enjoyed friendships, business deals, and even romances across family lines.

Unlike the political turmoil in Varoja, in Sal-Kala people could not remember a time when a member of the Laquino family did not act as the community's voice and leader. The elder Tazay Laquino watched the developments in Varoja with bemusement, content with whatever wealth trickled into Sal-Kala as a result of the growth of their neighbor city. Cursory excavations outside Sal-Kala revealed <u>four ancient sites</u> on the fringes of the village but they bore no artifacts. In fact, it turned out that several had been visible for years after a major sandstorm, but their importance was unrecognized due to their mundane appearance; they were nothing but a series of polished stones that only looked unusual under close inspection. It was only in 1163 that an Academy student by the name of <u>Hugh Antuma</u> broke with tradition and traveled to investigate the sites of Sal-Kala. He used a <u>water microscope</u> to reveal that each stone was covered in a minute flowing script that he began to decode. When Eras Bonneau heard of Antuma's discovery, he warned the young man about wasting his precious study time on meaningless research. When Antuma began giving impromptu lectures in the courtyards of Varoja on alchemical formulations he'd read in the stones, Bonneau's tone changed. He decried it as preposterous religious drivel that had no basis in natural law and threatened to throw Antuma out of the Academy. In response, Antuma gave a public demonstration of the <u>Water</u> <u>Whisper</u> technique he'd learned; Bonneau held true to his word and had him expelled from the academy. Antuma left in a fury, but not before taking a half-dozen scholars with him.

The diplomatic Tazay Laquino tolerated the presence of the impetuous Antuma in Sal-Kala, neither helping nor hindering him. Laquino was cautious not to draw the ire of Varoja, but also respected Antuma's right to study what he wished. To further complicate matters, in 1165, Antuma married <u>Caro Cuevas</u>, niece of <u>Livonia Cuevas</u> and head of the Cuevas clan, and brought her south to Sal-Kala. The girl was pale, gaunt, and rarely spoke. Though many reported the marriage to be a happy one, she died within two years of relocating to Sal-Kala under mysterious circumstances. After this event, Antuma withdrew from public view.

In 1167, Tazay Laquino died of natural causes. The leadership of Sal-Kala fell to the fiery <u>Kade Laquino</u>, Tazay's youngest son. He embraced Antuma in friendship and channeled as many resources as possible toward the study of Sal-Kala's ancient sites. This influx of funding led to the complete uncovering of the southwestern site, hitherto believed to be the least significant of the four. Antuma soon realized quite the opposite. The site's greatest offering was the smooth stones that served as the floor of an enormous temple that had once been known as <u>the Máolorian</u>. The study of the mysteries of the Máolorian has proceeded at the same meteoric rate as the Varojan Academy in its early years.

Governance *(approximately 400 words)*

Historically, the nomadic tribes of Tal-Vaz governed themselves using a simple system of a voice vote that appointed a leadership council, where they chose a single speaker to declare their decisions. The council featured both men and women who rotated through each role, including the most powerful position of speaker. A humble farmer was just as likely to be appointed as an accomplished warrior. This tribal system of governance continued as the region's two primary villages grew into towns and then cities, with the Gallego and Cuevas clans being the most prominent decision-makers in Varoja and the Laquino family assuming a perpetual leadership position in Sal-Kala. Because the region had little wealth, rivalries between the families rarely escalated to anything above petty bickering.

The rapid influx of wealth to the region has multiplied these tensions tenfold. The Cuevas clan, in particular, has been accused of needlessly expanding the role of the government, especially in the form of taxes on commerce and property. This expansion has been met with resistance from many in the community, but the Cuevas clan, along with the complicit Gallegos, have headed off more serious discontent by providing a wealth of social services for citizens of Tal-Vaz, most notably in free schooling, occasional public access to libraries, and subsidized tutoring by the city's many scholars. The Varojan families also take credit for improved water filtration, wastewater handling, and food storage lockers that keep perishables fresh for long periods of time.

Crime is kept in check with a moderate amount of policing. The tight quarters of the desert cities make any large-scale heists difficult, though petty crimes such as pickpocketing and especially confidence tricks are on the rise, primarily against foreigners. Drunkenness and vagrancy are also growing among non-natives, which has fueled some resentment among the lifelong citizens of Tal-Vaz. Street brawls are now a daily occurrence. Improved policing has not been a priority of either the Gallegos or Cuevases, which displeases the scholars of the Varojan Academy, who feel that thieves could loot the library at any time without a more robust police presence. Eras Bonneau has taken matters into his own hands by hiring mercenary soldiers to stand guard at the academy's gates.

Economy *(about 500 words)*

The strength of the Tal-Vaz economy has everything to do with trade related to the wonders emerging from remains of the ancient civilization upon which it was built. People travel great distances to visit the cities of Varoja and Sal-Kala to acquire the magical elixirs produced there; a new trend has started where visitors come only to hire away scholars to serve in royal courts or to be private tutors for members of the aristocracy across the length and breadth of Arvalon. The amount of wealth present in Tal-Vaz rivals any metropolis on the continent. With so much money and goods flowing through this strip of barren desert, the Cassius Trade Route is a prime target for brigands, and now only well-guarded and heavily fortified caravans make the trip. The route between Sal-Kala and Varoja is heavily traveled and the least susceptible to attack, though travelers who push through the cooler night hours take a significant risk.

Wealth is measured in both property and material goods. Historically, permanent residences of the nomadic people of Tal-Vaz were rare and of humble design. Now, the most visible sign of wealth is the towering palaces of the ruling families of Varoja and Sal-Kala that can be seen from miles around and would be impressive even among the largest cities on the continent. They are made all the more conspicuous rising high from their desert surroundings. Nomadic tribes also kept personal possessions to a minimum due to often being on the move. Therefore it is unsurprising that today, the wealthiest families choke the rooms of their cavernous palaces with furniture and bric-a-brac as well as devices of enormous value, often hung haphazardly on a wall or pushed into a corner.

The new wealth in Tal-Vaz has been highly concentrated in the hands of the traditional ruling families and, more problematically, among the newcomers and immigrant scholars. The high level of social services provided to the citizenry by the ruling classes ameliorates this tension somewhat, but more often it is channeled into resentment at outsiders who are seen by locals as not paying their fair share back into the community. The Cuevas clan does their bit to stoke these resentments, and both they and the Gallego clan do little to counter the distrust of Bonneaus, who are still considered foreigners even after several decades of being established in Varoja. Likewise, the Laquinos and Antumas in Sal-Kala are content to shift the cause of discontent to Varoja while downplaying their own full coffers.

Trade through Tal-Vaz continues to be brisk and consistent with no signs of slowing down, though the rate of growth seems to have plateaued. Still, the amount of ingenuity and invention being produced in Tal-Vaz hasn't tapered and the economic outlook is both very strong and stable, only rivaled by the major trading cities of the coasts.

Social Relations *(about 500 words)*

The people of Tal-Vaz pride themselves on their resiliency and commitment to equality among their people. As a people, they are slow to change their beliefs and customs, which has put a strain on the society given the rapid transformation of their region. Though class divisions have always existed in Tal-Vaz, it has never been a cause for social unrest as even the poorest members of the society were seen as contributors and thus cared for by the wider community. Never before has the wealthiest member of the society been so far above the poorest though, and the people of Tal-Vaz still struggle to cope with this new reality.

One of the most notable features of Tal-Vaz is the total equality of the sexes, which is unheard of in other parts of Arvalon. Many in Trammelore see the governance system of Tal-Vaz to be a guiding light in terms of guaranteeing equal rights for the sexes, while most Palustranian view it as a weakness, as much of their society is structured around strictly enforced gender roles. As a result, one of the reasons some travelers go to Tal-Vaz is to settle there on a permanent basis to take advantage of the greater social standing afforded to women.

The nomads of Tal-Vaz are less tolerant when it comes to issues of sexual expression. The attitude of many people toward same-sex relations could be viewed as a grudging acceptance to moderate disapproval. Virility is a source of pride for the desert dwellers, as is procreation. Outright harassment of consensual nonheterosexual relationships is rare, though subtler forms of discrimination are not uncommon. One example is that Tal-Vaz citizens prefer to do business with couples who have several children. The pressure for monogamous partnering is significant, as even widows of both sexes are often encouraged to find new mates after being allowed a short period of mourning, even if the women are beyond their childbearing years.

Tal-Vaz is beset by an outright mistrust of foreigners which is intensifying with each passing season. The sparsely populated desert region rarely saw visitors and never entertained them for an extended period, as most travelers were eager to continue their journeys and the people of Tal-Vaz were happy to see them go. The notion of Varoja and Sal-Kala as destinations in themselves rather than brief stopovers came as a genuine surprise to the region, and some have said they wished they'd done more to stem the flow of immigrants when it was merely a trickle. Now a large part of the population openly resents those who they believe have come to exploit the generosity of the cities. They view outsiders as corrupting their culture and traditions, particularly when Palustranians fail to give women the respect they deserve, and also for promoting false religion in Sal-Kala. As tensions between the families of Sal-Kala rise, the problems of xenophobia have increased and are worsening.

Cultural Influences *(about 1700 words)*

MILITARY

Maintaining a standing army is a foreign concept to natives of Tal-Vaz. For the majority of their history, the cities of the region had little that outsiders would covet, and the harshness of the desert made the expense of provisioning an army an unnecessary inconvenience. The nomadic tribes were far from peaceful and no strangers to bloodshed, but few battles featured more than a few dozen combatants and never lasted more than a day. Extended military campaigns, fortifying strategic locations, and laying siege to an enemy position are not concepts familiar to those in Tal-Vaz.

That is changing, however, primarily due to the Cuevas clan in Varoja, who have assembled a small army of a few hundred soldiers capable of defending the city from attacks or raids. Well over half of the army is made up of foreigners.

Many in Varoja call them mercenaries who care nothing for the city, while others think that it's only right that it should be foreigners putting their lives on the line to protect foreign wealth. The presence of the army is a hotly debated topic and a cause of much disagreement throughout society, especially between those who are aligned with the Cuevas house versus those who side with the Gallegos. The Bonneaus make it a point to remain neutral, but the Academy quietly provides some financial support with the understanding that soldiers will be stationed near the campus and Isodorus Library. This too polarizes opinions. Some in the Bonneau clan and members of the Academy argue this arrangement is tantamount to extortion and would rather risk being unprotected than have the name of the Academy sullied in such a way.

To the consternation of many, Sal-Kala has also mustered its own small army under the Laquino Clan, but most know who is behind it. Hugh Antuma is known for his hot temper and aggressive approaches to problem-solving. His maternal grandfather, Teódulo Colmos, was a highly decorated naval commander, and young Hugh attended one of the most prestigious military academies in Arvalon before pursuing scholarly studies. He maintains a martial mindset and composes long letters to his grandfather speculating on military stratagems involving sites around Tal-Vaz. The Sal-Kala army is a mix of natives and Antuma blood relations. Many fear that a Sal-Kala army could be read as a signal of aggression from Varoja and lead to further military escalation.

RELIGION

Tal-Vaz culture is unusual in its total lack of established religion. There are no churches, temples, or cults in the region. While neither Palustra nor Trammelore are known for their piety, travelers through Tal-Vaz who show any sign of their religious beliefs can expect a torrent of probing questions from the locals that border on the outwardly hostile. Both Varoja and Sal-Kala forbid the construction of any building intended for religious purposes and likewise will not permit any public area to be designated as a place of worship. This can cause friction between outsiders, especially those with deep-seated religious convictions who have relocated to the region. They are granted a small measure of freedom of religious expression, such as the wearing of discreet religious symbols, garb indicative of their faith, and private prayer in their own home or dwelling. This can be vexing for some foreigners from Trammelore, as the Nur branch of the Trandala religion emphasizes community and the shared celebration of the tripartite Holy Spirit of Earth, Sky, and Water. The Tal-Vaz people are unapologetic for their intolerance of religion, and this is one point upon which both the indigenous citizenry of both Varoja and Sal-Kala are in complete agreement.

With the discovery of the Isodorus Library, scholars now believe that the lack of an established religion in Tal-Vaz has deep historical roots. It can be traced to the ancient civilization that once thrived in the region, one that prized knowledge of natural laws over the ephemeral matters of the spirit. Though that civilization disappeared, the secular absolutism somehow survived, perhaps in even greater intensity. The discovery and study of the Máolorian have thus been a hotly debated issue throughout the Tal-Vaz region as it appears to be some sort of a religious site. Many Varojans have called for the site to be abandoned or even reburied, while extremists argue it should be destroyed. To complicate matters, the new knowledge emerging from the Máolorian confounds what is known about natural law, which some have labeled as witchcraft. As a rebuttal, Máolorian scholars claim that any sufficiently advanced form of natural law will be indistinguishable from "magic" for dullards and the narrow-minded, and those who see its use as magic or witchcraft are superstitious rubes themselves. Furthermore, Sal-Kala scholars say that one must distinguish between decoding the secrets of the Seven Sacred Limbs of the Máolorian and subscribing to any supposed spiritual subtext.

A widely held, though rarely discussed, belief is that the ancient Sal-Kalans violated some fundamental natural law with cataclysmic results. The apocalyptic event dried up the water, killed all the green growing plants, and ushered in a century of sandstorms that transformed the once lush region into a desert, scattered its people, and erased any record of their knowledge. Some independent scholars operating outside two schools spend their careers attempting to prove or disprove this theory.

TECHNOLOGY AND THE ARTS

Without question, Tal-Vaz is awash in technologies that are simultaneously ancient and yet advanced for the time. The stereotypical Tal-Vaz nomad, often lampooned in the political cartoons of Palustra, has long been signified by their use of simple tools that have many uses. For example, the patcho that combines the function of spoon, fork, serrated knife, hammer, and personal weapon, or the boola strap that is used as a lead for pack animals, cord for tying down caravan cargo, and climbing rope for rappelling cliffs or traversing steep rock outcroppings. The discovery of the Isodorus Library ushered in a new era of technophilia, especially for Varojans who witnessed the explosion of new tools, techniques and wonders coming out of the academy, the most famous of which is the Bone Dragon, a device that improved the speed of communication, followed by the Norium Wheel that combined water filtration and decontamination, and the Pantocosm that aided in desert navigation. These are but a fraction of the numerous inventions and processes to emerge from the Varoja Academy.

Aesthetics and art have practically no value in Tal-Vaz. A tapestry or sculpture must have some pragmatic, functional use in order for the typical Tal-Vaz citizen to find value in it. The wealthy of Tal-Vaz clutter their homes with gadgets and items as an ostentatious display of their riches. They regard portraiture, drawing, and painting as vain and useless. Travelers to the region find local cuisine to be insipid and lacking vitality. The local alcohol is pungent and an affront to the palate. Vendors offering sophisticated Trammelorean fare and Palustrian specialties have sprung up in both cities and are popular with the non-native population.

Magic

As a rule, the people of Tal-Vaz do not believe in magic in any form as this suggests the existence of the supernatural or something outside natural law. "Magician" in the language of Tal-Vaz is equivalent to "liar" or "deceiver." Illusionists and divinationists—those who claim to tell the future by reading palms or cards—have been run out of both Varoja and Sal-Kala in the past. Mirages and tricks of the eye can be fatal in the desert environment and thus the people of Tal-Vaz have no time for anything but the verifiable facts discovered through the empirical study of natural law.

It is no surprise the Máolorian has caused consternation for the natives, as the powers of the <u>Seven Sacred Limbs of the Máolorian</u> are poorly understood. They have been inscrutable for scholars wishing to work out the science behind the wonders. A real concern in some quarters of the Tal-Vaz population is that more and more people are beginning to adopt superstitions related to the Máolorian, such as <u>hearth tracing</u> to ensure a good night's sleep or <u>water kisses</u> to bring good health.

Among the scholars studying the Máolorian, there is a quiet minority who firmly believe in magic, the presence of otherworldly forces such as ghosts and spirits, and alternate planes of existence. For their own safety, they do not speak of their beliefs except among a close-knit circle of individuals. They interpret several passages inscribed in the Limbs to be veiled instructions on how to carry out a series of rituals in a ceremony called "the Máolorian." In this reading, the Máolorian isn't a place but a process. Such an interpretation adds clarity to certain passages but confuses others, and is a matter of enormous dispute among scholars. Those interested in researching this question out more are careful to disguise their intentions or risk expulsion from Tal-Vaz, or worse.

12

Designing Catalog Templates and Entries

While the metanarrative tells a story explaining how the world works and how it came to be that way, the *catalog* is where the fictional world takes shape in more concrete terms. This is the most individualized part of the collaborative worldbuilding project, where collaborators get a chance to flex their creative muscles without requiring group consensus, beside the standing obligation of maintaining consistency and coherency within the framework and structures of the world. If you're worried that an entry might not fit, you should get a second opinion from another contributor (or two) to ensure it doesn't conflict with some aspect of the world. Barring that exception, catalog entry creation tends to be solitary work.

The easiest way of building the catalog is using a *wiki*. Every time you create a new entry in the catalog, you will be creating a new *page* on the wiki. Wikis allow you to create *templates* so you don't have to start a new page from scratch. Templates populate the new page with all the *fields* you need to fill out. For example, a *character entry* usually has the character's name, gender, height, etc. Your group must decide what fields will be required information for each entry. This helps ensure consistency across the entire catalog so all entries of the five *categories* (*historical events, items, locations, characters,* and *groups*) will use the same standard fields for each category's *stat block*. In addition, every catalog template provides space for a *narrative description* that tells the story of the entry and how it fits into the world. If necessary, refer back to Chapter 6 for a refresher of the purpose for how the stat block and narrative description work in catalog entries, and review the different options you have when designing category templates.

Types, Tags, Links, Images

While there are five template categories so you can distinguish your items from locations and so on, there are also *types* within each category. Types help you further distinguish the kinds of entries within a single category. For example, you can have "industrial" or "residential" location entries—the entry *category* is a location, and the *type* of location is "industrial" or "residential." The variety and quantity of types for each category will depend on the kind of world you're building. Identifying types from the onset and using them in the Scope and Schedule Worksheet (Appendix C) ensures that you have a diverse set of entries for each category. This prevents your group from inadvertently creating twenty factories but only one apartment complex.

Categories and types also allow you to sort and organize your wiki's catalog entries through the use of *tags*. A tag is a single word or short phrase like "character" or "location" that is associated with the entry's page. In wikis, tags make it simple to generate a list of entries based on how they've been tagged. For example, if your character template inserts the tag "character" into each record as it's created, you can easily generate a list of every character in your catalog that separates them from items, locations, and other entry categories. If contributors add tags for "male" and "female," then you'd have the ability to generate lists of all your male and female characters. Contributors can add any tags for any category, type, or field that would be relevant. This should be a coordinated effort, however, as all contributors need to apply tags in a consistent fashion for them to be useful. All wiki platforms allow for tagging pages and automatically embedding tags in page templates. Refer to your wiki's support documentation to see how the platform handles tagging and tags in templates.

Another crucial aspect of the catalog is creating *hyperlinks* in the entries. Links create relationships between entries, and a single entry can have a dozen of links within it. A character's entry might link to the character entries for their family members and close associates, to the town where the character was raised, and even to the building in which the character works. The entry could link to entries for items that the character carries with them or to the groups to which they belong. This multitude of links allows readers to traverse the fictional world in a non-linear fashion, possibly stumbling across interesting connections they may not have come across otherwise.

Finally, catalog entries benefit from being accompanied by some sort of relevant *image*. The images should be of a consistent size and, ideally, a similar art style. Using contributor's own art is a great way to further personalize the catalog but it can be time-consuming to illustrate something for each entry. Searching for images on the Internet is faster, though it can sometimes be frustrating to find an image that imparts the right connotation. If you go down this route, be respectful of copyright. Major search engines such as Google

Images allow you to filter your searches by usage rights. Many great images are available for use as long as you provide attribution to the original artist. The site search.creativecommons.com simplifies searching for images published under fair use licenses and includes major image sites like Flickr, Wikimedia Commons, and Pixabay. The last consideration is for all contributors to use an agreed-upon image filter to help ensure a consistent look across the entire catalog. For example, running all images through a charcoal rub or watercolor filter can create a unique look for the site. Software such as Adobe Photoshop or free online tools like Gimp and Pixlr can be used to resize images to a consistent size and add a variety of filters to create a consistent visual aesthetic.

Keys to Writing Good Entries

The catalog entries are the raw material from which contributors will draw their stories, so it follows that the higher the quality of the entries, the better bits storytellers will have for inspiration. To write good wiki entries, contributors should follow a few pieces of standard advice for what makes for good writing. First, use concrete imagery that hits all five senses and uses descriptive language. Secondly, avoid passive constructions. For example, the passive "is running" or "was running" rely on the weak verbs "is" and "was," as opposed to the active verbs "runs" or "ran." Also avoid adverbs that prop up weak verbs, which are usually identifiable by their -ly endings; for example, "walked confidently" versus the stronger single verb, "strode." While these small technical details might seem trivial, in truth they matter a great deal in terms of keeping a reader's interest and allow writers to pack more punch into every paragraph, sentence, and phrase.

For example, a location entry might describe a small shack where a social pariah lives on the outskirts of town. The beginning writer often doesn't give the reader much to imagine the location. Such entry descriptions tend to be short with bland language, something like this 69-word example:

> Mad Mike's Shack is a small shack a mile outside of town. It is made out of wood and looks like a strong breeze could tip it over. It is very dirty and it smells terrible. He uses barbed wire to keep people out and uses simple traps and alarms to alert him if anyone is approaching. He has a dog that barks if it smells or hears anything.

While that's not terrible, some tightening of the language and adding more concrete imagery can elevate the entry and create a deeper sense of place for this location. For example, this 117-word entry provides more style and sensory details:

> Two miles south of the city of Passole stands a dilapidated shed known as Mad Mike's Shack. Constructed of rusty corrugated steel and two-by-fours bound with wire and nails, the structure threatens to collapse at any moment. The area reeks from Mad Mike's pit toilet, rotting food scraps, and fish bones that have accumulated over the years. His dog, a Siberian husky named Judo who has matted fur and bloodshot eyes, paroles the perimeter of Mad Mike's "property" and will attack intruders on site. Mike has strung barbed wire around the area along with crude traps that will trigger wind chimes or other sounds to alert them that they have an unwelcome visitor because all visitors are unwelcome.

This improves on the first example in a number of ways. It uses more active, interesting verbs, and grounds the location in concrete details that give the reader's imagination something to work with. To use just one example, "smells terrible" could be many different smells, but the detailed mixture of a pit toilet, rotten food, and fish should be enough to turn a reader's stomach.

Of course, in order to get from the first example to something that more closely resembles the second is through careful revision. For your first drafts, jot down whatever comes to mind and don't think too long or hard about the language. Once you've captured your basic mental picture, then go back and examine the verbs and the imagery. Give it a few passes to clean up and tighten language and layer in imagery that evokes as many of the senses that you can. This is both good writing practice for contributors as each entry becomes its own compact writing and revision exercise, and it also provides more detail for anyone who wishes to incorporate the entry into their story later on. Take time with your entries and polish them to make them shine.

Historical Event Templates

Historical events mark turning points in your world's history. The metanarrative paints the broad historical picture, but major events can be significant enough to warrant an entry in the catalog that provides more in-depth detail. This is particularly true if an event happens over a long duration—for example, a military conflict spanning many years—or an era of intellectual flowering that lasts a half-century. Such events are sure to have a number of important characters, locations, items, and groups mentioned in them.

Historical Events: Types

Historical events usually don't require types. Often a collaboratively built world only has a half-dozen of significant events and they are easy enough to distinguish. In certain cases, such as in worlds with long complex histories, you might find it useful to add different types of events. In that situation, here are some possible suggestions for types of historical events:

- Historical (generic default type for all events)
- Natural (earthquakes, floods, major storms, droughts, blights, diseases)
- Political (elections, coups, formation of new political parties, changes in laws)
- Conflict (foreign wars, civil wars, guerrilla wars, cold wars)
- Discovery (geographic locations, breakthroughs in science, thought, technology)

Historical Events: Stat Block and Tags

The stat block for historical events usually only has a few required fields, normally a mix of dates, spans of time, and brief text. A historical event can be a single moment (e.g., the sinking of the Lusitania on May 7, 1915) or a range of time where the exact beginning and end dates might be fuzzy (e.g., the Renaissance, the 14th to 17th centuries); an event could happen in a very specific location (e.g., the construction of the Eiffel Tower in Paris, France) or over a large geographic area (e.g., the Cultural Revolution across the nation of China). The stat block should give a condensed look at where and when the event took place. To accomplish this, the suggested minimum fields for historical event templates include:

- **Event name:** Descriptive name for the event
- **Date:** Date of event, either specific or a range of time
- **Location:** Location of where the event happened, either specific or broad

Optional fields include:

- **Type:** Historical, natural, political, conflict, discovery, or others
- **Major figures:** Optional links to relevant character entries
- **Other events:** Optional links to other event entries

As with types, historical events usually don't need any tags beyond the category "Event." One possibility for needing tags for historical events is if there are a series of entries connected to some larger-scale event that already has an entry. To use a primary world example, the historical event "Storming of the Bastille" might also be tagged with "French Revolution."

Historical Events: Narrative Description

Remember that if the description of the historical event is short, it can reside in the metanarrative without the need for a separate historical event entry. However, if it is a momentous event that spawns many sub-events and features a cast of important characters or happens across many locations, it should be split off into a historical entry as not to overwhelm the metanarrative. The event narrative should describe the event itself and connect its relevance to the world, most specifically where it fits in the sequence of major events that shaped the world. The narrative section for a historical event should be at least 350 words and may elaborate on information found in the metanarrative or in other entries.

Building Tal-Vaz, Historical Event: Discovery of Isodorus Library
(about 1000 words)

Event: Discovery of the Isodorus Library

Date: 16th day of the 10th moon, year 1140

Location: Varoja, Varojan Academy

Major figures: Eras Bonneau

Related events: Discovery of the Máolorian

Figure 12.1 Isodorus Library

The most important event in the recent history of Tal-Vaz is the discovery of the Isodorus Library in the city of Varoja. This directly led to the explosive economic growth and complete transformation of the region. Prior to the library's discovery, the region offered little besides a few nights' respite from the harsh desert in one of the region's two small cities, Varoja to the north or Sal-Kala to the south. Few visited the region save for travelers passing through on the Cassius Trade Route between Trammelore and Palustra.

In 1133, a goatherd fell through the roof of an ancient, one-room workshop on the western edge of Varoja's borders, the first evidence that an older civilization had once lived in Tal-Vaz. Over the next four years, <u>four more sites</u> were discovered: another to the west not far from the workshop, one within the city's border to the north, another far to the east, and a final site on the southern side of the city, which appeared to be a scholar's or writer's room due to some odd writing implements and a row of books, the contents of which had mostly turned to dust. Later discoveries suggest that this southern site was the quarters for the rector of the Isodorus Library, a theory corroborated by several texts that describe the rector's frugal nature and austere living conditions.

Two decades passed with minimal investigations for other sites. This is due both to the remoteness of the Tal-Vaz, the lack of interest among locals, and the hazards of underground exploration in a desert, such as cave-ins at the great cost of human life. Scholars across <u>Arvalon</u> saw little interest in an expensive excavation in a desert backwater that promised to uncover very little. However, in 1134 an aspiring young scholar named <u>Eras Bonneau</u> began his studies at <u>the Palustrade</u> of Palustra, one of the oldest continually operating academies in the world. Scholars at the Palustrade chose one or more areas of study: oration, divinity, art and aesthetics, mechanics, natural law, and antiquity. Bonneau studied the confluence of the last three and became enamored with the beachside excavations of inlets and coves lining the <u>Saibur Sea</u>, a common burial ground for the sailor-explorers of bygone ages. He apprenticed on three separate sites, learning the sophisticated excavation techniques developed at the Palustrade, but grew frustrated at the political bureaucracy preventing him from declaring his own excavation site. He learned of the desert discoveries of Tal-Vaz in the year 1137. By 1138 he was promoted from apprentice to journeyman excavationist, and in 1139 he set out with a small team and a caravan of equipment to make his reputation.

Bonneau spent his first six months in the region poring over every map of Varoja and Tal-Vaz that he could find and visited each of the sites dozens of times in order to form a mental map of what might lay beneath the sand. Reasonably sure he had calculated the center of the old civilization, he purchased a small dilapidated basket shop that had an unusually deep cellar, a site near where the famous <u>Varoja Academy Clock Tower</u> now stands. From here, Bonneau began his excavations using a technique known as branch mining, where his team dug parallel tunnels ten yards apart of the same length. After 50 days of digging and with Bonneau at the end of his funds and on the edge of despair, one of the workers' picks punched through the wall into what would be the <u>Sixth Point</u> of the Isodorus Library, which housed books on the physical sciences.

Bonneau was exhilarated by the find and did not yet know that the Sixth Point was in the worst condition of all wings of the library. Only after a week of slow exploration did Bonneau uncover the opening to the domed central chamber, also called the Chorus, which had seemed to survive the centuries virtually unscathed. Placing their torches in the ornate wall sconces invoked the Blazing Night installation across the ceiling, an engineering marvel that used a network of mirrors that gave the viewer the sensation that they were standing outside beneath the stars rather than inside a building. Apocryphal stories say Bonneau fell to his knees and wept until his eyes ran dry.

At Bonneau's insistence, no study of the library's artifacts would begin until they had finished tracing the site's perimeter. Invigorated by their find, the team excavated the boundaries of all six Points of the library in a little over ten days, hardly stopping to eat or sleep. Like the Chorus, the Fifth Point was in pristine condition and seemed hardly touched; First Point and Fourth Point suffered minor damage but Second Point was in much rougher shape, with Third and Sixth Points being in states of serious disrepair with caved-in ceilings and crumbled furniture. The foreign word or name "Isodorus" was inscribed over each arched doorways into each Point and was etched in the center of the floor in the Chorus.

A combination of loyalty, bribes, and threats kept the extent of Bonneau's discovery a relative secret for the better part of two years. By 1145 though, it was widely known throughout the continent that a major archaeological site had been discovered in Tal-Vaz, though only clan relations and close friends of the Bonneaus had set foot inside. The first artifact from the Isodorus Library, the Bone Kite, made its public appearance in 1150; and by 1157 the cluster of buildings on the square near the excavation site had begun to be referred to as Varoja Academy. Understandably, much of the attention swung to deciphering the documents in the library rather than completing the excavation. The final bits of earth were removed from Sixth Point, ironically the first room discovered, in 1163, officially ending the excavation of the site.

Item Templates

Broadly considered, an *item* is anything that is neither a person nor a place. This is usually a physical object, but it could also be something more abstract like a piece of information, a scientific theory, or a religious rite. Item entries usually have some property that makes them unique or noteworthy; however, the nature of certain fictional worlds can make a mundane item notable. For example, a hamburger from a fast-food chain wouldn't make a good entry for your urban fantasy world, but a freeze-dried hamburger packet on an interstellar space cruiser might be a worthwhile entry. Likewise, a bottle of hydrogen peroxide found in a typical drugstore wouldn't be interesting in a cyberpunk world, but it might be of enormous value for a character scavenging in a post-apocalyptic world. Items should be notable for their uniqueness, their usefulness, any custom modifications, or if the item belongs to a specific person. To use just one example, swords are common in the world *A Song of Ice and Fire,* but the greatsword Ice is notable for being the ancestral weapon of House Stark and is made of rare Valyrian steel.

Items: Types

Below are some recommended item types followed by sample items of that type. Choose the categories that best represent the kind of world you're making and add other categories that suit your purpose. As always, feel free to adapt, revise, and add your own.

- **Agricultural:** hoe, seeds, fertilizer, wire fencing, tractor, thresher, pick, shovel, saw
- **Armor:** plate mail, leather jacket, motorcycle helmet, bulletproof vest, riot gear
- **Artistic:** painting, sculpture, literature, musical instruments, brushes, sheet music
- **Clothing:** casual clothes, athletic clothes, formal wear, uniform, outerwear
- **Domestic:** dish, vase, decoration, bed, desk, bookshelf, lamp, dresser, microwave
- **Electronics:** mobile phone, supercomputer, tablet, microphone, terminal, drone
- **Equipment:** scuba gear, wetsuit, space suit, rappelling gear, paddle, life preserver
- **Explosives:** grenade, TNT, pipe bomb, Molotov cocktail, chemicals, C-4, nuclear bomb
- **Industrial:** workbench, sandblaster, forge, boiler, drill, bellows, forklift, gears, vat
- **Magic:** scroll, staff, spell book, wand, crystal ball, magic rings, cloak of invisibility
- **Medical:** stints, splints, braces, antibiotics, medicine, hypodermic needle, oxygen mask
- **Religious:** relic, symbol, robes, holy books, artwork, sacramental items, jewelry

- **Scientific:** microscope, magnifying glass, telescope, petri dish, centrifuge, test tube
- **Survival:** water purifier, multi-tool, thermal blanket, flare gun, compass, canteen
- **Transportation:** bicycle, pack animal, motor vehicle, glider, jumbo jet, streetcar
- **Weapon, melee:** baseball bat, sword, golf club, knife, spear, hammer, ax, mace
- **Weapon, ranged:** handgun, rifle, shotgun, bow, crossbow, grenade launcher

Items: Stat Block and Tags

The item stat block mostly has to do with the entry's physical properties, i.e., its general size, weight, and worth. Items are often, but not always, things that can be possessed, carried, or owned by a character or can be found only in certain locations. Some items can only be used in conjunction with other items. For example, a magazine of bullets does little good without an automatic rifle and vice versa. Here are the fields commonly used in item stat blocks:

Item name: Descriptive name for the item
Item type: One of the predefined item types
- **Size:** Numeric (e.g., 3 ft. high, 6 in. long) or descriptive (e.g., football-sized)
- **Weight:** Numeric (e.g., 14 lbs.) or descriptive (e.g., very heavy, almost weightless)
- **Value:** Numeric (e.g., $13.00, 1,540.00) or descriptive (e.g., cheap, expensive, priceless)
- **Condition:** Descriptive (e.g., brand new, used, worn, damaged, not functional)
- **Rarity:** Descriptive (e.g., common, uncommon, scarce, rare, extremely rare, legendary)
- **Location:** where the item can be found
- **Links** listing associated historical events, items, locations, characters, and groups

Items should always be tagged by the category "Item" and the item's specific type. Other common tags include an item's value and rarity, making it easy to generate a list of expensive or rare items. If the item is only found at a specific location—for example, a space telescope only found in one specific laboratory—it can be useful to add a tag using that location's name.

Items: Narrative Description

When creating an item entry, think about why that item is notable in your fictional world. An item's narrative description should tell a story. Where did it come from? How is it used? Who uses it? What are its features? Think about how the item might look, touch, taste, smell, and feel. Is it heavy? Rough or smooth? Hot or cold? Item narrative descriptions are generally the shortest of all entry categories, but an item entry should be a minimum of 150 words, with a typical entry weighing in around 300 words on the low side. The description section for items of great importance can run to 1000 words or more.

Building Tal-Vaz, Item Entry: Desert's Hammer
(about 450 words)
Tags: Item, Medical, Religious, Drug

Item Name: Desert's Hammer

Type: Medical, Religious, Drug, Psychotropic

Size: Marble-sized

Weight: 0.5 ounce

Value: Very expensive

Condition: Spongy while in earth, turns brittle soon after

Rarity: Very rare in Tal-Vaz, extremely rare elsewhere

Location: Found throughout Tal-Vaz, surreptitiously sold at Ojoveja's Curiosis in Varoja

Figure 12.2 Desert's Hammer

Appearance Description

Desert's Hammer is a small, nondescript mushroom the size of a marble. The mushroom's cap bends down toward the stem giving it a spherical appearance, though when the cap is drawn back its shape resembles a hammer, which explains its name. Like all mushrooms, Desert's Hammer grows in dark, moist places, which are very rare in the arid Tal-Vaz region. It has a musty odor and taste. Once plucked, the mushroom begins drying out almost immediately, and it will turn brittle and crumble within a single day. The mushroom holds together better if kept in its soil and put in a tightly sealed glass jar, but it is difficult to execute the transfer without disturbing it. When expertly harvested, Desert's Hammer can remain intact for up to two weeks. All attempts to cultivate the mushroom under controlled conditions have failed.

Effects

The mushroom is best known for its hallucinogenic properties, which diminish severely as it dries. A single thin slice can send a user on a psychedelic trip lasting hours, during which the senses are distorted and feeling of the passage of time grossly expands or contracts. Large doses increase both the intensity and duration of the experience, which can be psychologically crippling or even fatal for the novice user. However, monks of religious orders who wander the desert searching for Desert's Hammer have been known to swallow an entire mushroom whole and experience no permanently harmful effects other than the protracted mind-expanding episode.

Uses

Once dried, Desert's Hammer can be boiled in water to make *meneyado tea*, a drink with very mild sedative properties. It is often used as pain relief for the wounded or dying, though some people drink it during social occasions, as other cultures would drink wine or beer.

Most nomads view the psychedelic trip as a foolish indulgence and either leave the mushroom where they find it undisturbed or quickly sell it to foreigners traveling the Cassius Trade Route. The price skyrockets if the mushroom is found within a few days' travel of either Palustra or Trammelore, where aristocrats will pay top dollar for as much as they can get their hands on. Nobles have been known to host impromptu week-long parties to take advantage of an unexpected delivery of a few fresh caps of Desert's Hammer.

Besides its recreational use, Desert's Hammer is most often associated with the Palustran order, the Monks of Marci. Marcian Monks swear vows of poverty and wander the desert seeking the mushroom's effects to gain a deeper understanding of the nature of reality. They are common figures of fun represented in crude jokes, low art, and comedic street theater in Palustra and Trammelore for their behavior under the influence of the mushroom.

Location Templates

Locations are where the action happens in your world. Every story told in your world will happen in at least one location, if not several simultaneously. This is because locations act both as hosts of sublocations and are sublocations themselves. For example, the cantina from *Star Wars* is named Chalmun's Cantina and it is found within the city of Mos Eisley, which itself is a location within the planet of Tatooine, which is in a location of the galaxy known as the Outer Rim. Each one of those locations—Chalmun's Cantina, Mos Eisley, Tatooine, Outer Rim—functions as its own individual location entry, with its own stat block and characteristic narrative description. For example, the Outer Rim is comprised of all the backwater worlds in the galaxy; Tatooine is a desert planet with few resources; Mos Eisley is a large spaceport populated with many smugglers and criminals; Chalmun's Cantina is a dive bar where those criminals go to find work and escape the blistering heat. The job of the location entry is to convey those connotations and information in concrete details relevant to that level.

Locations: Types

Location types are extremely important for creating a rich and diverse world. Characters in your world will need to sleep, eat, work in different places. They need to visit places for entertainment, to heal themselves if they are sick or injured, and to tend to their spiritual side. There are locations where innovators invent the future and where political dissidents plot to overthrow the government. Some locations produce food, other locations sell food, and other locations dispose of food refuse. Some locations feel like paradise, while others are hell on earth. One character might feel uncomfortable in a location where another character might feel most at home. A priest may recoil at finding himself in a brothel, and a crime lord may shudder if she finds herself in a church. A good location should both have a story and help make a story.

Here are suggestions for different types of Location entries of different shapes and sizes. Add your own or customize this list:

- **Agricultural:** crop farm, cattle farm, dairy farm, poultry farm, fish farm
- **Celestial:** galaxy, solar system, star, black hole, planet, moon, asteroid, space station
- **Commercial:** store, stall, bank, mall, flea market, restaurant, masseuse, repair shop
- **Criminal:** gambling den, brothel, fighting den, bootleggers, drug den, hideout
- **Cultural:** museum, theater, concert hall, sculpture, archaeological site, ancient building
- **Educational:** school, university, library, institute, trade school, scroll shop

- **Geographic:** river, mountain, desert, forest, ocean, lake, plain, savanna, valley
- **Government:** assembly building, town hall, courtroom, jail, police station, fire station
- **Industrial:** factory, mill, mine, railyard, oil derrick, slaughterhouse, forge
- **Medical:** hospital, doctor's office, apothecary/pharmacist, back-alley clinic
- **Military:** military base, barracks, outpost, fort, station, naval yard, training area
- **Recreational:** amusement park, nature preserve, national park, pub, dancehall
- **Religious:** church, temple, mosque, holy ground, cemetery, religious site, shrine
- **Residential:** apartment, family home, hotel, dormitory, gated community, palace
- **Transportation:** airport, seaport, bus depot, train station, spaceport, stables

Locations: Stat Block and Tags

The location stat block should convey some basic details that can be expanded upon and further explained in the narrative description. If it's a building, is it the size of a small restaurant or a shopping mall a city block long? Is the location a small country nestled among mountains, or is it a nation that's size spans a continent? Other pertinent questions the stat block answers include how many people can typically be found at the location and its overall shape and condition. Is it a dilapidated shack or an opulent mansion? For larger land masses, is it a region with a coastal jungle or does it consist of snow-swept peaks?

- **Location Name:** Descriptive name for the location
- **Location Type:** One of the predefined location types
- **Site:** Describes where the location resides in relation to other entries (e.g., a neighborhood in a city, a nation on a continent)
- **Size:** Expressed numerically (e.g., 1000 square feet) or descriptively (e.g., three city blocks, or a large planet)
- **Population/Inhabitants**: Usually expressed numerically with a short description (e.g., 10,000,000 citizens)
- **Condition:** Current physical shape of the location (e.g., pristine, worn down, ramshackle, meticulously maintained)
- **Terrain:** Physical features of the land (e.g., temperate forests, coastal, mountainous, desert)
- **Links** for associated historical events, items, locations, characters, and groups

The tags for locations should always include their category of "Location" and also their type. It can also be useful to add tags if the location resides within a larger location entry; for example, tagging cities with the name of the common region or country to which they belong.

Locations: Narrative Description

When writing a location entry, describe its past first—where it came from, why it is significant—and then go on to explain how the location looks and feels at the *point of the present*. When describing the location, run through the five senses. Does the location look drab or vibrant, or is it well-lit or shadowy? Is it cluttered or austere? What aromas waft in this place's air and what causes them? What sounds might someone hear in this location—crashing waves, the chatter of birds, or the breeze whispering through leaves? Might someone smell the scent of the salt sea, the aroma of sizzling garlic, or the acrid stench of burning tires? Is the location generally hot or cold in temperature? Dry or humid? Is the terrain rough, hard, moist, or soft? Invoking the different senses immerses readers in the description. Location entries should be a minimum of 250 words, though the typical length is between 500 and 1000 words.

Building Tal-Vaz, Location: Ojoveja's Curiosis
(about 600 words)
Tags: Location, Varoja, Commercial

Name: Ojoveja's Curiosis

Type: Commerical

Location: Central Varoja, Tal-Vaz

Size: 1400 square feet

Condition: Showing signs of age but sturdy

Inhabitants: Manu Ojoveja, usually 10–20 shoppers when open

Figure 12.3 Ojoveja's Curiosis

Ojoveja's Curiosis is a shop off the central square of Varoja, run by the owner-proprietor Manu Ojoveja of Clan Ojoveja. The shop is divided into three rooms of equal size and a fourth tiny room wedged in the northeast corner that functions as Manu's office. The three rooms are packed with items for customer perusal, and the office has only Manu's cash box and a ladder with a trap door to the second level, leading to Manu's garishly decorated personal quarters.

History

For most of its existence, the structure was little more than a small storage space for his father's modest grain trading business. Manu spent much of his younger days hoisting grain sacks on and off pack animals and standing at the counter waiting for merchants to pass through the town's center looking to trade. Manu's father was a simple man with few plans for the future beyond having his son continue the meager family business.

Following his father's death in 1147, Manu ended the grain-trading business and converted the space to a storefront. He experimented with different business ideas starting with a courier service and then tried his hand in silk trading, but both businesses eventually failed, nearly bankrupting him. In a last-ditch effort to save himself from financial ruin, he began peddling some of the oddities from the library down the road. The trinkets were small-scale prototypes made by scholars in an effort to model the wonders described in various works in the library. The scholars cast them off as trash or sold them to Manu for cheap, which he then sold in his store to the delight of children and travelers looking to acquire unique knickknacks as mementos of their time on the Cassius Trade Route. As the stream of travelers through Tal-Vaz increased, Manu's business expanded. He bought the adjacent spaces to the store and added a second level. The store is now two stories tall and is a veritable hive of activity from noon to night. He named the store "Ojoveja's Curiosis," using the plural form of an Old Varojan pejorative word that means "worthless object of curiosity" as a kind of self-effacing joke.

Description

Each of the three rooms is lined with shelves, tables, and racks overflowing the shop's wares. There is no system of organization, and no items have prices listed as Manu prides himself on his bartering. The items themselves have little practical use. Almost all of what he sells he does so on consignment, playing the role of middleman between scholars, who are busy with their research, and the purchasing public. For several years he has retained a small group of artists who will reproduce copies of the models and diagrams designed by the scholars. Business is always brisk.

The shop's exterior is adorned with a narrow, sun-bleached cloth awning and a badly faded hand-lettered sign. The interior walls are painted a light red. The store is open from dusk to mid-morning, then closes through midday as the tight confines and poor air circulation make the space oppressively hot. It reopens at dusk and the cycle repeats. The linen covered windows provide light when the sun is up, and <u>chemiluminescent chandeliers</u> light the store during the evening.

Controversially, Manu has begun selling more and more work drawing on the scholars of the <u>Máolorian</u>, drawing the ire of rival shopkeepers in <u>Sal-Kala</u> as well as Varojans who view such works with disdain and disgust. Manu is also known as a broker of the psychoactive mushroom <u>Desert's Hammer</u>, but only on the rare occasion he comes to possess it. He sometimes sells ordinary dried mushrooms passed off as Desert's Hammer to gullible tourists.

Character Templates

Characters bring your collaborative worldbuilding project to life. They are the movers and actors in your world, the ones who experience it firsthand, immersed in its glory or gloom. They breathe its air, fight its battles, and shape its future. They eat, sleep, bleed, bear children, and die in your world. They celebrate personal victories and mourn their defeats. It's through their eyes that the world's complexity shines through. This is all to say: characters are very important.

Think about characters as existing in three classes: *perspective characters* (referred to as PCs), *non-perspective characters* (referred to as NPCs), and indistinct characters who only exist as a *group* (discussed in the next section). The only thing that distinguishes between these three classes of characters is the level of detail provided in their entries. Nameless group characters are in the background, going about their daily business in the world. For example, a town will have dozens of merchants and barkeepers, and the king's army has hundreds of soldiers, but not every one of them needs a name. Keep in mind, however, that every living, breathing person in your fictional world indeed has a name and a life story. You could pick out an individual merchant, barkeeper, or soldier, give them a name and flesh out their personality. Once you do this, the person ceases to be an anonymous member of the group and instead becomes an NPC.

An NPC is a character we know a good deal about. They may be the last scrupulous politician in the land, the chummy tavern owner who knows all of the town's gossip, the taciturn mercenary seeking employment, or the wisecracking pilot eager to show off her skills. These are the people who have notable lives. They have a handful of prominent personality traits, a few easily identifiable motivations, and a thought-out backstory. Their character entries should reveal their innermost hopes, fears, and desires. Most of the character entries in your catalog, and by extension your world, will be engaging, conflicted, and compelling NPCs. As you add people to your world, you may find that an individual NPC's story intrigues you and seems to go deeper than the rest. Follow that path. Let that NPC tell their life story. If you listen well and write that story down, they're well on their way to becoming a PC.

PCs are the *primary characters* in the world. They are the protagonists of the world's stories waiting to be told, the ones through whose perspective we see and experience the world. Their position as a PC has nothing to do with power. A compelling PC is just as likely to be a street urchin struggling to survive than be the lord of the world's most powerful nation. Of all the character entries in the world, we both know the most about PCs, but we also want to continue to learn about them. When you write your stories in your world, you will put your PCs under stress. Good storytellers give their protagonists difficult, sometimes seemingly insurmountable, tasks. We put daunting obstacles in their path to see what they do. Sometimes they succeed and grow as characters. Other times, the challenge is more than they can bear and they break or even perish. We might grieve for them, but we thank them for living interesting lives and giving us a good story. If you put in honest work when creating PCs, you won't have to search hard for conflict. In most cases, your PCs' conflicts will emerge simply from their existence in the world. As you develop their personalities and attributes and where they fit in the social order, it should be clear what aspects of the world will cause them to feel tension, uncertainty, and even fear.

In the early stages of creating catalog entries, avoid getting too attached to a single PC. A PC functions like any other shared piece of creative property in your collaborative project. Any other contributor might want to adopt, adapt, or add to a PC you created. This is a good thing. Your world and the PC will be better for it. Create two or three PCs to avoid getting too close to any single one. You also want to guard against shaping parts of the world specifically for an individual PC's benefit. For example, don't create a location entry of a mountain goblin den, an item entry for a magic goblin-killing sword, and a character entry for a PC who just so happens to own that sword and know about that den. This always feels overly convenient and thoroughly false when you enter the storytelling phase. Rather, the best approach is for contributors to focus on creating a handful of genuine, fascinating PCs with complex, conflicted lives. And who knows, maybe a story will emerge organically about a hero journeying to clear out a goblin den.

Characters: Types

Characters don't fit easily into single types as easily as locations and items. Instead, every field in the stat block functions as its own type with a range of possibilities. The most important part of thinking through character types with the stat block fields is to ensure you're creating a diverse array of characters for use in your storytelling, and that the character population reflects the structures of the world that you've created. This will be very important when it comes to distributing the character entry assignments among the contributors, so you don't wind up with too many characters of one race, class, gender, or other factors that relate to their social standing.

The best way of approaching a number of these fields is to treat them as demographic categories and to consider what percentage of the population fits into each category, and then think about how your character entries will reflect those demographics. The percentage of your character entries need not match your world's demographics exactly, but in most cases it should strive to be representative. In a world where a small group controls most of the resources, your character entries should reflect those demographics. If your group creates twenty-five character entries, five could be very wealthy, five could belong to different levels of middle class, and the remaining fifteen would be very poor. That allows you to both tell stories from a variety of class perspectives while also being true to the demographics—if most of the world is poor, it makes sense that most of your characters would be poor too.

Characters: Stat Block and Tags

Most, if not all, of the below fields, should be used for NPC and PC entries:

- **Name:** Most often birth name, but could include nicknames or serial numbers.
- **Age:** Should determine the youngest allowable age for PCs/NPCs and general population breakdown among age groups, usually by ten-to-fifteen-year brackets. While it can be described narratively (e.g., very old) it's better to provide a specific age (e.g., 93) so age relationships may be more immediately and unambiguously established.
- **Sex and/or Gender:** Usually male or female, but can include a range of other options depending on the nature of the world.
- **Race and/or Species and/or Nationality:** Can mirror primary world census data, but may have a much wider range of options depending on the world's

genre. This could include a number of alien species, monsters, robots, and races within those species.

- **Class:** Usually divided among five broad economic classes: the very rich, the upper middle class, the lower middle class, the working poor, and the underclass or lowest class of society. Remember that not all worlds will define class by economic status alone.
- **Sexual Orientation:** Wide range of options, with heterosexuality often being the most common orientation but allowing for multiple types of sexual orientations.
- **Occupation:** Depends on the specifics of the world, but should include a wide range of possibilities that include a range of professional and management professions, service jobs, manual labor jobs, as well as politicians, public servants, and members of the military. Sometimes it will make sense to use demographics to determine the number of entries for a given profession—for example if the world has an overwhelming number of people pressed into military or religious service—and other times the characters' professions can be left up to individual contributors.
- **Appearance:** A few short sentences (no more than three to five) providing a brief visual description of the character. May include distinguishing features such as tattoos, piercings, injuries, etc. as well as the style of dress (e.g., unkempt, fashionable).
- **General Disposition:** A few words or phrases that sum up the character's mood and outlook (e.g., grumpy, optimistic, energetic).
- **Motivation(s):** One or two of the character's primary motivations (e.g., protection of family, attainment of wealth, seeking revenge).
- **Links** for associated historical events, items, locations, characters, and groups.

Tags for characters should, at a minimum, include the categories of "Character" and either "NPC" or "PC." After this, it depends on a combination of what's most important in your world and the thoughts of the collaborators. Gender, race, and class tend to be useful tags to sort out different groups of characters. In worlds with clearly defined professional roles, each character's occupation can also be worthwhile to tag. Another useful tag would be any important group membership, such as being a member of a prominent family or a political affiliation. Remember, the tags must be used in a consistent fashion by all the contributors for each entry or entries will be lost. For example, if one person uses the tag "female" and another uses "woman," or one uses "soldier" and another uses "military," these characters will only show up in one list and not the other. Inconsistent tagging can result in characters' entries being obscured or lost in the catalog, so it's wise to limit the number of required tags per entry and make sure everyone is tagging them using the agreed-upon terminology.

Characters: Narrative Description

The only difference between NPC and PC narratives are their length and the depth of detail provided. A typical NPC narrative should be a minimum of 250 words and usually closer to 500; a PC narrative should be at least 1000 words and will often run much longer. The narrative begins with a broad description of the character, similar to a *metanarrative lead*, which describes the character's distinguishing physical characteristics, notable skills or abilities, and a general overview of their personality and disposition. It also includes the character's position within the social structures of the world and any pronounced motivations. The opening paragraph often functions as little more than the written description of the information found in the stat block.

The second section of the narrative description recaps the character's history—where they were born, their early life and education (if any), any significant family or romantic relationships growing up, as well as how they acquired any of their notable skills. Other factors to consider are any life-changing experiences they may have had, either positive or negative. In total, this portion of the narrative explains characters' formative years and helps the audience develop some understanding of how or why the character has the attitudes, beliefs, and emotions that they do. This section often has many links to different items, locations, and other characters, and historical events, especially if they were raised in a time of chaos, crisis, or change. Whereas this might be covered in a few short sentences for an NPC, for a PC this could be several paragraphs of information.

The third paragraph of the narrative should bridge the character's past to where the character is in the *point of the present*. If the character is a young teenager, this section could be quite short since not much time has passed since their formative years. In contrast, if the character is elderly, then whole decades of the person's middle-aged years would require recapping. Again, for an NPC, this might be done in brief, whereas a mature PC could have whole life phases described in greater detail. The final section of the narrative gives a sketch of the character at the *point of the present* in the world—literally where they're at, what they're doing, their greatest fears, and what they most want at this stage of life, their specific goals, challenges, motivations.

Change is an engine for most stories, so PCs should always possess some capacity for some kind of change. Characters should neither be completely hopeless nor should they have the world at their feet. Good characters are always plagued with problems. Sometimes it's relationship trouble with a spouse, a child, a sibling, a lover, or a friend. Other times it could be political or financial trouble that complicates a character's life, where they face serious setbacks in their plans for the future. Social relations and cultural influences can also cause their share of complications, where the character can be struggling to promote some kind of wide societal change or prevent one from happening. If a character's life seems to be stable, connect them to something or someone that would be a legitimate threat to their wellbeing; if a character's life feels too sedate or stalled out, connect to other characters, groups, or imminent social changes that would disrupt their routine and get them moving again, even if it's against their will. Characters who have no fight in them, and conversely those who easily win every fight, tend to be dull. Compelling stories revolve around characters who are engaged in some type of struggle.

Building Tal-Vaz, NPC: Keekay Casille
(about 450 words)
Tags: Character, Varoja, Guardian

Name: Keekay Casille (**KEY-kay ca-SEEL**)

Age: 27

Gender: Male

Race: Tal-Vazan

Class: Middle

Occupation: Guardian

Appearance: Tall, athletic build, physically imposing, handsome

Positive traits: Athletic, Loyal

Negative traits: Biased, Naive

Motivation(s): Protecting Darija Gallego

Locations: Varoja, Gallego Compound

Notable Relationships: Darija Gallego

Affiliated groups or factions: Clan Gallego

Figure 12.4 Keekay Casille

Description

Keekay Casille is a tall, athletically built man who exudes confidence and whose physical presence dominates a space. He tends to speak only when spoken to, though he is always quick to laugh and share a joke. His relaxed manner suggests he can handle any situation. He rarely sits; his most natural position is standing against a wall or rock, his arms loosely folded, one bent leg beneath him almost as if he could spring into action in a split second. His presence is a great comfort to his friends, though his calm confidence can make others nervous.

History

Casille is the embodiment of the idealized Tal-Vazan nomad. Raised in Clan Casille sworn to Clan Gallego, young Casille stood out among his peers both in his quickness of thought as well as the speed of foot and strength of arm in physical challenges. Casille demonstrated excellence with the bow, blowgun, and knife, and was unrivaled wielding the <u>karma</u>, the pair of short spears that can be used in melee combat or as thrown weapons. Before he reached the age of manhood, he had been singled out by <u>Darija Gallego</u> for grooming as her personal protector. By the time he reached the age of twenty-one, he matched or had bested his instructors in their specialties and began teaching students of his own.

Present

His name is legendary throughout Tal-Vaz and beyond. It has been said that <u>Clan Gallego</u> can attribute the stability of its power purely through the reputation of Casille. In training exercises, he has defeated as many as eight trained warriors attacking him simultaneously using a devastating combination of tactics, speed, and strength. His retinue of warriors serves under him with a fierce loyalty that borders on fanaticism. They would fight to the death to receive even a word of his praise.

The enemies of Clan Gallego know that if they are to topple Clan Gallego, their greatest obstacle is Casille and their greatest weapon against him is time. The desert ages one quickly and Casille has already lost some of the spring in his step. Furthermore, his knowledge of battle tactics is limited to one-on-one combat and skirmishes between clans. Some feel that a more learned strategist, most likely from the military universities of Palustra, may be able to dupe Casille into pressing an attack to the point at which he is overextended and vulnerable. This seems at least plausible, especially if he were baited by a "foolish foreign-type" as Casille makes no attempt to hide his disdain for those who come from outside Tal-Vaz, believing that they hold no respect for the desert or for the hardened nomads who have for centuries called it home.

Group Templates

Groups are essentially collections of characters who share some common connection. Everything from a suburban knitting circle to a revolutionary paramilitary organization is a group. For the purposes of a collaborative worldbuilding project, group membership should be relevant to larger issues at play in the world. Groups draw characters together and create connections between them. They provide logical reasons why characters would know each other, either as friends, acquaintances, or enemies. A group might be where lifelong friendships are forged or where bitter rivalries are born. One group's members might be united in a larger struggle, while another group could be splintered by infighting.

A group might have been formed last week, or it might be centuries old. A group might be casual and open, or it could be private and have a rigorous membership application process. Groups might proudly publish a list of their constituents or they could be tightly guarded secret societies. Group activity can be limited to operating out of a neighborhood pub or could be a multinational collective with branches on every continent. Groups may be growing in power, or they may wistfully remember their past glories. In order to understand a group and what membership means for its constituents, we need to comprehend its trajectory—where it came from, what power it might wield, and where it might be headed.

Groups: Types

Groups may be of more than one type. For example, in the United States, the VFW (Veterans of Foreign Wars) organization is both social and political in nature, as it provides services to former soldiers who served in the nation's military. Consider what the group does for its members: does it provide a service, a sense of identity, or afford members some privileges? Some possible group types include:

- **Economic**: Economic groups often form at the opposite ends of the socio-economic spectrum, with country clubs and closed estates on one end for the wealthy, and street gangs in economically depressed neighborhoods on the other. Economic groups are most notably in societies with clear class distinctions and stratification of wealth and can overlap with political and professional affiliations.
- **Familial:** Clans or tribes are often organized around bloodlines, as are feudal or monarchical societies that have strict lines of descent for rulers.

Organized criminal organizations, businesses, and politics often have strong familial components to them.

- **Military:** The different branches of military service, as well as deployment in specific locations or battles, can form tight bonds between soldiers who serve that remain strong long after they have been retired for active duty. Elite military groups can carry significant amounts of prestige among both other soldiers as well as the public at large.
- **Political:** Political parties are one obvious option, but other political groups may form around specific social or cultural concerns, especially when inequalities are an issue. A character who is a member of a political group should see this as a defining part of their life rather than the affiliation of whoever they voted for in the last election.
- **Professional:** Professional groups form around careers and vocations as guilds, trade unions, or business leaders. Professional groups usually have clear economic or political motivations attached to them, promising to improve the lives of their members through some sort of economic or social change.
- **Religious:** Religious groups are associated with various belief systems and the branches and sects within major religious traditions. Religious groups are often politically or socially motivated, either to care for the poor or to uphold specific types of cultural values. In some cases, religious groups may be formally connected to the government or military.
- **Social:** Social groups often deal with interests and pastimes that don't necessarily cross over the other group types. For example, a Sunday morning football league brings people together around sport and may draw participants from a wide range of social and cultural groups. Social groups can bring together people from different backgrounds and perspectives.

Groups: Stat Block and Tags

The stat block is normally quite compressed to convey the basics about the group. While some of the details about Groups can be expressed categorically, the most important information will be in the narrative description. Common fields for group stat blocks include:

- **Name:** Group name or nicknames (including derogatory or pejorative ones).
- **Type:** Economic, Familial, Military, Political, Professional, Religious, Social, or others of your choosing.

- **Dates Active:** A year or specific date the group was founded. Can also include year dissolved or disbanded if relevant.
- **Membership:** Numeric value indicating the number of members or affiliates in the group.
- **Location(s):** Headquarters, satellite locations, meeting places, and other significant places with links to all relevant location entries.
- **Important Members:** Links to character entries for any key figures, such as high-ranking officers or notable members.

Similar to historical events, groups rarely use tags beyond their category "Group." One exception is if the group has a unique affiliation with a specific location, but often you can get by without any additional tags for groups unless other contributors feel that they would be necessary or useful.

Groups: Narrative Description

The narrative must situate the group within the wider social structures of the fictional world, and ideally position them in clear tension or opposition to other groups, characters, or other aspects of the world. Group narratives should be a minimum of 250 words but could be much longer given the group's history and importance.

Building Tal-Vaz, Group: Varojan Scholars
(about 428 words)
Tags: Group, Varoja, Isodorus Library, Varoja Academy

Name: Varojan Scholars

Type: Academic, Educational

Dates active: Around 1165 to present

Membership: About 200

Location: Varoja, Varoja Academy, Isodorus Library

Important members: Enzon Mirande (founder), Sabine Saubon, Eras Bonneau, Trillus Fandue

Figure 12.5 Varojan Scholars

Description

The buildings located near the edges of the Isodorus Library excavation site began to be known as the Varoja Academy as early as 1157, though it would be years before Eras Bonneau began formalizing educational plans and forming cohorts of scholars in the ways of the centuries-old Palustran universities. Enzon Mirande, one the first scholars to answer Bonneau's call to join him in Varoja, initiated another old tradition, that of the Scholars Group. In 1165, he started referring to anyone who studied at the library as a Varojan Scholar and spoke about the group's philosophy and avenues of inquiry as though they had existed for hundreds of years. While many of his contemporary scholars found the name pretentious, unearned, and unnecessary, newcomers to the Varoja Academy appreciated being welcomed into a familiar social structure steeped in intellectual history.

Like the Palustran academic orders of old, scholars took a nominal pledge to pursue knowledge for knowledge's sake and not let their avenues of study be influenced by politicians, merchants, religious leaders, or anyone who would benefit from the research being devoted to any specific cause. And like the Palustran academic orders of old, it sounded good in theory but made little difference in actual practice. The Scholars Group's purpose is to publicize the intellectual business of the institution and insulate the Academy against charges of benefitting some aspects of society more than others. While such a rationale might have once seemed preposterous, it has kept the Academy in the background during increasingly anxious times. Mirande's move proved to be worthwhile after all.

Throughout the calendar year, the Varojan Scholars host debates and public lectures, though almost no one outside the Academy shows any interest in them. They tend to be on esoteric topics and quickly descend into arguments over minute details. However, they are well attended by the scholars themselves who, to a person, heartily enjoy them.

As the Academy is mostly Palustran males, so too is the Varojan Scholars group. One charge against the group is that it can be cliquey and not represent the views and ideas of all members equally, though Mirande, who acts as its de facto leader, shrugs off these criticisms and does little to resolve them. He spends most of his time working to depoliticize the Academy and the Scholars from current affairs, and whenever he is seen outside his quarters, he is usually in quiet conversation with Eras Bonneau.

Strategies for Catalog Development and Management

Before you begin creating catalog entries, your group should develop a catalog management plan using the Scope and Schedule Worksheet (Appendix C).

To begin, choose a minimum number of entries your group wants to have in the catalog. As a general rule, regardless of group size, this should be at least 75 entries across all categories. Having this minimum number of entries will give you plenty of different angles to explore the world. While 75 entries might sound daunting, most groups easily eclipse this number. Creating catalog entries tends to be both fun and addictive. Momentum builds fast when building out the catalog as good entries invite contributors to branch out the narrative in many different directions. A single catalog entry links to many other entries, and often the introduction of a new wrinkle in the narrative description inspires another dozen entries that you didn't know you needed. Usually, it's harder to stop making entries than it is to hit your minimum.

This phenomenon can be very exciting creatively, but it can also lead to unwanted sprawl and a lack of focus. It can also lead to the unintended proliferation of only certain types of entries. For example, if a contributor creates a location for a monastery, she might get on a roll and create four more religious locations, two religious items, and a half-dozen different monks as characters. Suddenly, this one location has spawned twelve new entries and this supposedly minor religious order now constitutes a fifth of the entire catalog.

The Scope and Schedule Worksheet helps your group manage the catalog, both by ensuring there will be diverse entries created across categories and types, but also to rein in some of the creative impulses that can overwhelm the project. Creating an abundance of entries is by no means a bad thing, provided that the contributors spread the work as evenly as possible and do not violate the scope they had all agreed to from the start.

Steps for Completing the Scope and Schedule Worksheet

1. Fill in the ballpark number of catalog entries your group wants to create, with 75 being the minimum. Divide this total by the number of contributors in the group to get the number of entries each person will need to create. You can also approach this the other way, where each contributor agrees to create at least one historical event, one group, and then five entries each for items, locations, and characters. For a group of four, that's already 68 catalog entries.

2. Break out the total number of entries into different categories. For example, if you have 100 entries, you may want 30 characters, 40 locations, 20 items, 5 historical events and 5 groups. These are all ballpark numbers that will

undoubtedly change once the contributors get rolling, but it gives you an initial target.

3. For location and item entries, determine the minimum number of each type that you want. For example, if you create 25 locations, you might want at least 3 commercial, 3 educational, 3 governmental, 3 industrial, 3 medical, and 3 religious. That accounts for 18 of the 25 location entries, leaving the remaining types to be determined by each contributor during the creation process. Repeat the process for item entries. For characters, determine the number of NPCs and PCs for each contributor. For example, with 25 characters, at least 5 could be potential PCs (one for each contributor) with longer, more detailed narrative descriptions, and the other 20 would be NPCs.

4. Review your metanarrative for all the underlined terms the group decided would need catalog entries. Match the items, locations, characters, events, and groups against that list of entries. Contributors can volunteer to create specific entries they're most interested in, and multiple contributors should be encouraged to work on entries together.

5. Find a mutually agreeable deadline for the wiki entries to be completed. Entries wind up serving as short writing exercises in themselves. A good plan is for contributors to commit to working on one or two each day.

6. Pick a time shortly after the agreed-upon deadline to meet to discuss the catalog and the worldbuilding project as a whole. At this point, you can either arrange for another round of wiki entries or conclude worldbuilding and move onto the storytelling phase.

Building Tal-Vaz: Populating the Catalog

The group meets to discuss the catalog entries. Bryan searched through the metanarrative and copied all of the underlined terms and he announces that they have 43 potential wiki entries: 2 events, 17 items, 10 locations, 9 characters, and 5 groups. Cassandra hands each contributor their own copy of the Scope and Schedule Worksheet and suggests that they all agree to write a minimum of five entries each for items, locations, characters. That gives them 60 entries right off the bat, 15 shy of the minimum recommended 75 entries. They all feel comfortable that once they start plugging things into the worksheet they'll have no problem reaching the recommended minimum and beyond.

They start with the 20 items. Bryan looks at his list taken from the metanarrative and says they already have 17 items identified, with 9 of them being mechanical contraptions from Varoja and 6 are magical things from Sal-Kala. The other two items are pieces of equipment. That's almost all their allotment for items, but they know they need other types too. They scan through the list of items types from the book and decide that they should have at least a few from domestic items, equipment, medical, transportation, and weapons—at least 3 each, for another 15 items. Cassandra says they know where those extra wiki entries they needed are going to come from! They start divvying them out: Aaron and Bryan each will write one magical item entry and Cassandra and Karly each volunteer to do two; everyone agrees to do two of the mechanical devices. No one has strong feelings on the rest of the categories so they just go around the circle with each of them being assigned that type of item. Aaron takes a domestic item, Bryan a piece of equipment, Cassandra a medical item, Karly a transportation item, Bryan a weapon, and so forth until all the items types are claimed and entered into their Scope and Schedule Worksheets.

They repeat the process for the 20 locations. Aaron reads from his list that they have ten locations identified but they include several geographic area types: the continent, the region, and the names of the two focal points of Varoja and Sal-Kala. The other two locations in the metanarrative are the Isodorus Library (educational) and the Máolorian (religious). They look through the list of location types and decide they need a residence for each of the 5 ruling families and at least a few districts in each city, so that gives them another 11 locations. Cassandra says they also really need merchant shops and Karly adds they need a few military outposts. Aaron asks if anyone wants any specific locations and Karly says she wants to claim the residence of the Antuma clan. Bryan wants to work on the Isodorus Library. Karly asks if anyone minds if she grabs the Máolorian. Cassandra says she'd like to work on it too, but Karly should get it started. They pencil these in their worksheets and then go around the circle again divvying up the remaining geographic areas, residential areas, merchants, and military locations.

The final category to be divided up are the characters, and everyone wants to claim one of the nine people mentioned from the metanarrative for their PCs. Aaron reads aloud the characters' names: Hugh Antuma, Eras Bonneau, Teódulo Colmos, Ando Cuevas, Caro Cuevas, Livonia Cuevas, Darija Gallegos, Kade Laquino, and Tazay Laquino. Karly immediately says she wants Hugh Antuma and Caro Cuevas since she has a whole star-crossed lover story already worked out. Cassandra says that she's not sure that's a good idea, and maybe someone else should develop one of those characters to keep it from feeling too contrived. Karly starts getting huffy but Cassandra quickly volunteers to do whichever one Karly prefers, and she says she'll work with her so the character isn't too far afield of what Karly wants. Aaron and Bryan agree, saying that sharing the characters is more in the spirit of the project anyway. Karly's shoulders slump. She's not happy, but says she'll take Hugh and Cassandra can have Caro. Cassandra thanks her and promises to make it work. Bryan wants Eras Bonneau and Aaron takes Kade Laquino. They divide the remaining characters, and Karly suggests they just list Teódulo Colmos in Hugh Antuma's entry instead of giving him his own entry.

For the remaining 12 characters, they agree to have at least 5 merchants and 5 prominent scholars, 3 from Varoja and 2 from Sal-Kala. Bryan says that 20 characters feels like far too few people given how much they have going on, and Cassandra agrees but says they should start with this and add more later. After all, all of these main characters are going to have spouses, advisors, and friends and it could get out of hand fast. Aaron says that, on second thought, he doesn't want his PC to be a member of the nobility. He'd rather develop a soldier character, maybe a bodyguard. Bryan says that's up to him. They quickly deal out the merchants and scholars to each contributor.

They review the metanarrative list. The only things outstanding are the events of the discovery of the Isodorus Library and the Máolorian, and the job of writing up a group entry for each of the five families. They agree to do this in pairs: Bryan and Cassandra will write the Isodorus Library event and Aaron and Karly can do the one for the Máolorian. Cassandra and Karly will team up for the Cuevas and Antuma family pages, and Bryan and Aaron agree to do the Bonneaus, Gallegos, and Laquinos. They take a collective deep breath, review their worksheets, and confirm they understand what to do. They look at a calendar and pick a date in three weeks that they should target finishing all of their entries.

Bryan says that he knows he's going to need more entries. Can they all agree that they can create extra entries, but no more than five additional entries per category? Everyone thinks that sounds reasonable. Bryan reminds everyone to keep in touch on the project and check in if there's any question about entries that might cause some inconsistencies in the narrative. Everyone says they're all excited to get started and begin sharing some ideas for what they might do with their entries.

Transitioning to Storytelling

Once your group completes their catalog entries you've agreed upon, you can begin thinking about finishing off the worldbuilding project and moving to telling stories in your collaboratively built world. Some people may wish to keep developing the catalog with new entries, while others may be impatient for the storytelling phase. Keep tabs on the catalog's progress and be ready to gently apply the brakes as you approach the agreed-to number of catalog entries. While a robust catalog assists you in your storytelling endeavors, it can go on forever unless the group agrees to a hard stop at some designated point.

This is where worldbuilding stops, if only momentarily, and the storytelling exercises begin. At this point, contributors are usually full of unique story ideas to begin developing. The next chapter introduces a number of strategies for structuring stories drawn from the collaboratively built world.

13

Storytelling and Gaming in Collaboratively Built Worlds

At this point in the process, you should be the proud co-owner of a sprawling fictional world. You know everything there is to know about it, from its oldest history to its present-day demographics; you can explain the social forces at play, how they came to be, and what parts of the world are currently undergoing some change; you can easily identify the most interesting items, the most important locations, and you can see the world through the eyes of many different types of characters. Most importantly, things are happening in this world. It is a deep well of imaginative possibility waiting to be drawn from, containing a plentitude of stories waiting to be told. In fact, all this possibility can be daunting. This chapter gives you some points of entry for setting stories in motion in your new world.

For Writers

For the purposes of this book, a writer is anyone who produces print fiction of any length (flash fiction, short stories, novellas, novels) as well as screenplays, graphic novels, webcomics, video shorts, or any other kind of creative endeavor that involves crafting a structured story that has characters, a setting, and a plot. This section primarily focuses on writing print fiction, but the concepts apply to any storytelling medium you choose. Of course, the most straightforward approach to storytelling in your world is to simply pick a PC you like and start writing about their lives using whatever details from the catalog that get your creative juices flowing. You likely already have plenty of material for a steady stream of solo authored short stories or longer works of fiction.

However, keep in mind that your world is full of links to other people's creations. Why not connect your stories too? Writing networked stories can be a lot of fun if the contributors lay down some ground rules and there are a number of ways for writers to connect their works. For example, here are a few ways to tie stories together. One way is for all the contributors to write a vignette or short story set at the moment of a major historical event, each from a different PC's perspective. Reading these stories in succession can bring insight to the many different ways people in the world experienced that event. Another idea is to work in pairs or threes to tell the stories of groups of characters—of siblings, spouses, coworkers, comrades-in-arms—and track them together as their stories progress over a period of weeks, months, or a year. Plenty of novels and stories follow different sets of characters through the story; to use the examples from this book, *The Lord of the Rings* tells the story of Sam and Frodo taking the One Ring into Mordor while also following the adventures of Merry, Pippin, and the other members of the fellowship. *The Empire Strikes Back* and *Return of the Jedi* do something similar, where the characters' individual story arcs weave in and out as Luke, Leia, Han, Chewbacca come together, split up, reunite, and then split again. *A Game of Thrones* switches between the perspectives of six different members of House Stark, the perspective of Tyrion Lannister, and also that of Daenerys Targaryen from across the sea. In the context of a collaborative worldbuilding project, the only difference is that each new perspective character could have a different author.

Perhaps the most ambitious goal is to write a series of novels in your shared world. The popularity of National Novel Writing Month (NaNoWriMo) has steadily grown, and there are more people trying their hand at novel writing than ever before. A collaborative worldbuilding project can be great preparation for NaNoWriMo as it gives you plenty of material to draw from and story ideas to get started. If you can convince other members of your group to take up the challenge with you to write novels set in your shared world, then you have a built-in critique group when it comes to trading drafts and revising what you've written.

Whether you're writing short stories or novels, if you publish your works online, you can create literal connections between the stories by linking to your world's catalog entries. This allows the audience to move between the stories and the worldbuilding catalog, and you can use timestamps or other narrative devices to create links between the different stories you're writing as well. You could also publish your work in a serial fashion in monthly installments using a blog or another social media platform.

Sometimes shifting to the storytelling phase can feel surprisingly overwhelming. With so much information out there, it can be difficult to find a way into the world. Below are some specific prompts to help you get started. You can also use these as writing exercises to help you stretch your imagination and flex your storytelling muscles. Remember, if you have an open worldbuilding project that's published on the Internet, there's no need to overload your fiction with the specifics of the world. Readers who want more information about how the government or economy works, or any other fine details, can always check out the wiki. Focus on the characters and their problems for your stories and let the details about the world come in as necessary.

Prompt 1: Historical Events

During the worldbuilding process, you should have identified a number of different historical events that helped shape your world in some significant way. Historical events have witnesses who are either viewing them afar or are caught up in the immediate action. Find or make a PC and position them in and around one of the nearest historical events. Run through a few different possible starting points—a day before the event, the moment of the event, or days or weeks after the event. Think about how the PC fits in the world, and how their place in it changes after the major historical event. How does this alter things emotionally for the PC? How is the PC connected to the historical event? What decisions does the historical event force the PC to make? How might the historical event impact the PC's future? Explore the answers to these questions through stories.

Prompt 2: Draw Random Entries from the Catalog

For a fun challenge, randomly draw one PC, two NPCs, two items, and two locations from the catalog and write a story that incorporates all of them in a nontrivial way. You can bring in as many other entries as you like, but you must include those seven. This approach forces you to think through all kinds of juxtapositions between the entries. Think about it like a puzzle. How would the PC have found themselves at these locations? How would they feel about being there? Does it make sense for the story to begin in one location and end in the other? How would the PC feel about the randomly selected NPCs? Would they get along well, or be at odds with each other? Find the greatest point of tension among the entries you've randomly drawn and begin developing the story thread from that.

Prompt 3: Group Conflicts

Among your group entries, you should have a few groups that want to change something about the world, or perhaps they fear the changes happening in the world. Find a simmering sense of conflict between two or more groups and crank it up to a boil. Either some event has happened, or is about to happen, that will change the group dynamics forever. Find a PC who is a member of one group and situate them within the conflict. Are there factions forming within the group threatening to tear it apart? Or is the group demanding absolute unquestioning loyalty to the cause? In either case, how does your PC feel about it? Is the PC helping one side over the other? Does the PC have something to lose or gain by the changes in the world? Is the PC trying to resist or hasten this change? How will the changes in the group change the PC's relationship to other NPCs or to the PC's family members and close friends? Think through several possible ramifications and imagine the emotional states of the PC as the story hurtles toward one conclusion or the other.

Prompt 4: Character Conflicts

Your PC entries should have several points of tension you can play with. Begin with looking at the PC's connections to other characters and think about how you might heighten these tensions. Lovers can quarrel over all kinds of issues, children fight with parents and siblings, employers and coworkers can cause all kinds of stresses, or could it be that someone the PC cares very much about can be in danger? Put your character in a tight spot where they need to make some kind of sacrifice. What is it, and how do they feel about being in that situation?

Another avenue is to consider a similar set of questions, only instead of relationships consider the PC's motivations and find a genuinely difficult choice for them. For example, force the PC to choose between career advancement and a family member, or between their loyalty to a friend and their devotion to a political cause. Look again at the structures of the world and find the greatest point of potential conflict between the world and the character. Use that source of tension as a catalyst for a story.

Prompt 5: Life-Changing Moments

Just as historical events contribute to the point of the present of the world, personal events shape the attitudes, beliefs, and dispositions of PCs. Isolate the two or three most important moments of a PC's life and write about the emotions the PC felt as it happened. What choices did the PC make that led to this moment? What's the snap decision the character needs to make in this moment of crisis? What feelings does the PC have before, during, and after the life-changing event? To the best of your ability, show how this moment helped to define the PC the audience sees in their character entry.

Prompt 6: Relations and Genealogies

Find a PC you think is particularly interesting and identify one of this character's closest family relations. This might be a parent, child, sibling, spouse, or any other close relation who is either not an entry or an NPC entry. Take this second character and develop them into a complete PC in their own right. Tell a story about the original PC through the eyes of your newly created PC. For example, it could be the perspective of a doting parent reflecting on their child's accomplishments; or it could be from that of a resentful child who holds a grudge for some perceived slight. Use this new perspective to consider new angles of the original PC's personality. What kinds of things do others think about this PC that they themselves might not realize?

These are just a few ideas to get you started. You'll find that as you begin to write stories in this world, more storytelling opportunities will present themselves. Go wherever the inspiration leads you. For as much work as your group put into building the world, there's always another back alleyway to explore.

For Gamers

This section addresses two kinds of gamers: players of role-playing games and game designers who create all types of games. As explained throughout this book, the collaborative worldbuilding methodology is built on concepts drawn from role-playing games and role-playing game catalogs. It also uses game-like mechanics when it comes to randomizing the structures of the world. Therefore it should come as no surprise to learn that the structures of collaborative worldbuilding projects lend themselves to being used in and for games too.

Role-Playing Game Campaigns

It can be enormous fun to have a group of role-playing gamers collaboratively build a world as a setting for their campaigns. For one, this makes good sense within the fictional space of the game. The players will become knowledgeable about and connected to the world, just as their characters in the game ought to be. There are two big differences to consider when building a world for a role-playing game campaign: 1) the design of the catalog template, particularly the stat block; and 2) the amount of information about that world that's known only to the game master.

Role-playing games require more precise statistical information when it comes to the entries in the catalog, and this usually means using more numeric fields in the stat block. This is because those numeric fields usually plug into dice rolls to determine if character actions are successful or not. For example, imagine a character entry for an NPC who is a grizzled space marine who wears expensive body armor. If you're writing fiction, those broad details along with everything else in the catalog entry should give you enough information to bring the NPC into the story. In an RPG, however, the players need to know exactly how tough that body armor is and what kind of weapons can penetrate it. Be aware that filling out complete numerical stat blocks from scratch for every entry can be tiresome work. A good alternative is to create templates with some of the base values already filled in. You could create a template prefilled with average human stats and then simply bump values up or down to customize the NPC. This saves time and fatigue, though adding too many prefilled template types can also clutter your wiki.

The other major thing to consider is what type of information is for the GM's eyes only. A monster's stats, the floorplan of a dungeon, or the duplicitous nature of the town mayor are the kinds of things that the players of the campaign shouldn't know since these discoveries are a big part of what makes playing RPGs so much fun. Some wikis allow granular permissions which can restrict access to pages based on the user's account, so the GM could make certain pages inaccessible to the players. If your wiki doesn't feature this administrative feature (and many of the free sites do not), another strategy is to set up a second wiki where only the GM can create or view pages. In this case, the GM can copy the same catalog templates to the second site so it has the same look and feel. After the campaign ends, the GM could open the site up to public viewing so the players can see what other information had been hidden from them. The final way is simply for the GM to handle these affairs in electronic documents or physical notebooks. While this is the easiest approach, it does have the drawback that none of the GM's contributions are added to the wiki.

Another plan would be to blend the worldbuilding project with online campaign management software like Obsidian Portal.[1] The worldbuilding project serves as a great way to build camaraderie among players and for them to get a deep sense of the world that they're exploring, while the campaign management software can track the group's adventures.

Game Development

Many of today's sophisticated videogames, as well as tabletop and board games, feature elaborate backstories and detailed settings. Just as in novels, films, and other media, a richly described world can add new dimensions to the story and, in the case of games, of gameplay.

The collaborative worldbuilding project should occur during the pre-production phase of the game development cycle. Game designers approach the game design process differently based on the kind of game they're developing, but in most cases the team will draft a master game design document. One common element of this document is a description of the game and its setting. While the game development process will be most often driven by its core game mechanics rather than its story or its world, a well-thought-out, detailed world can add to the overall experience of gameplay.

The first stage of the worldbuilding process, that of building the world's foundation by establishing its framework and developing its structures, can be followed as described in this book. The main difference between worldbuilding for a game and for other purposes is that the catalog of entries will likely be smaller. Overscoping is a significant issue in game design, as problems include the desire to add too many features and too many complex game mechanics. A large-scale world can complicate things further by offering too many potential paths for players to follow and the temptation to create more NPCs than are necessary. Using the Scope and Schedule Worksheet can be a useful tool for tempering the worldbuilding impulse and restricting the number of characters and locations that will be incorporated into the game. As always, it's wise to start small and expand outward.

As with role-playing game catalogs, the catalog entries for your collaboratively built world might hold technical information about the person, place, or thing that exists for the team's use in the primary world. For example, entries on The Fallout Wiki each contain reference identification numbers that are used by the game engine as well as characters' and items' numeric stats, such as a character's strength or the amount of damage a weapon deals.

Beginning with a collaborative worldbuilding project early in the game design process can help designers think through the logic of their game world and give them some fresh ideas on tired genres. More often than not, designers find new and interesting connections between the setting and the mechanics, and the addition of an inspiring character, location, or item can lead to unexpected new directions for the game that improves upon the original concept.

For Educators

Worldbuilding exercises can be used in a wide range of courses that deal with any kind of fictional world. They can also be a useful tool for building representations of specific historical periods, or using the system to model social forces in different contemporary locations around the globe. Variations of this worldbuilding process have been used successfully in creative writing, literature, history, and political science courses, and hopefully more disciplines will see the value in this methodology.

The easiest way to use the system is to have students use the system or card deck to build models of worlds, whether they're worlds they encounter in short stories, books, films, games, or news articles. They can perform this task individually or in small groups. Through discussion, the class soon comes to realize that there is very little consensus on the numeric and trending values for each category, and the numbers mean little without some frame of reference. The worldbuilding model provides an easy way for students to begin thinking about and discussing the many different and competing social forces at play in any given culture at a given time. It works as well as for analyzing *Pride and Prejudice* as it does for a critical viewing of *The Godfather*, or coming to terms with the contemporary political situation of Pyongyang, North Korea, or understanding the culture of the Antebellum era of the southern United States.

The worldbuilding system was originally developed for use in creative writing classes in order to increase student engagement with each other's work, as well as enticing them to think more critically about how writers represent fictional worlds in their fiction, regardless of whether those worlds are similar or very unlike our own. It also required them to think through the different subject positions of the characters in the world, and from whose perspective those stories would be told. Some of my creative writing courses have been divided between a single collaborative worldbuilding project and role-playing sessions, where students first build a world together but then shift to controlling the decisions of a single character who lives in that world. Other courses have focused on building multiple worlds over the course of the semester so students can explore many different genres and note their similarities and differences. Without exception, both ways these have been deeply engaging learning experiences for the students and their instructor alike.

This book's companion website, collaborativeworldbuilding.com, features resources for educators along with links to examples of students' collaboratively built worlds. I encourage educators to peruse the site and design at least one unit of a course around collaborative worldbuilding exercises. Use the contact page on the website to let me know how it went, share links to student projects, and to troubleshoot anything that went wrong during the process. Of course, feel free to modify the instructions in this book however you see fit. The most important thing is for the worldbuilding project to work for you and your students.

Coda

Building Worlds Together

This is a book about building fictional worlds. The worlds readers build will be radically different than the everyday world in which we live and breathe. With the guidance provided in these chapters, your fictional worlds should have richly developed histories, complex social forces at play in different societies, and they will be populated with hundreds of compelling people, places, and things. The world should hold infinite possibilities for storytelling. My hope is that this book helps you accomplish that goal.

However, this book has another equally important purpose in the space of our primary world, the one we inhabit. I hope this book can bring people together, and I hope it creates space for dialogue around difficult questions, especially for people who may see our world in very different ways. In order for a collaborative worldbuilding project to succeed, it requires respect, patience, and compromise from every contributor. Worlds are not monolithic, and they are not univocal. They are fluid and transitory, and we know it to be true that whole cultures' attitudes and opinions and beliefs shift over time. A world's history is not a single incontrovertible narrative, but rather an aggregation of a number of subjective viewpoints, where the points of greatest overlap suggest to us some broad truths. It could be argued that we reach the deepest understanding of a given place in a given time if we listen to the stories of the people who live there. This is true for understanding our place and our time as well.

In today's world that seems so bitterly divided, there is no better time for us to find new ways to listen to each other, to work together, and to seek common ground. Perhaps one way is through shared creativity, and together we can roll up our sleeves and get to work building a better world for tomorrow.

Appendix A

Worldbuilding Structures Worksheet

COLLABORATIVE WORLD BUILDING

Name of World _____

🏛 GOVERNANCE

GOVERNMENT PRESENCE
① ② ③ ④ ⑤ Ⓣ Ⓢ

RULE OF LAW
① ② ③ ④ ⑤ Ⓣ Ⓢ

SOCIAL SERVICES
① ② ③ ④ ⑤ Ⓣ Ⓢ

ECONOMICS ⑤

ECONOMIC STRENGTH
① ② ③ ④ ⑤ Ⓣ Ⓢ

WEALTH DISTRIBUTION
① ② ③ ④ ⑤ Ⓣ Ⓢ

AGRICULTURE & TRADE
① ② ③ ④ ⑤ Ⓣ Ⓢ

◉ CULTURAL INFLUENCES

RACE RELATIONS
① ② ③ ④ ⑤ Ⓣ Ⓢ

CLASS RELATIONS
① ② ③ ④ ⑤ Ⓣ Ⓢ

GENDER RELATIONS
① ② ③ ④ ⑤ Ⓣ Ⓢ

SEXUAL ORIENTATION RELATIONS
① ② ③ ④ ⑤ Ⓣ Ⓢ

SOCIAL RELATIONS ♫

MILITARY INFLUENCE
① ② ③ ④ ⑤ Ⓣ Ⓢ

RELIGIOUS INFLUENCE
① ② ③ ④ ⑤ Ⓣ Ⓢ

TECHNOLOGY INFLUENCE
① ② ③ ④ ⑤ Ⓣ Ⓢ

ARTS & CULTURE INFLUENCE
① ② ③ ④ ⑤ Ⓣ Ⓢ

NOTES

FRAMEWORK WORKSHEET

Scope and Perspective Description

Historical Events

Timeline

METANARRATIVE			CATALOG						SCOPE AND SCHEDULE		
Contributor Name	Metanarrative	Due Date	Item Type	Item Name	Location Type	Location Name	Character Type	Character Name	Events/Groups	E/G Name	Due Date

Glossary

agriculture and trade: a substructure of *economics* that indicates the level of natural resources and briskness of buying and selling of goods and services within a society.

arts and culture: a substructure of *cultural influences* that indicates the level of importance a society places on visual arts (painting, sculpting, photography, etc.), performing arts (theatre, dance, music), literary accomplishments, culinary arts, and more.

audience: readers who are not *contributors* but will become familiar with the *collaborative worldbuilding project*, either directly through access to the *wiki* or through the stories set in the *fictional world*.

breadth: an aspect of *scope* that estimates the physical size of a *fictional world*; e.g., whether the world is the size of a large metropolitan area, a continent, a solar system.

catalog: repository for all *characters, locations, items, groups*, and *historical events* in a *fictional world*, usually kept as individual entries on a *wiki*.

category: one of five kinds of *catalog entries* that includes *items, locations, characters, historical events*, and *groups*.

characters: representation of a person in a *fictional world*, either as a member of *group*, as a *non-perspective character*, or a *perspective character*.

class relations: a substructure of *social relations* that indicates the various levels of equality between people of different social hierarchies, most commonly divided by wealth and income.

closed project: a *collaborative worldbuilding project* where the *contributors* are the only intended *audience*.

coherence/coherent: an effort to ensure that aspects of the *fictional world* make logical sense in relation to each other.

collaborative worldbuilding project: the construction of a large-scale *fictional world* that involves significant input from more than one person.

collaborator: see *contributor*.

consistency/consistent: an effort to ensure aspects of the *fictional world* that are compatible and follow a universal set of rules that pertain to that world.

contributor: any participant in a *collaborative worldbuilding project*.

cultural influences: one of the four *structural categories* that describe the social forces at play in a world, made up of the *substructures* of *military influence, religious influence, technology influence*, and *arts and culture influence*.

depth: an aspect of *scope* that indicates the level of detail about a *location* within a *fictional world*.

document sharing: online software that allows group access to files for real-time editing.

economic strength: a substructure of *economics* that indicates the level of available wealth in the society, which includes currency but also the total value of all goods and services.

economics: one of the four *structural categories* that describe the social forces at play in a world, made up of the *substructures* of *economic strength*, *wealth distribution*, and *agriculture and trade*.

fantasy: a genre of *speculative fiction* where the *fictional world* tends to be based on supernatural elements such as the use of magic and the presence of mythical creatures.

field: a discrete piece of information captured in the *stat block* in a *catalog entry*; e.g., each *character* entry has a field for the character's name, a field for their gender, a field for their occupation.

fictional world: a world separate and distinct from our *primary world*.

first-person perspective: a mode of storytelling in which a narrative is told from the perspective of a *character* in the *fictional world* speaking directly about themselves using words like "I" or "my."

first stage: the beginning of a *collaborative worldbuilding* project where *contributors* choose a *genre* of fiction, determine their intended *audience*, and establish a *framework* for their *fictional world* and develop its *social structures*.

focal points: *locations* with a significant amount of *depth* and usually where stories are set in a *fictional world*.

foundation: a combination of a *collaborative worldbuilding project*'s *genre*, *audience*, *framework*, and *structures*.

framework: part of a *fictional world*'s *foundation* that includes its *scope*, *sequence*, and *perspective*.

gender relations: a substructure of *social relations* that indicates the various levels of equality between people of different genders, most commonly divided between males and females.

genre: a type of fiction that exhibits a certain set of features, characteristics, or commonalities with other works, usually under the umbrella of *speculative fiction* for *collaborative worldbuilding* projects.

genre-blending: incorporating aspects of two different genres of *speculative fiction* into a *fictional world*.

governance: one of the four *structural categories* that describe the social forces at play in a world, made up of the *substructures* of *government presence*, *rule of law*, and *social services*.

government presence: a substructure of *governance* that indicates the level of government involvement and authority in the daily life of its citizens.

group: all the *contributors* of a *collaborative worldbuilding project*.

groups: within a *fictional world*, an assemblage of *characters* bound together by some association or cause.

historical events: significant turning points in a *fictional world*, as recorded on its *timeline*.

historical fiction: fictional set in our primary world that attempts to faithfully follow the historical record.

historical world: representation of a world that once existed in our *primary world* that attempts to follow the historical record and contains none of the elements of *speculative fiction*.

horror: a *genre* of fiction that seeks to frighten, scare, or unsettle the *audience*, often through supernatural means.

items: any individual article or thing that exists in a *fictional world* that is not easily identifiable as either a *character* or *location*.

limited access: a *collaborative worldbuilding project* where certain portions of the *fictional world* are restricted to viewing and editing by a smaller subset of *contributors*.

locations: physical places within the *scope* of a *fictional world*.

map: a visual representation of the *fictional world* that encompasses most if not all of its *scope* and *focal points*.

metanarrative: the story of a *fictional world* that describes its major *historical events* and provides an in-depth overview of the *structures* and *substructures* that make up the social forces at play at the *point of the present*.

metanarrative lead: a synopsis of the *metanarrative* that highlights the most prominent features of the *fictional world*, and usually functions as the introduction to a *collaborative worldbuilding project* on the front page of a *wiki*.

military influence: a substructure of *cultural influences* that indicates the level of importance a society places on its armed forces, generally indicated through the number of military *locations* and how many *characters* have affiliations with military institutions.

narrative description: part of a *catalog entry* that richly describes how that *item, location, character, group,* or *historical event* fit within the wider context of the *fictional world*.

neutral point of view (NPOV): an attempt to provide an unbiased and fair representation in the *narrative description* of a *catalog entry* that includes all of the most significant views on that topic.

non-perspective character (NPC): a *character* who has been significantly fleshed out with a name, physical attributes, personality traits, and motivations, but not to the same extent as a *perspective character (PC)*, and functions as a background or secondary character in a narrative.

open world: a *collaborative worldbuilding project* that is entirely visible to a public *audience*.

participants: see *contributor*.

people: see *characters*.

perspective: part of a *collaborative worldbuilding* project's *framework* that describes the point of view from which the *audience* is learning information about the *fictional world* in the *metanarrative* and *catalog entries*.

perspective character (PC): a well-developed *character* who is created with the intent of becoming a protagonist of a story set in the *fictional world* of a *collaborative worldbuilding project*, and therefore has a complete personal history, physical attributes, personality traits, attitudes and opinions, and more.

places: see *locations*.

point of the present: a place on the *timeline* of a *fictional world* that represents the "now" of a *collaborative worldbuilding project* and most likely the period in which stories set in the world will be told.

primary world: the shared reality in which we live our daily lives.

race relations: a substructure of *social relations* that indicates the various levels of equality between people of different races, most commonly divided by ethnicity and skin color.

religious influence: a substructure of *cultural influences* that indicates the level of importance a society places on organized religion, generally indicated through the number of religious *locations* and how many *characters* have affiliations with religious institutions.

rule of law: a substructure of *governance* that indicates the level of enforcement of a society's laws, including the policing of laws, having established courts to pass judgment on the accused, and a system for meting out punishment to the guilty.

science fiction: a genre of *speculative fiction* where the *fictional world* tends to be based on futuristic technologies, extrapolations from social sciences, and other thought experiments founded on reason rather than supernatural powers.

scope: part of a *collaborative worldbuilding* project's *framework* that describes the *breadth* and *depth* of your fictional world, or its approximate size and level of detail.

second stage: the latter half of a *collaborative worldbuilding project* where *contributors* design *templates* and begin populating the *catalog* with a number of *items, locations,* and *characters*.

sequence: the order of major *historical events* on your *fictional world*'s *timeline*.

sexual orientation relations: a substructure of *social relations* that indicates the various levels of equality between people of different sexual orientations, most commonly divided by individuals' sexual, emotional, and romantic attraction to different genders.

social relations: one of the four *structural categories* that describe the social forces at play in a world, made up of the *substructures* of *race relations, class relations, gender relations,* and *sexual orientation relations*.

social services: a substructure of *governance* that indicates the level of services provided by the government to its citizens, usually emphasizing education and healthcare but includes transportation, parks, and public works.

speculative fiction: umbrella term that covers the fiction genres of fantasy, science fiction, and horror, where some rules of our *primary world* have been bent, altered, or broken.

stage one: see *first stage*.

stage two: see *second stage.*

stat block: the portion of a *catalog entry* that lists primarily categorical information that is often represented numerically and adds a degree of *consistency* to the *fictional world.*

structural categories: the four basic categories that describe the social forces at play in a world, including *governance, economics, social relations,* and *cultural influences* and the 14 *substructures* that fit within it.

structures: see *structural categories.*

sublocations: locations that are nested within other *locations*; e.g., a neighborhood within a city or a planet within a star system.

substructures: the aspects of a society that describe the social forces at play in a world and fit within the four broad *structural categories.* The substructures are *government presence, economic strength, wealth distribution, race relations, class relations, gender relations, sexual orientation relations, military influence, religious influence, technology influence,* and *arts and culture influence.*

technology influence: a substructure of *cultural influences* that indicates the level of importance a society places on the production of new technologies, generally indicated through the number of technology-centered *locations* such as factories and labs, and how many *characters* have affiliations with technology-related institutions.

termination points: the beginning and ending of a *fictional world's timeline.*

things: see *items.*

third-person perspective: a storytelling mode in which a narrative is told from a disembodied perspective that is not necessarily bound to any one *character* in the *fictional world.*

timeline: a broad record of a world's most significant *historical events* placed in chronological order between two *termination points.*

types: different varieties within *categories* of *catalog entries.*

wealth distribution: a substructure of *economics* that indicates how evenly the total amount of goods and services is spread through a society.

wiki: an online encyclopedia that can usually be viewed and edited by a public audience; e.g., Wikipedia, Wikia fan sites.

world: some narrow portion of human life that attempts to capture a specific location in a moment in time.

worldbuilding: the act of creating a *fictional world,* or otherwise attempting to reconstruct a specific historical moment in time.

Notes

1 Introduction to Collaborative Worldbuilding

1 Mark Wolf, *Building Imaginary Worlds: The Theory and History of Subcreation* (New York: Routledge, 2012).

2 M. John Harrison, "Very Afraid," Uncle Zip's Window, January 27, 2007, http://web. archive.org/web/20080410181840/http://uzwi.wordpress.com/2007/01/27/very-afraid/.

3 Lincoln Michel, "Against Worldbuilding," Electric Literature, April 6, 2017, https://electricliterature.com/against-worldbuilding–700e4861c26b.

4 Ibid.

5 Joan Gordon, "Reveling in Genre: An Interview with China Miéville," *Science Fiction Studies*, November 2003, www.depauw.edu/sfs/interviews/mievilleinterview.htm.

6 "Tolkien Gateway," Tolkien Gateway, accessed June 2, 2017, http://tolkiengateway. net/wiki/Tolkien_Gateway.

7 "Encyclopedia of Arda," Encyclopedia of Arda, accessed June 26, 2017, www.glyphweb.com/arda/default.php.

8 "Wookieepedia," Wookieepedia, accessed June 26, 2017, http://starwars.wikia.com/ wiki/Main_Page.

9 "A Wiki of Ice and Fire," Wiki of Ice and Fire, accessed February 13, 2016, http://awoiaf.westeros.org/index.php/Main_Page.

10 "Fallout Wiki," Fallout Wiki, accessed August 26, 2016, http://fallout.wikia.com/wiki/ Fallout_Wiki

2 Worlds, Worldbuilding, and Collaborative Worldbuilding

1 Chuck Wendig, "25 Things You Should Know About Worldbuilding," Terrible Minds (blog), September 17, 2013, http://terribleminds.com/ramble/2013/09/17/25-things-you-should-know-about-worldbuilding/.

2 J.R.R. Tolkien, Humphrey Carpenter, and Christopher Tolkien, *The Letters of J.R.R. Tolkien: A Selection* (Boston: Houghton Mifflin Co., 2000); and Christopher Tolkien, *The Complete History of Middle-Earth* (London: HarperCollins, 2001).

3 Michael Kaminski, *The Secret History of Star Wars* (Kingston, ON: Legacy Books Press, 2008); and J.W. Rinzler and Charles Lippincott, *The Making of Star Wars: The Definitive Story behind the Original Film* (New York: Ballantine Books, 2007).

4   George R.R. Martin, "Last Year (Winds of Winter)," Not A Blog (blog), January 2, 2016, https://grrm.livejournal.com/465247.html.

3 Audience and Genres

1   John Clute et al., "Encylopedia of Science Fiction," *The Encyclopedia of Science Fiction*, n.d., www.sf-encyclopedia.com/.
2   John Clute and John Grant, "Encyclopedia of Fantasy," *The Encyclopedia of Fantasy*, accessed June 27, 2017, http://sf-encyclopedia.uk/fe.php?id=0&nm=introduction_to_the_online_text.

4 Frameworks of Fictional Worlds

1   All books on the craft of creative writing will address the issue of perspective, or point of view, at one point or another. I have found the most thorough discussion of the topic in the following texts, all of which I recommend for considering different perspective viewpoints for both worldbuilding and telling stories set in the collaboratively built world: Alexander Steele, Thom Didato, and Gotham Writers' Workshop, *Gotham Writers' Workshop Fiction Gallery* (New York: Bloomsbury, 2004); Josip Novakovich, *Fiction Writer's Workshop* (Cincinnati: Story Press, 1995); Alice LaPlante, *The Making of a Story: A Norton Guide to Creative Writing* (New York: W.W. Norton, 2007); Janet Burroway, Elizabeth Stuckey-French, and Ned Stuckey-French, *Writing Fiction: A Guide to Narrative Craft* (Boston: Longman, 2011).
2   "Wikipedia: Neutral Point of View," *Wikipedia*, December 14, 2016, https://en.wikipedia.org/w/index.php?title=Wikipedia:Neutral_point_of_view&oldid=754855206.
3   "World War II," *Wikipedia*, December 9, 2016, https://en.wikipedia.org/w/index.php?title=World_War_II&oldid=753780098.
4   "Causes of World War II," *Wikipedia*, September 19, 2017, https://en.wikipedia.org/w/index.php?title=Causes_of_World_War_II.
5   J.R.R. Tolkien and Christopher Tolkien, *The Silmarillion* (New York: HarperCollins, 2001).
6   J.R.R. Tolkien, *The Hobbit, Or, There and Back Again* (New York: HarperCollins, 2012).
7   J.R.R. Tolkien, *The Fellowship of the Ring: Being the First Part of The Lord of the Rings* (Boston: Mariner Books, 2012); John R.R. Tolkien, *The Two Towers Being the Second Part of The Lord of the Rings* (Boston: Mariner Books, 2012); J.R.R. Tolkien, *The Return of the King: Being the Third Part of The Lord of the Rings* (Boston: Mariner Books, 2012).

8   George Lucas, *Star Wars: Episode IV – A New Hope* (20th Century Fox, 1977).

9   George Lucas, *Star Wars: Episode V – The Empire Strikes Back* (20th Century Fox, 1980); George Lucas, *Star Wars: Episode VI – Return of the Jedi* (20th Century Fox, 1983).

10 George Lucas, "Star Wars: A New Hope Script," Internet Movie Database, accessed May 19, 2017, www.imsdb.com/scripts/Star-Wars-A-New-Hope.html.

11 George R.R. Martin, *A Game of Thrones* (New York: Bantam Books, 1996).

12 George R.R. Martin, Elio Garcia, and Linda Antonsson, *The World of Ice & Fire: The Untold History of Westeros and the Game of Thrones* (New York: Bantam, 2014).

13 Joanna Robinson, "Why the Latest Game of Thrones Spin-Off News Is the Most Exciting Yet," Vanity Fair, September 20, 2017, https://www.vanityfair.com/hollywood/2017/09/game-of-thrones-bryan-cogman-prequel-spin-off-five.

14 Tolkien, *The Fellowship of the Ring.*

15 "The Legendary Star Wars Expanded Universe Turns a New Page," StarWars.com, accessed September 14, 2016, http://www.starwars.com/news/the-legendary-star-wars-expanded-universe-turns-a-new-page.

16 "Abeir-Toril," *Wikipedia*, December 7, 2016, https://en.wikipedia.org/w/index.php?title=Abeir-Toril&oldid=753446411.

17 Wizards of the Coast, *Sword Coast Adventurer's Guide* (Renton, WA: Wizards of the Coast, 2015) 7.

18 Matt Forbeck and Ed Greenwood, "Volo's Guide to the Forgotten Realms," in *Volothamp Geddarm's Dungeonology: An Epic Adventure through the Forgotten Realms* (London, UK: Studio Game, 2016).

5 Structures and Substructures of Fictional Worlds

1   George R.R. Martin, *A Song of Ice and Fire* (Random House, 2013).

2   J.R.R. Tolkien and Christopher Tolkien, *The Silmarillion* (New York: HarperCollins, 2001); J.R.R. Tolkien, *The Hobbit, Or, There and Back Again* (New York: HarperCollins, 2012); J.R.R. Tolkien, *The Fellowship of the Ring: Being the First Part of The Lord of the Rings* (Boston: Mariner Books, 2012); John R.R. Tolkien, *The Two Towers Being the Second Part of The Lord of the Rings* (Boston: Mariner Books, 2012); J.R.R Tolkien, *The Return of the King: Being the Third Part of The Lord of the Rings* (Boston: Mariner Books, 2012).

3   Tolkien, *The Return of the King.*

4   Michael Moorcock, "Epic Pooh," *Revolution SF*, accessed September 29, 2017, www.revolutionsf.com/article.php?id=953.

5   *Star Wars: The Clone Wars* (Cartoon Network TV series, 2008–2015).

6   John Jackson Miller, *Star Wars: A New Dawn* (New York: Del Ray, 2014); James Luceno, *Catalyst: A Rogue One Novel* (New York: Del Rey, 2016); Jason Fry, *Servants of the*

Empire: Edge of the Galaxy, vol. 1 (Glendale, CA: Disney Lucasfilm Press, 2014); Jason Fry and Greg Weisman, *Servants of the Empire: Rebel in the Ranks*, vol. 2 (Glendale, CA: Disney Lucasfilm Press, 2015); Jason Fry, *Servants of the Empire: Imperial Justice*, vol. 3 (Glendale, CA: Disney Lucasfilm Press, 2015); Jason Fry, *Servants of the Empire: The Secret Academy*, vol. 4 (Glendale, CA: Disney Lucasfilm Press, 2015).

7   Claudia Gray, *Lost Stars* (Glendale, CA: Disney Lucasfilm Press, 2015); Chuck Wendig, *Star Wars: Aftermath* (New York: Del Rey, 2016); Chuck Wendig, *Star Wars: Aftermath – Life Debt* (New York: Del Rey, 2017); Chuck Wendig, *Star Wars: Aftermath – Empire's End* (New York: Del Rey, 2017).

8   Wendig, *Aftermath*; Wendig, *Life Debt*; Wendig, *Empire's End*; *Star Wars Rebels* (Cartoon Network TV series, 2014–2018); Fry, *Servants of the Empire*; Fry and Weisman, *Servants of the Empire: Rebel in the Ranks*.

9   Luceno, *Catalyst*.

10 Rafi Letzter, "An Economist Explains What's Really Going On in 'Game of Thrones,'" *Business Insider*, accessed May 24, 2017, www.businessinsider.com/game-of-thrones-is-all-about-economics–2016–4.

11 Moorcock, "Epic Pooh."

12 "Middle-Earth in Numbers", *Lord of the Rings Project*, accessed April 3, 2017, http://lotrproject.com/statistics/.

13 Timothy Zahn, *Thrawn* (New York: Del Rey, 2017).

14 J.J. Abrams, *Star Wars: Episode VII – The Force Awakens* (Walt Disney Studios Motion Pictures, 2015); Gareth Edwards, *Rogue One: A Star Wars Story* (Walt Disney Studios Motion Pictures, 2016).

15 Fry, *Servants of the Empire*; Cavan Scott, *Star Wars: Adventures in Wild Space*, 6 vols., Adventures in Wild Space (Glendale, CA: Disney Lucasfilm Press, 2016); Gray, *Lost Stars*; James Luceno, *Tarkin*, 2015; Zahn, *Thrawn*.

16 Paul S. Kemp, *Lords of the Sith* (New York: Del Rey, 2016).

17 Wendig, *Empire's End*.

18 "Star Wars Rebels."

19 Mark Waid et al., *Star Wars: Princess Leia* (New York: Marvel Comics, 2015).

20 George R.R. Martin, *A Dance with Dragons* (New York: Bantam, 2011).

21 "Star Wars Rebels."

22 Fry, *Servants of the Empire: Imperial Justice*.

23 "Star Wars: The Clone Wars."

6 Catalogs of Fictional Worlds

1   For a more comprehensive history of the precursors to the RPG and its gradual development, see Jon Peterson, *Playing at the World: A History of Simulating Wars,*

People and Fantastic Adventures, from Chess to Role-Playing Games (San Diego, CA: Unreason Press, 2012). Shannon Appelcline's and John Adamus's four-volume *Designers & Dragons: A History of the Roleplaying Game Industry* (Silver Spring, MD: Evil Hat Productions, 2014) also provides valuable insight into the growth and evolution of the tabletop RPG in both the United States and the United Kingdom over four decades.

2 Peterson, *Playing at the World.*

3 Gary Gygax and Jeff Perren, *Chainmail: Rules for Medieval Miniatures*, 3rd ed. (Tactical Studies Rules (TSR), 1975), 28.

4 Gary Gygax and Dave Arneson, *Dungeons & Dragons Volume 1: Men & Magic*, 1st ed., vol. 1 (Lake Geneva, WI: Tactical Studies Rules (TSR), 1974), 4.

5 Ibid., 1: 3, underline in original.

6 Ibid., 1: 5.

7 Ibid., 1: 4.

8 Ibid.

9 Gary Gygax and Dave Arneson, *Dungeons & Dragons Volume 3: The Underworld & Wilderness Adventures*, 1st ed., vol. 3 (Lake Geneva, WI: Tactical Studies Rules (TSR), 1974), 10.

10 Gygax and Arneson, *Dungeons & Dragons Volume 1: Men & Magic*, 1: 10.

11 Gary Gygax and Dave Arneson, *Dungeons & Dragons Volume 2: Monsters & Treasure*, 1st ed., vol. 2 (Lake Geneva, WI: Tactical Studies Rules (TSR), 1974).

12 Ibid., 2: 10.

13 Ibid., 2: 3.

14 Gary Gygax, *Monster Manual*, 1st ed. (Lake Geneva, WI: TSR Hobbies, 1978), 2.

15 Ibid.

16 Ibid., 4.

17 Gary Gygax, *Advanced Dungeons & Dragons, Players Handbook* (Lake Geneva, WI; New York: TSR Hobbies; Distributed in the U.S. by Random House, 1978), 5.

18 Ibid., 6.

19 Ibid., 38.

20 Ibid., 6.

21 Ibid.

22 Gygax and Arneson, *Dungeons & Dragons Volume 1: Men & Magic*, 1: 10.

23 Gygax, *Advanced Dungeons & Dragons, Players Handbook*, 18.

24 Ibid., 18–33.

25 Ibid., 33–34.

26 And digital games too.

27 Mike Mearls et al., *Monster Manual* (Renton, WA: Wizards of the Coast, 2014), 6.

28 Ibid., 4–12.

29 The nine options are: lawful good, lawful neutral, lawful evil; neutral good, true neutral, neutral evil; and chaotic good, chaotic good, and chaotic evil.

30 From the entry for the *Steam Mephit*. Mearls et al., *Monster Manual*, 217.

31 Ibid., 318.

32 Ibid., 286–87.

33 Mike Mearls et al., *Dungeon Master's Guide* (Renton, WA: Wizards of the Coast, 2014), 273–79.

34 Mearls et al., *Monster Manual*, 165.

35 Ibid., 211.

36 Ibid., 170.

37 Ibid., 203.

38 Ibid., 165.

39 Ibid., 207.

40 Ibid., 167.

41 Ibid., 290.

42 Ibid., 203.

43 Ibid., 325.

44 Ibid., 235.

45 Jeremy Crawford et al., *Player's Handbook* (Renton, WA: Wizards of the Coast, 2014), 122.

46 Mearls et al., *Monster Manual*, 195.

47 Ibid.

48 Ibid.

49 Ibid.

50 Ibid.

51 Wolfgang Baur and Steve Winter, *Hoard of the Dragon Queen: Tyranny of Dragons* (Renton, WA: Wizards of the Coast, 2014); Steve Winter, Alexander Winter, and Wolfgang Baur, *The Rise of Tiamat* (Renton, WA: Wizards of the Coast, 2014).

52 Mike Mearls and Inc Wizards of the Coast, *Volo's Guide to Monsters* (Renton, WA: Wizards of the Coast, 2016), 63–70.

53 Ibid., 165–67.

54 "John Hancock," Fallout Wiki, accessed June 2, 2017, http://fallout.wikia.com/wiki/John_Hancock.

55 "Sullust," Wookieepedia, accessed June 2, 2017, http://starwars.wikia.com/wiki/Sullust.

56 George Lucas, *Star Wars: Episode VI – Return of the Jedi* (20th Century Fox, 1983).

57 "Nauglamír," The Tolkien Gateway, accessed June 2, 2017, http://tolkiengateway.net/wiki/Nauglam%C3%ADr.

58 "War of the Ninepenny Kings," A Wiki of Ice and Fire, accessed June 2, 2017, http://awoiaf.westeros.org/index.php/War_of_the_Ninepenny_Kings.

59 Carl Bialik, "These Authors Know the 'Game of Thrones' Backstory Better than George R.R. Martin Does," *FiveThirtyEight*, December 18, 2014,

https://fivethirtyeight.com/features/these-authors-know-the-game-of-thrones-backstory-better-than-george-r-r-martin-does/; "Meet the 'Game of Thrones' Superfan Who Knows Westeros Better than George R.R. Martin," accessed October 10, 2017, www.salon.com/2014/04/28/meet_the_game_of_thrones_superfan_who_knows_westeros_better_than_george_r_r_martin/.

60 "Fallout Bible," Fallout Wiki, accessed October 2, 2017, http://fallout.wikia.com/wiki/Fallout_Bible.

61 "How a Pen and Paper RPG Brought 'Star Wars' Back from the Dead," Glixel, accessed May 24, 2017, www.glixel.com/news/how-a-dd-style-rpg-brought-star-wars-back-from-the-dead-w457301.

62 Ibid.

63 "Star Wars Legends," Wookieepedia, accessed June 5, 2017, http://starwars.wikia.com/wiki/Star_Wars_Legends.

64 "How a Pen and Paper RPG Brought 'Star Wars' Back from the Dead."

8 Before You Begin Your Project

1 "Remarks by Packers' White Draw Criticism in Wisconsin," *The New York Times*, March 26, 1998, www.nytimes.com/1998/03/26/sports/pro-football-remarks-by-packers-white-draw-criticism-in-wisconsin.html.

10 Developing the Structures

1 For one such study, see Christopher F Karpowitz and Tali Mendelberg, *The Silent Sex: Gender, Deliberation, and Institutions* (2014), http://public.eblib.com/choice/publicfullrecord.aspx?p=1689374.

11 Writing the Metanarrative

1 "World War II," Wikipedia, December 9, 2016, https://en.wikipedia.org/w/index.php?title=World_War_II&oldid=753780098.

13 Storytelling and Gaming in Collaboratively Built Worlds

1 See obsidianportal.com.

Index

Page numbers in **bold** refer to figures, page numbers in *italic* refer to tables.